What Should I Do

This is a question that is all too common when it comes to careers. Even the most established professionals look for different colored parachutes to open or add to their existing career. If you are questioning your career or looking for a new job, this book is for you. It will help you to define your own creativity, see the best path to career success, and identify how your skills and life experience fit into the complete picture. It even shows what kind of building is best for you to work in! Finally, here is a book that opens your window of opportunity and lets you in on the larger spiritual mission in light of your work abilities.

If you are a professional astrologer and clients have repeatedly asked you for help in their career decisions, this book provides a unified and comprehensive method for analyzing a client's birth chart and the impact of current conditions on career. It provides a map for navigating the complex considerations that impact career choices. Numerous lists, tables, and case studies assist you to quickly find the appropriate astrological factors in any chart.

Charting Your Career is unusual in its direct approach to the very questions that we all ask about our careers. It considers each area generally, provides specific delineations of astrological data, and includes examples in the form of case histories and client interviews. Many fresh insights and approaches, gleaned from the author's psychological and astrological counseling practices, have been combined with traditional astrology techniques to provide a concrete method that the career seeker, professional astrologer, or client will find useful in their career search.

About the Author

A professional astrologer for twenty-five years, Stephanie Jean Clement, Ph.D., has been a board member of the American Federation of Astrologers since 1991. She has lectured and given workshops in the U.S. and Canada on psychological counseling and astrology. Stephanie's published books include *Twin Angles; Decanates and Dwads; Counseling Techniques in Astrology; Planets and Planet-Centered Astrology;* and *Consciousness and the Midheaven.* In addition, she has published numerous articles on astrological counseling, charts of events, and counseling techniques.

Stephanie's Ph.D. in transpersonal psychology has prepared her to work with clients in defining their creative potential and refining their creative process. This work is the source of her personal insights into vocation in terms of both practical considerations and spiritual mission. She developed a therapeutic technique for overcoming writing blocks and taught writing at Naropa Institute, a contemplative college in Boulder, Colorado, where she was an associate professor and librarian.

To Write to the Author

If you wish to contact the author or would like more information about this book, please write to the author in care of Llewellyn Worldwide, and we will forward your request. Both the author and publisher appreciate hearing from you and learning of your enjoyment of this book and how it has helped you. Llewellyn Worldwide cannot guarantee that every letter written to the author can be answered, but all will be forwarded. Please write to:

Stephanie Jean Clement
℅ Llewellyn Worldwide Ltd.
P.O. Box 64383, Dept. K144–9
St. Paul, MN 55164-0383, U.S.A.

Please enclose a self-addressed, stamped envelope for reply or $1.00 to cover costs.
If outside the U.S.A., enclose international postal reply coupon.

CHARTING YOUR CAREER

The Horoscope Reveals Your Life Purpose

STEPHANIE JEAN CLEMENT, PH.D.

1999
Llewellyn Publications
St. Paul, Minnesota, 55164-0383 U.S.A.

FIRST EDITION
First Printing, 1999

Cover design by Anne Marie Garrison
Interior design and editing by Eila Savela

All horoscope charts in this book were generated using WinStar © Matrix Software.

Library of Congress Cataloging-in-Publication Data
Clement, Stephanie. 1944–
      Charting your career : the horoscope reveals your life purpose / Stephanie Jean Clement.
      — 1st ed.
          p. cm.
      Includes bibliographical references and index.
      ISBN 1–56718–144–9
      1. Astrology and vocational guidance.   I. Title.
BF1729.V63C54 1999
133.5'8331702—dc21   99–16565
                                       CIP

Llewellyn Publications
A Division of Llewellyn Worldwide, Ltd.
St. Paul, Minnesota, 55164–0383, U.S.A.
www.llewellyn.com

Printed in the United States of America

Contents

Illustrations

Introduction

The word vocation comes from a Latin root, *vocare*, meaning to call. If we are called to a vocation, what is the mechanism of that calling? Who calls? Is it Spirit? This is not a question to be taken lightly, as it is the thrust of philosophical debate throughout history, and no one has responded in a totally satisfactory way. However, by gathering the terms we use for calling and the thoughts of the cultures in which those words originated, we can get a pretty good idea of how calling works.

Plotinus, a follower of Plato, agrees fundamentally with Hindu precepts when he suggests that choosing to incarnate in a certain family circumstance is consistent with the personal calling of the individual. He concludes that:

- the individual soul recognizes the call, both before birth and during the present incarnation
- the individual will choose to align the entire life with the calling and
- all events or accidents throughout one's life can be seen as part of the pattern of fulfillment of the calling—they either contribute directly or cause challenges to the path.

Historical references to calling use the terms *daimon, character, fate, soul, destiny, image, genius, vocation,* or *mission,* more or less interchangeably. I will use most of these terms, because multiple views of calling can be incorporated into career considerations to good effect. We can discover our individual missions through the use of natal astrology. I will discuss how to implement that mission, using the energies of current progressions and transits. Finally, the heliocentric chart provides a clear statement of mission on the spiritual plane, and how that mission is translated through the geocentric chart.

Psychologist James Hillman indicates that the calling does not go away, no matter what we do. We cannot avoid it. He also states that modern psychology has relegated calling to religion or parapsychology, and has chosen to address the neurotic symptoms of individuals who have not aligned well with their missions. Current vocational counseling techniques depend as much on the counselor's personal mission as they do on concrete evaluations of the client's daimon. Much of the power of Hillman's writing lies in the fact that he recognizes the daimon as a fully manifested facet of personality from birth. Small children can have an adult vision of their calling. For those of us who have not pursued our mission to our satisfaction, this book is designed to go back to a time before the daimon was repressed or ignored in order to identify its nature. Then we will bring that innate sense of purpose forward to the present and give it new life by examining those careers that suit its energy in our current circumstances.

The daimon is not a child and must not be insulted by treating its desires childishly. Most of us can remember moments in childhood when we had a grand idea that was not taken very seriously by the people around us. They may have given us toys instead of real grown-up tools, or they may have said, "You will probably change your mind a hundred times before you are done." I personally remember people saying that they thought it was "nice" that I wanted to become a teacher, and then telling me how to be a good wife and mother, or a good scientist. I knew even then that they did not know how important teaching was to me. Even in first grade I was measuring my teachers against a model of teaching that was to form the essence of my being.

Back to the initial question—who calls? I believe we call ourselves. We come into this lifetime with the greater part of our character in place, whether we remember choosing it or not. Because we are born with this character, and the sense of mission it implies, astrology is well able to evaluate the potential which we can fulfill, as well as the path of that fulfillment. Astrology places us in the context of the larger universe and provides the template into which we pour our experience, thoughts, and feelings. It shows the probable path and challenges along the way. It reveals what we have chosen for ourselves and how we may pursue our choices.

This book is designed to explain how the geocentric chart shows the individual character and personality as they affect career choices. Case histories of Mata Hari and Peggy Fleming will be used throughout the book to illustrate astrological considerations and demonstrate how the personal daimon influences us to follow our chosen path. Other charts will be used to illustrate specific principles. The uses of the heliocentric chart to define personal mission outside the context of ego are included as well. I hope to uncover how we can engage in a career consistent with mission, or at least find one that accommodates an avocation that will not let us rest until we fulfill it, too.

Chapter One

Skills and Talents

Perhaps the most joyful experience for an astrologer is to see a client bloom and grow into their talents and skills. Certainly the counselor wishes to see a transition from painful situations through discoveries which bring success. This is as true for vocational searches as it is for emotional self-discovery. There are numerous methods for the astrologer to trace the threads of individual talents and skills. This chapter will address them one at a time, with a case history summary to demonstrate how they can be used in concert to reveal patterns of potential. We will consider what creativity is and how you can use astrology to discover it. You will also find helpful hints about consciously stimulating your creativity or the creativity of the people around you.

What Is Creativity?

You may be wondering how creativity affects your career. Perhaps you don't feel that the work you do is very creative, or perhaps you have creative pursuits that are not part of how you earn money. I feel it is very important to find the creativity within each of us. I believe that all people have creative capacities. I do not limit my definition of creativity to painting, music, or dance. I encourage my clients to expand their definition of creativity to include more activities.

We see creativity as the production of something new and different. Sometimes we think of God creating the world. Another definition of creativity involves climbing the ladder of success and gaining fame, the way that movie stars do. A third definition involves renewal, as when Mother Nature makes plants come up in the spring. A fourth definition involves trickery. We find this kind of creative activity in stories from all cultures. Brier Rabbit is creative when he pleads with Brier Fox, "Please, please, please don't throw me in that there briar patch." Legends of stealing fire from the gods reveal the creative minds of heroes.

My personal definition of creativity makes it an essential part of human development. Without it, I doubt children would learn to walk, language would not have developed, and we would not be able to mold the environment to suit our needs.

Creativity doesn't need to involve anything really new. Human beings as a group already know enough—we have enough facts. It is the reexamination of what we know that will be the most important creative work for us. When we can integrate the information we presently have at hand, then we can begin to resolve problems, such as pollution, abuse, and hunger, which threaten to destroy the planet. We can also apply that knowledge to the pursuit of truly satisfying vocations.

In addition, the goal of creativity need not be fame or position. I see my brother creating beautiful furniture and I am aware of the pure satisfaction involved for him, as well as for the people who buy the furniture. I watch a child draw, and I know the picture isn't for anything except the pleasure of making it. Creativity, a human virtue, is its own reward. Creativity should be considered a cardinal virtue, one to be treasured and encouraged everywhere.

Astrologically we see an emerging psyche in the natal chart. The person begins with a certain potential, goes through some period of time, picking up advantageous and detrimental baggage, and then pursues "life." He or she emerges from life's processes in a renewed form, still the same individual, but with a fresher sense of selfhood, a greater clarity of vision, and closer contact to his or her creative capacity.

"Buddhists, as well as Jung, and the alchemists, perceive that the major task to accomplish is the redemption of the divine spark within" (Moacanin, *Jung's Psychology and Tibetan Buddhism,* 92). For the Buddhist, this statement deals with a deity hidden in the unconscious. For Jung, the task is realization of the Self. The alchemists spoke of the redemption of the *anima mundi.* For Arthur Young, the process involves an informed return to a greater degree of freedom and light. What is your sense of this task for yourself? For me, the goal is to understand my whole being as an active force in the universe, not separated from the One Mind by any ignorance or error of thought or action.

Creativity is the expression of an ideal which we each find within ourselves. We each have that *prima materia* which is unique and deserves to be polished and refined. Arthur Young identifies the sense of purpose in human process, Carl Jung speaks of this process as individuation, and eastern religions address questions of enlightenment. All of these speak directly to the creative expression of our manifested individuality and its participation in Unity.

Astrology provides several potent methods for investigating creativity. These methods deserve careful examination. With your own chart in front of you, consider each technique carefully as you read the following descriptions.

Abilities Associated with the Planets

Each planet indicates vocations that are attractive, but sometimes the house or sign placement is not ideal for its pursuit. Still, the abilities are there and may be combined with other skills in a profession not usually associated with the planet being examined. Here, as with all areas of vocational astrology, it is the synthesis of many factors that results in the best vocational counseling. In accordance with the inclusion of heliocentric astrology as a tool for the vocational astrologer, each planet contains abilities associated with its higher spiritual expression. The sign the planet occupies, then, reveals the variable expressions of these qualities. Where vocation is concerned, it is essential to consider all levels of expression, as no vocation will be completely satisfying unless it addresses the complete person.

The Sun: *candidness, confidence, will power, dignity, loyalty, determination, self-consciousness, boldness, generosity, and ambition.*

The Sun deals with form and personality at the most basic level, with the soul and consciousness on the intermediate level, and with life energy on the highest spiritual level.

The Moon: *instinct, sensitivity, magnetism, romance, assimilation (mental and physical), protectiveness, rhythm, dreams, flexibility, and imagination.*

The Moon influences us by transmitting thoughts and feelings to the inner recesses of the mind. The Moon is not so much an active energy as a conduit. Hence the sign of the Moon is paramount, as it indicates the tone of the energy filtered through the Moon to the personality. The Moon shows the less conscious activities of the mind. Its strong influence occurs on the personality level. Earth's Moon serves to illuminate the hidden side of the geocentric personality. The moons of other planets serve the same role vis-à-vis that planet.

 Mercury: reason, discrimination, precision, analytical ability, resourcefulness, efficiency, refinement, versatility, communication, and expression.

The sign Mercury occupies indicates the form that self-expression takes most easily. Mercury is important on the practical level because it reflects what we know through how we communicate, and it reflects the energy of the sign it occupies and of the planets it aspects, seeming to take on their qualities in the process. Mercury's role as mediator is key to vocation. It indicates how the individual will respond to outside influences—what kind of expression we can expect from an individual. It also mediates the higher spiritual voice from deep within, allowing us to hear and interpret that voice. Mercury will aggravate us until we adjust our outward expression to suit our inner spiritual mission.

 Venus: artistic and musical ability, gentleness, rhythm, courtesy, appreciation, charm, sociability, awareness of relationships, and cooperation.

Venus serves to reveal the harmony of our thoughts, actions, and relationships. The impulse to relate things is at the foundation of knowledge. The things themselves simply exist—it is intelligence that brings them together in meaningful ways. Venus' sign and its aspects indicate how personal values are developed and the form they are likely to take.

 Mars: courage, independence, definiteness, enthusiasm, frankness, boldness, devotion to a task, determination, and assertiveness.

Mars shows how the urge to accomplish and build will be expressed. It also indicates where the war for self-mastery will be waged, and aspects to Mars indicate the weapons in this battle.

 Jupiter: generosity, expansiveness, broad-mindedness, optimism, idealism, understanding, vision, and confidence.

Jupiter reveals the natural potential to receive and to spend. Its aspects show the skill with which these activities are carried out.

Saturn: *caution, sincerity, attention to detail, punctuality, observation, self-discipline, patience, diplomacy, endurance, and compassion.*

Saturn reveals our understanding of structure, and its aspects show how we tend to operate within structure.

 Uranus: *innovation, independence, originality, ability to change, sense of adventure, intuition, and scientific approach to tasks.*

Uranus brings equilibrium, but only after turmoil. The ability to bring thinking and intuition together can be seen through aspects to Uranus.

 Neptune: *sensitivity, responsiveness, subtlety, abstract reasoning, creativity, musical talent, ability to inspire others, and sympathy.*

Neptune is impressionable, and because it is impressionable, it gives the ability to read beyond the obvious into the true nature of a situation. Yet it can also allow us to avoid the truth by clouding the issue.

 Pluto: *will, power and will power, candidness, zeal, coercion, spirituality, understanding of the life/death cycle, interest in group activities, capacity to allow ideas to ferment, sexual awareness, indifference, intemperance, ability to regenerate, and passion in all things.*

Pluto reflects the force and power of our nature. Thus it reveals by its sign the principal way we seek to establish our worth—both in terms of material possessions and in terms of self-esteem.

Dignities

Traditional astrology has provided a system of rulership and dignities that is useful in determining the strength and the relative level of constructive energy of each planet. Each planet has a certain standing in each house and sign—an advantage in some signs and a disadvantage in others. The planet has an advantage when in a sign of its dignity or exaltation, while there is a disadvantage in the signs of detriment or fall. The house rulers are determined from placing Aries in the First House, Taurus in the Second, and so on, with the house ruler being the ruler of the sign that is found there.

Domal Dignity

A planet has domal dignity in the sign it rules (also referred to as domicile). The planet has power there, and things indicated by the planet and sign are strengthened. The strength has no innate constructive or destructive qualities. These qualities are only developed by the individual through experience and practice. Thus, if an individual has primarily beneficial experiences and learns from them well, then the planet is strongly constructive, while if the experience is negative and the lessons learned are neurotic or defensive, then the planet is strongly destructive or counterproductive.

Detriment

The sign of detriment is always opposite the sign that a planet rules. The planet is at a disadvantage, in that there is some opposition to its efforts. For many people the ultimate result of planets in detriment is that the person strives to develop the qualities of the planet and, therefore, finds success by overcoming limitations. An alternative outcome is that the person gives up on the planet and never learns to express its energies completely.

An example of a planet in a dignified sign but a detrimental house is Mars in Scorpio in the Seventh House. As Mars has dignity in Scorpio, it is strong. But if Mars is placed in the Seventh House, it is in a detrimental position, as Mars is in its detriment in Libra. The position is detrimental because Mars cannot function at its full, most constructive level in Libra. There is, no doubt, an urge to associate with others and a desire for teamwork. At the same time there is a strong tendency toward the less positive expression of Mars—a tendency to depend too much on mood and feeling, and toward directness that can be harmful to the social flow. Thus, Mars has the possibility of rising to its best expression because it is in Scorpio, but suffers by being in the Seventh House.

Exaltation

Each planet expresses best in its sign of exaltation. The individual is sure to rise to a higher position where such planets are concerned, developing the innate talents and skills to great advantage. Because of this fact, even less constructive aspects tend to bring positive results. There is no logical formula for determining exaltation. For all of the planets visible without a telescope, the sign of exaltation is sextile or trine to the sign of dignity. For the outer planets, the exaltation is square to the sign of dignity. For Pluto the choice between Leo and Aquarius has not yet been determined. People with

Pluto in Aquarius include Daniel Webster, Martin Van Buren, Washington Irving, Zachary Taylor, Jacob and Wilhelm Grimm, Davy Crockett, Lord Byron, Arthur Schopenhaur, James Fenimore Cooper, Gloachino Antonio Rossini, Percy Bysshe Shelley, John Keats, and James Polk. People born between 1938 and 1958 have Pluto in Leo. We have fine examples of literary and political and philosophical giants from those born in the eighteenth century, but no clear examples to show the opposite. By the same token, we have many examples of limited success among those Pluto in Leo types, but no historical perspective on the potentially exalted success of others.

The important thing to remember is that each planet finds a sign in which it can express its energy fully and constructively. As a student it seemed odd to me that this sign was not the sign the planet was most closely tied to, but was another sign. Now this seems consistent with the fact that we often cannot express the sun sign fully, but do a more constructive job of expressing the Ascendant, or Rising Sign, as we have the ability to choose the qualities we will express, where we simply are the Sun sign.

Fall

In the sign opposite exaltation a planet is said to be in its fall. Here the planet falls from favor and must apologize for its position. Thus a planet in its fall is disadvantaged. The individual must strive harder to express that planet's qualities well, and may never feel as successful in that area of life. There will be a felt need to make excuses, even when one's actions are perfectly satisfactory. Clearly this is not a favorable position for the work place.

Accidental Dignity

A planet has accidental dignity when it falls in an angular house. This accidental standing diminishes through succedent and cadent houses. Thus angular planets will always tend to be more powerful. This is because they are associated with the Ascendant—the expressed personality, and the Midheaven, the understanding of self. The determination of accidental dignity is wholly dependent on an accurate birth time, and therefore is of no use when the birth time is suspect.

Sign Rulership: Expression of Abilities Through the Signs

Aries: I Am.   *Ruler:* Mars

Creative: *confident, courageous, proud, ambitious, enthusiastic, audacious, spontaneous, and inspired and inspiring.*

Neurotic: *egotistical, dictatorial, overbearing, impatient, resentful, sarcastic, jealous, selfish, and coarse.*

Taurus: I Have.   *Ruler:* Venus

Creative: *determined, persistent, generous, patient, retentive, stabile, enduring, and thrifty.*

Neurotic: *stubborn, possessive, sensual, vain, secretive, lazy, and attached.*

Gemini: I Think.   *Ruler:* Mercury

Creative: *alert, adaptive, restless, sensitive, tolerant, creative, active, resourceful, and open-minded.*

Neurotic: *worried, indecisive, impatient, nervous, fretful, unemotional, experimental, and diffuse.*

Cancer: I Feel.   *Ruler:* The Moon

Creative: *emotional, maternal, sympathetic, intuitive, dramatic, prudent, artistic, inspired, expressive, and cautious.*

Neurotic: *self-indulgent, possessive, frivolous, timid, lazy, dreamy, and touchy.*

Leo: I Will.   *Ruler:* The Sun

Creative: *recognized, ambitious, impulsive, persistent, aggressive, outspoken, devoted, and fearless.*

Neurotic: *conceited, overbearing, arrogant, cruel, snobbish, indulgent, dictatorial, stubborn, and selfish.*

Virgo: I Analyze.   *Ruler:* Mercury

Creative: *cerebral, scientific, honest, cautious, detailed, practical, dexterous, and precise.*

Neurotic: *fault-finding, apathetic, nervous, indecisive, skeptical, egotistical, and diffident.*

Libra: *I Balance.* **Ruler:** *Venus*

Creative: *sociable, just, neat, artistic, inoffensive, romantic, idealistic, harmonious, and impartial.*

Neurotic: *dependent or codependent, temperamental, moody, indecisive, and impatient.*

Scorpio: *I Desire.* **Ruler:** *Pluto*

Creative: *healing, sacrificing, creative, determined, forceful, tenacious, aggressive, and trustworthy.*

Neurotic: *jealous, rebellious, suspicious, sarcastic, cruel, violent, excessive, and indulgent.*

Sagittarius: *I Aspire.* **Ruler:** *Jupiter*

Creative: *athletic, religious, philosophical, reverent, zealous, cheerful, honest, and magnanimous.*

Neurotic: *dogmatic, fanatic, gullible, undisciplined, conceited, indulgent, and indolent.*

Capricorn: *I Utilize.* **Ruler:** *Saturn*

Creative: *cautious, conservative, systematic, dutiful, dependable, faithful, industrious, and efficient.*

Neurotic: *fearful, resentful, selfish, melancholy, rigid, suspicious, pessimistic, and secretive.*

Aquarius: *I Know.* **Ruler:** *Uranus*

Creative: *humanitarian, sociable, freedom-loving, scientific, metaphysical, detached, cooperative, persistent, and altruistic.*

Neurotic: *exploitative, eccentric, exacting, impetuous, rebellious, undemonstrative, and reclusive.*

Pisces: *I Believe.* **Ruler:** *Neptune*

Creative: *romantic, idealistic, universal, sensitive, mystical, sympathetic, and compassionate.*

Neurotic: *moody, hypersensitive, indecisive, secretive, impractical, negative, and discontented.*

The standing of a planet by sign and house is an indicator but not a controller of fate. Saint Theresa had no planet in its own sign, but she had the Venus in Pisces in the Twelfth House and the Sun in Aries in the First, both in double exaltation. Yet she had Neptune in Aquarius in the Eleventh (fall), and Jupiter in Gemini in the Second (detriment). Exaltation in this case serves as an indicator of her potential.

Jesse Jackson also has the Moon exalted in Taurus. He has Mars in its own sign, Aries. Yet the Sun is in fall by sign and detriment by house, and Mercury falls in the Twelfth House. He also has Neptune in detriment in Virgo and Jupiter in its detriment, Gemini. No one has all of the planets well or badly placed, and it is the effort of will that determines which energies will be developed constructively.

Balance of Planets in the Elements

Each of the five elements is representative of our various bodies' density: earth/physical, water/emotional, air/mental, and fire/spiritual. Ether is that state of being which transcends any understanding based upon material considerations. The four traditional elements "constitute different modes of operation of the One Power which, for us inhabitants of the solar system, has its primary source in the Sun" (Rudhyar, *Astrology and Personality*, 328). The Sun is the Buddha energy or ether, that which both contains and interpenetrates the whole universe.

Pythagoras described the pentagram as a union of four and one. Chinese and Tibetan astrology have settled on a five element system as well. Western astrology accommodates the five by placing the fifth element in the center of the mandala or chart. Although different five element systems seem to contradict each other in many ways, out of them I have found a combination which works for me. My conclusions are based on two things: inherent logic, and definitions of the elements as indicators or metaphors for the creative process which can then be read in the quintile aspect patterns in astrological charts.

The Creative Process of Fire

Fire is "the primordial Energy of the Divine manifesting in Matter, at so early a stage that it is not yet definitely formulated as Will" (Crowley, *The Book of Thoth*, 188). The impulse to be is found in fire, but without noticeable substance. First we identify the descent of spiritual energy into the creative word. New potentialities emerge. Second, fire contains the creative force of authority, emerging as it does directly from Unity. It

Saint Theresa
March 28, 1515
Avila, Spain
05:30:00 AM LMT
ZONE: +00:00
004W42'00"
40N39'00"

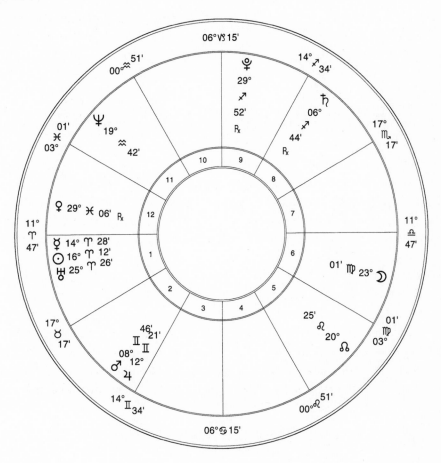

Geocentric
Tropical
Koch Houses

Figure 1. Saint Theresa's Natal Chart.

Jesse Jackson
Oct 08, 1941
Greenville, SC
09:00:00 AM EST
ZONE: +05:00
082W23'00"
34N51'00"

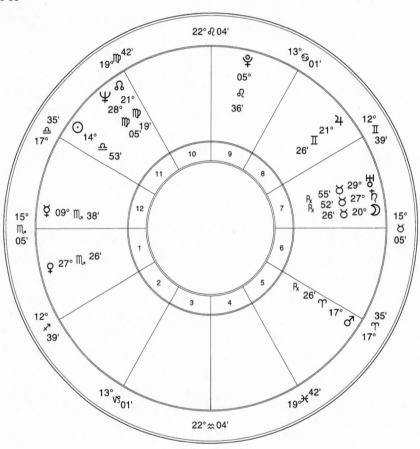

Geocentric
Tropical
Koch Houses

Figure 2. Jesse Jackson's Natal Chart.

will also provide the authority to merge once again into Unity as we ascend toward creative expression. The creative healing force of heat is the third aspect of fire. And finally there is the creative ability to look into the future and to pursue purpose. A key phrase for the fire of creative process is *to arouse*.

Vocational Significance of the Fire Element

Planets in fire signs indicate, aside from the nature of the planet itself, these personality traits:

- high-spiritedness or dispiritedness
- self-confidence or diffidence
- zest or apathy
- enthusiasm or despondency
- overexertion or lethargy
- intuition, optimism, and inspiration
- self-motivation, dedication, courage, and energy
- egotism, restlessness, and unrestrained desires.

The Creative Process of Earth

Earth represents the dharmic creativity of service. This kind of creativity is based on our understanding of the material plane, and the understanding of our own nature. Earth represents the creative capacity to identify what is. First, we can be ourselves. Then, we can exercise creative discrimination. Third, we can exercise the creative ability to lead and to assume our full authority. Finally, we can exercise the will to integration, which is the ultimate expression of alchemical earth. A key phrase for the earth of creative process is *to materialize*.

Vocational Significance of the Earth Element

Traits indicated by earth planets include:

- pragmatism or impracticality
- stability or instability
- sensuality or asceticism
- security or dispossession
- workaholism (values tied up with vocational considerations)
- cynicism (if fiery inspiration is absent)
- bigotry or narrow-sightedness.

The Creative Process of Air

The power of intellect expresses creatively through the positive, open mind. First, we find the creative ability to be aware of what is hidden. The mind allows us to experience the revelation of unconscious energies and submerged psychic structures. The creative objectivity of the air process permits us to balance what we perceive by applying thought. The creative force of social action will continue beyond an individual lifetime. Finally, we are able to creatively project an ideal into form through the air process. A key phrase of the air process is *to make known*.

Vocational Significance of the Air Element

Air planets indicate these tendencies where vocation is concerned:

- intense perception or obtuseness
- contemplation or recklessness
- intellectualism or anti-intellectualism
- discernment and judgment or lack of perspective
- rationality or irrationality
- adaptability or inflexibility (nervous exhaustion due to inflexibility)
- physical grounding or spaciness
- overspecialization or dilettantism.

The Creative Process of Water

The creative process of nourishment belongs to water. It sustains and integrates; it has the power to respond and to feel. Water can creatively reorient itself; water changes its shape to fill whatever container. Water can creatively widen experience; it flows and spreads itself as far as possible. This expansion of consciousness allows for commingling, interchange, and is indicative of interpersonal commerce. Water represents the creativity to be found in controlled passion. A key phrase for the process of water is *to nourish*.

Vocational Significance of the Water Element

Planets in water indicate these traits:

- emotional balance or imbalance
- empathy or insensitivity
- self-awareness or emotional confusion

- psychic ability and intuition or distrust of these sources of knowledge
- stoicism or intense fear of pain
- loving, compassionate, and devoted
- self-absorbed, histrionic, and extremist
- ability to eliminate toxins from the body or accumulation of toxicity.

Concentration of Air and Fire

When planets are concentrated in fire and air signs, the creative process focuses on idealistic, aspiring, optimistic, and often not very realistic ideas. There may be a limited ability to rejuvenate and lack of emotional depth. The individual is good at creative visualization. It may be easier to relate to men.

Concentration of Earth and Water

This creative combination results in great depth of personality, seriousness, endurance, and self-protectiveness. The individual may be motivated by fears, feelings, conditioning, security, and unconscious factors. There can be a tendency to become stuck in traditional roles. The individual may be able to manipulate people and the environment, and may relate to women more easily.

Concentration of Air and Earth

This combination is not so incompatible, as the rulers are the same (i.e., Taurus and Libra ruled by Venus, Virgo and Gemini ruled by Mercury, Capricorn and Aquarius traditionally ruled by Saturn). It is a good combination for business, as objectivity is combined with practical ability to get things accomplished. The individual is usually able to work with others, but prefers practical and intelligent coworkers.

Concentration of Air and Water

This combination of elements indicates a strong pull between intellect and emotion. There is often an ability to achieve depth of thought but also to maintain objectivity. The person is physically and psychologically sensitive, and it is easy to create imbalance. With a fertile imagination, creative skills, healing ability, and counseling skill, such a person can tune in on subtle energies and perceptions and to talk about them. These individuals require freedom of activity. They are often interested in arts and other creative activities.

Concentration of Fire and Earth

This is a very creative combination, but often indicates the steamroller type. It is the concentration of elemental energy that is needed to turn clay into pottery or dough into bread. Initiative and practicality combine to produce sustained powerful energy. It may be difficult to balance pride with humility, or generosity with conservatism. These individuals may sometimes be insensitive, not very self-reflective, or careless. They do have the ability to conserve and direct their personal energy.

Concentration of Fire and Water

This concentration of planets indicates an excitable, impulsive, emotional nature with a likely lack of logical thought patterns. There is an all-or-nothing approach to life with the consequent lack of restraint. There can be severe mood swings, and these people are unpredictable at times. This is a good combination for work that involves convincing others, such as entertainment or sales. The pressure cooker energy can explode from time to time.

Elements in the Astrological Chart

You may already be familiar with the following information on the signs of the zodiac and the elements they represent. If not, please take this opportunity to examine them in the context of the creative process. Each represents a particular phase of the creative process, based on its element *and* its quality (cardinal, fixed, or mutable). Thus each element expresses through each quality in one of the signs.

In exploring vocational significance, I feel it is the balance of elements that is most important. Each person is a blend of the elements. No one is exclusively one element, and no one is truly without the influence of an element. How they balance each other affects how we operate most comfortably in the world, and therefore can influence the career path we select.

Elements and Modes Through the Signs

Aries: Cardinal Fire

There is an inspired, creative, ambitious, even aggressive accumulation of wealth, difficult to satisfy. Egotism may cover a need to appear larger than one feels.

Taurus: *Fixed Earth*

There is a practical, determined, patient, and industrious approach to accumulation of money and material goods. A selfish appearance may cover a need to provide for personal security.

Gemini: *Mutable Air*

There is a mentally alert, versatile, cooperative, yet detached attitude toward money and material things. Vacillation in decisions covers an unwillingness to control the flow of one's financial affairs.

Cancer: *Cardinal Water*

There is an independent, ambitious, dramatic, and somewhat emotional approach to financial affairs. Self-indulgence masks sensitivity or an inner wish to nurture others.

Leo: *Fixed Fire*

There is a stable, determined, enterprising, even dignified tone where money and material things are concerned. An overbearing demeanor masks basic generosity and fairness.

Virgo: *Mutable Earth*

There is a utilitarian, modest, conservative, and mentally alert style of money-handling. An argumentative or fearful style masks profound honesty and a tendency toward self-denial.

Libra: *Cardinal Air*

There is a cooperative, humane, active, and enthusiastic attitude toward money and material things. Apparent extravagance reflects the desire to protect the creative spirit.

Scorpio: *Fixed Water*

There is persistence, one-pointedness, devotion, and secrecy involved in financial affairs. Sarcasm or cruelty covers an emotionally inspired competitive courage and drive.

Sagittarius: *Mutable Fire*

There is a retiring, adaptable, courageous, and idealistic approach to earning and using money. An apparent impracticality where money is concerned masks a sense of vision that goes beyond the material.

Capricorn: *Cardinal Earth*

There is an ambitious, materialistic, workman-like, or aggressive approach to handling money. A suspicious or unsympathetic attitude masks a moral and conscientious concentration of energy.

Aquarius: *Fixed Air*

There is a mentally versatile, perhaps intuitive, sense of money management, yet detached and lacking practicality. Impetuous or eccentric spending reflects an altruistic, "who cares" attitude.

Pisces: *Mutable Water*

There is a restless, responsive, romantic, or visionary attitude toward money and material things. Reclusiveness or impracticality covers a desire to insulate oneself from the outer world.

Quintile Patterns

Western astrology accommodates the five elements through the quintile aspect system. The creative process becomes evident in quintile aspects and their patterns. Just as the Tibetan Buddhist family system points to the fact that each family is in the space between elements, the quintile aspects between planets in the signs can be interpreted as the process which occurs in the movement between elements.

The perfect quintile pattern will contain one planet in each of the four traditional elements with one element doubled. The diagram included here shows the quintile star patterns, indicating how energy flows through the chart mandala; it also indicates ways to balance the energy we find in individual charts which do not contain uniform pentagram patterns.

Two basic quintile forms appear in mandalas. One is a triangle made up of quintiles and biquintiles. The second is the pentagram, the five-pointed star. This would have five quintiles around the outside, and five biquintiles forming a star on the inside. (The quintile aspect is 72 degrees, while the biquintile aspect is 144 degrees.)

A perfect star of quintiles and biquintiles always involves two planets in signs of the same element: this first aspect always stands for the Buddha energy, or the energy of the space in which the pattern exists. "The ether of space is the field in and through which the energies from the many originating Sources play" (Bailey, *Esoteric Astrology*, 9). Ether, then, provides the container in which the creative process can occur.

B. T.
March 13, 1966

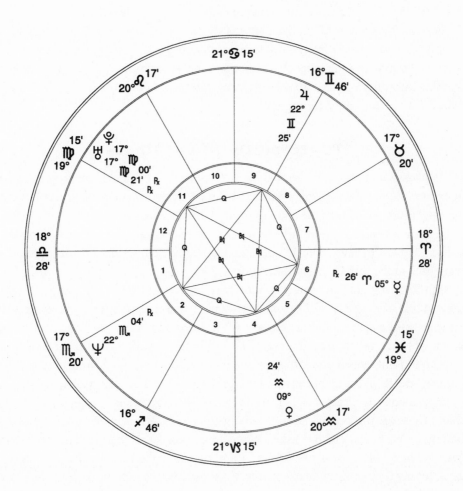

Geocentric
Tropical
Koch Houses

Figure 3. B. T.'s Natal Chart: Quintile and Biquintile Aspects.

Quintile aspects demonstrate a quintessential order by the forms they create. A mandala composed of quintiles moves directly around the circle, producing a pentagon. Biquintiles, on the other hand, produce a movement through the mandala, forming a pentagram, or five-pointed star. Quintiles describe one transit around the chart, while the biquintiles require two revolutions to complete the star.

The creative process of change begins with the ether, or mind. The end result is mind after it has been through the fully creative process. Astrologically we study a person by examining the natal chart, a map of individual potential, and we end with the same map, having been affected by progressions and transits. Yet the individual retains his or her essence throughout.

Progressions and Transits

When planets and planetary combinations (aspects) are contacted by progression or direction, there is a sustained period of time when that planet's or aspect's energy becomes more available to the conscious mind. Because we can only direct our energy in one or a few directions at any given time, we may allow some of our talents and skills to "lapse." However, they do not disappear. A strong progressed contact can bring them back to the surface for consideration.

Transiting contacts are generally shorter term. The outer planets transit at a rate close to that of progressed or directed inner planets. Transits of the inner planets are active only for a matter of hours or days, while the outer planets can have an effect for up to eighteen months. Transits generally are indicators of events on the material level. If conditions have been developing on the progressed (psychological) level, and if the potential exists (in the natal chart), then transits are timers or trigger of actual events.

Progressions or directions can stimulate creative potentials revealed in the natal chart. These are the periods of time when you are concentrating your thoughts and feelings on particular creative urges. When an appropriate transit focuses the energy, you tend to act on those urges. Keep in mind that a natal quintile aspect can be activated by any transiting contact—that is, the transiting planet can form any aspect to the natal planets in quintile to each other. This is reflective of the human tendency to think about things for some time before taking action. In fact, we often spend more time in the thinking, planning process than we do in action.

As with other factors in the vocational analysis of a chart, creativity ebbs and flows. One key to success is to know when and how to release the creative energy. Astrology certainly helps to provide a sense of where you are in the ebb and flow, and to indicate the most potent timing opportunities.

Chapter Two

The Fifth House

The Fifth House, the natural house of the Sun, is often described as the house that rules love affairs, gambling, hobbies, and children. Considering that the Sun is the most significant object in any horoscope, this list does not do justice to the Fifth House, which in fact can be said to address creativity in three forms: creation, recreation, and procreation. This list must be examined in depth to understand the importance of each activity to happiness, and to life itself. Otherwise love is reduced to casual affairs, recreation becomes an obsession with games, and procreation is unfulfilling and even destructive.

An examination of the processes involved in these three expressions of life will reveal the deeper needs of the individual and how they may be satisfied. It is interesting to note that the word *love* in English is used to cover an enormous range of human feelings. In Spanish there are two verbs: *amar* and *querer*. These differentiate between the feelings of unconditional positive regard for the loved one and the feelings of desire to be with that person. In Greek there are three words: *eros, agape,* and *philia*. Naturally, it is difficult to describe the subtleties of difference. Hindus have more than twenty words to describe love! There are English synonyms, but all lack the "heart"—the depth—of terms in other languages. *Affection, fondness, warmth,* and *liking* all suggest light and passing feelings. *Attachment, desire,* and *attraction* focus on the purely physical attributes of relationship.

It is not that we do not experience the subtle variations that love brings into our lives. An entire genre of soap operas has developed around the feelings we have for others and how we express them. Rather, we are often confused about our feelings. Parents say that they love us, yet they punish us for real or perceived shortcomings. Friends say that they love us, yet sometimes choose to go away when we need them the most. Lovers say that they love us, yet hurt us in the most poignant ways. To understand the Fifth House, we must sort out the issues of love and its results. Creation, recreation, and procreation all are results of our deepest feelings of love.

Love is an outpouring of positive thought and action. It is the unconditional positive regard that we seek from others. We seek to give that kind of unconditional positive love to others as well. When we are at our creative best, we pour our very hearts into the work, and we recognize the creative works of others that exemplify an outpouring of positive feeling. This is not to say that the only true expressions of love are aesthetically beautiful. It is the poignancy and the lasting value of works of art that demonstrate the love and care that went into their production, whether or not they suit our individual aesthetic tastes.

The Sun and Leo rule the heart. The positive, dynamic expressions of love I am talking about come from the heart—the metaphorical center of our being. The Sun is the source of life as we know it on Earth, and serves as a metaphor for the heart as the source of individual physical lives. The physical heart and its functions serve as a metaphor for the mental, emotional, and spiritual love we experience.

So, how does all of this relate to vocation or career? Because intimate expressions of sexuality are generally considered to be private and inappropriate in the workplace, this discussion will not address individual sexual inclinations. However, the same inner voice that leads us to seek sexual contact also inclines us toward other creative activities, and that is significant in terms of career. Each individual experiences the urging of the daimon, or inner voice, and each individual must, in the end, follow it. The daimon is the truest source of our unconditional positive regard for ourselves. It never lies to us, is never jealous of our success, and never boasts of its deeds. It is never arrogant, rude, irritable, nor resentful. It never rejoices in our mistakes.

The daimon is relentless. It never gives up on us, regardless of what we do. It absorbs all of our thoughts, feelings, and actions, and then reflects back a beacon of light that is consistently aimed at the goal. This inner voice never gives up. We need to listen to this voice. It is the best and truest source of information that will help us to be happy and successful. It speaks to all three of the creative processes. It tells us how and what to create to achieve our highest purpose. It tells us how to play well, considering our personal limitations. It tells us what procreative role we should pursue. In terms of vocation, it guides us ever closer to the exact actions that will satisfy our personal needs.

The range of creative expression is huge. It can include competitive activities such as sports, or legal battles, or the desire for one's company to produce the best widgets with the fewest "lemons." It can include writing in a private journal, encouraging the inner dialog with the daimon, or it can involve publication of art, writing, or musical works. As we come to see all of life's activities as creative possibilities, we also come to understand the personal daimon and learn to listen to its urges. We incidentally become truer friends, lovers, and parents because we have learned to value the inner voice in others as well as in ourselves.

Astrology provides the Fifth House map to help us understand the inner personal urges—our creative potential—and the processes that are most readily available for fulfilling those urges. Astrology also shows where we are challenged in terms of creative expression. Where vocation is concerned, this kind of information is useful because it allows us a more objective method for finding the best that life has to offer.

Some people find the proper career early in life and pursue it energetically, perhaps even ecstatically, for many years. Others always seem to be seeking the right job with the right company and the right income, and they are only satisfied for a short time, and then move on to something different. Some people do not move on, but become more and more depressed with work that does not satisfy the inner daimon.

All events or accidents in your life can be seen as integral pieces in the fulfillment of your calling. The challenges are there to show that you are somehow missing the best path, while the joys are there to show that you are indeed moving in the right direction. We each call ourselves to the best path, and therefore you are the best and only judge of how you are doing. When you find that you are unhappy, the Fifth House is a good source of information about what will work better for you.

Examination of the Fifth House shows the astrological considerations that bear on the question of creativity. What you find in the Fifth House can then be carried into your work environment, your career choice, and even into the way you earn a living. In fact, you must consider your creative process in order to fully achieve the goal of satisfying your inner self. Delineation of the Fifth House will include:

- sign on the Fifth House cusp
- the ruler of the Fifth House
- aspects of the ruler to planets in the Fifth House
- planets in the Fifth House and their aspects and
- progressions, directions, and transits to the ruler and planets in the Fifth House.

What Pleases You

The sign on the Fifth House indicates what naturally pleases you. You may think that you already know this, but a serious look at the Fifth House may reveal information that surprises you. We so often come to believe that our pleasures are those of our parents, our mates, and our friends. This is simply not the case. Rather, we choose friends who share the same pleasures, and we teach our children how we please ourselves. The sign on the Fifth House cusp indicates what pleasures are emphasized in one's life and work. When a second sign occupies the Fifth House, that sign indicates a second set of pleasures that may tend to arise later in life to demand our attention.

Sign on Fifth House Cusp

Aries: Creativity revolves around the moment of inspiration. Like a small child, you thrill to the moment of discovery, the inception of a new plan, the desire to forge ahead, and passion for all that is new. Your creative process may not be evident to others at first, but there is action nonetheless. Like a brooding hen, you warm and protect your initial ideas with the assurance that they will produce a worthwhile product. It is this initial stage of creation that most pleases you, and you like to be the idea person. You need the silent moment for the idea to take root because dissipation of the energy too soon can prevent real progress.

Taurus: You invigorate the creative process by sensing the form a project may take and fostering the development of that form. You strengthen the creative ambiance by consolidating the resources needed, providing creative structure to the growth process, and persevering when others may falter. You thrive on the comfortable knowledge that growth continues even when not much can be seen on the surface. You take the greatest pleasure in surpassing the painful moments of doubt and seeing activities through to a more comfortable outcome. "We did it," can become your mantra.

Gemini: Your creativity lies in the ability to diversify an idea. You could have been the original fractal designer, taking one idea and working it into many. You thrive on sharing creative process with others, and brainstorming is your forte. You have the capacity to take a broad view of things, not becoming overly attached to details. When you come back down to earth, you bring with you the sense of space in which to implement your ideas.

Your greatest pleasure lies in sharing your experience, and you work well in situations where teamwork is encouraged.

Cancer: Your creative power lies in the ability to rest with thoughts and feelings, to allow them to run their course without interference. Your fertile mind is able to soak up facts; you thrive in situations where you can apply that knowledge to problem solving. You tend to immerse yourself in projects, and may need to take a moment out for yourself to enjoy the process. You take pleasure in the fact that you can manifest stillness even in the midst of an intense work effort. You are at your best creatively when you work with the natural direction of life, not fighting the currents around you.

Leo: You have the will to create and the stamina to see a process through to completion. You are self-reliant. Your urge for offspring can focus on children, or it can be directed toward some other manifestation in the material world. You thrive on the process of bringing ideas to fulfillment, on the heat of production, if you will. You want assurance that your works will survive you in some way. Your creative heat is like an oven that bakes bread or fires pottery. You recognize that creativity takes a certain amount of time and cannot be rushed. You take the greatest pleasure from the pregnant process of development, whatever the line of work you pursue.

Virgo: Your creative strength lies in the ability to analyze situations and see beyond the obvious. You are able to accumulate data from sources that others may overlook, digging deep into the meat of a problem. You are the ultimate systems analyst, whatever the system may be. You can test the end product, finding pleasure in discovering its best qualities as well as its correctable faults. Others may have had the idea to produce diamonds from coal; you are the one who can see and measure the results in detail, thriving on the final refinement into true gems.

Libra: Your creative eye focuses on refinement and elegance, both in the process itself and in the result. For you means do not justify the ends if the means are messy and undignified. The ends are satisfying only when they have the stamp of quality that elegance suggests. You thrive on the creation of glamour around your work, but not if it detracts from its meaningfulness. You take the greatest pleasure in partnerships, and therefore work best in situations where you have someone with whom to share projects. You are able to balance the objective and subjective perspectives in your creative work.

Scorpio: You are often at your creative best when others cannot see anywhere to go. You have a somewhat ruthless ability to hang on and survive, and, in fact, you thrive on crises. You understand the cycle of birth and death, and can see past the end of a cycle. Your creative work demands steady attention to achieve a complete transformation. Your greatest pleasure is found in work that achieves the birth of something new and wonderful out of something old and dead. Your feelings are always an integral part of your creative process.

Sagittarius: Creativity for you involves the spiritual side of life. You find pleasure in being inspired and in inspiring others to fulfill their greatest potential. You are quietly creative, immersed in thought. You seek to blend your experience of the physical world, your educational process, and your intuition into a spiritually pleasing, creative admixture where nature and art co-mingle. You are the individual who can see beyond the initial idea, through the building process, and, yes, past the completion of a project. You are able to envision the effect of your work on the world and to transform creative energy into a spiritual tool.

Capricorn: Your creativity lies in the ability to focus on yourself and your personal process. Your serious attitude toward life, the planning and striving for success, form a large part of your creative life. You thrive in the midst of change because you are able to keep one eye on the job and the other on the larger goal. You take the greatest pleasure from taking the materials at hand and producing concrete results. Never one to wait until the optimum conditions exist, you make conditions change to suit you. Your self-control is not the result of lack of emotion, but rather emerges from your self-examination and understanding.

Aquarius: You are a master planner, able to wait for just the right moment to take action. Your creative talent lies in acting decisively when that moment arrives. You are a good observer of human nature, yet you can maintain a suitable distance when that is required. You thrive is situations where you can remain detached enough to see the overall picture, and you desire a certain freedom. If you are able to analyze your inner feelings and thoughts, your creativity is unlimited. You find pleasure in your ability to convince others of your viewpoint.

Pisces: Your creativity grows from a place of serenity where you can see the goal and the path as part of a seamless unity. Because you do not approach life piecemeal, career considerations must be part of the unity or you will not be happy. You thrive in situations where you participate in the larger vision of the future and not isolated to contend with the details. Your intuition is a vital part of the creative process. Your greatest pleasure comes in situations where you can creatively demonstrate the compassionate side of your nature.

Life's Pleasures

Each of us naturally chooses activities that appeal to us. We also choose the part of an activity that has the greatest appeal. The planetary ruler of the Fifth House is an indicator of the activities you tend to find most pleasing, and by extension, what work activities will captivate your attention most easily. Its house position indicates the area of your life where you seek pleasure most naturally. The sign occupied by the ruler reveals the strategies you are most likely to employ to satisfy your creative impulses. As you consider these, remember that these are not the only ways for you to demonstrate creativity. They are simply the basic, bottom line approaches to satisfaction that you tend to utilize.

House of Planetary Ruler of Fifth House

First House: You are most creative when you are both the source of the ideas and the implementer. You are quite capable of designing and developing products, as well as producing results in your chosen field.

Second House: You require a comfortable setting in which to work if your creativity is to be maximized. However, what is comfortable for you may include unusual settings where you must roll up the shirt sleeves and dig into the work.

Third House: Your creativity works best in areas where communication flows freely. Thus any career that involves travel, computers, or any form of communication will appeal to you. You can manage two or three projects at one time.

Fourth House: You can be quite happy working at home amid familiar surroundings. Some of your best ideas appear while you have your feet up, relaxing in your own easy chair. Your creativity may seem like it came from your parents' generation—it is that solid.

Fifth House: Young people can inspire your creativity. Their natural capacity for the new and interesting pushes your thought process. You may also do well in sports, either as part of a team or as an individual participant. Activity is the key, not competition.

Sixth House: You need a designated area where you can stash your personal belongings, situate yourself, and dig into the work. You may find that you like an office with a door to leave open—or to be closed when you choose.

Seventh House: Your creativity works best in partnership with others. You may feel stifled by overly assertive supervisors and even resent any appearance of control by others. Yet you may also feel isolated if no one is around to share in the creative process.

Eighth House: Your creative process can be expressed in situations where change is the name of the game. The unusual appeals to you and you see transformation as the primary creative outcome.

Ninth House: Your creativity involves the transcendental or spiritual in some way, so you seek positions that enhance your ability to see the larger picture and to mold it. You may become a powerful teacher who facilitates creativity in others.

Tenth House: Your creative process can manage the most public demonstrations. This is probably because you do your homework ahead of time, but you are known for the results you achieve, not for behind the scenes activities.

Eleventh House: You are a huge asset in any crisis, as you are at your most creative under pressure. Whether working with a group or alone, you are able to think your way through difficulties and come out on top of most situations.

Twelfth House: Your creative efforts blossom in private, where you are allowed to try out ideas without concern for what others may think. There is plenty of time for them to evaluate your work when you are finished, if you are in the optimum working situation.

Sign of Fifth House Ruler

Aries: Your creative process is complemented by assertive energy. You can take the initiative when it is necessary, and you have a penetrating mind. You bring enthusiasm and energy to your work, and can be spontaneous. You sometimes seem too forceful to others.

Taurus: You like to focus on practical considerations and leave daydreams to others where work is concerned. You measure success in terms of results. Results for you include completion, harmony, and dependability, all managed in a timely manner.

Gemini: Your mental creativity is certainly a career asset. Generally open-minded, you are also able to speak your mind. You can be a valuable mediator in difficult situations. Avoid the appearance of superficiality in your work or your speech.

Cancer: You bring a decided dramatic touch to your work, and this keeps you interested and interesting. Often your impressions of situations are right on the mark, so don't discount them. You can add an artistic touch to the final product.

Leo: While the approval of others is nice, it is self-approval that you ultimately need. You are able to carry off the dignity required in stressful situations. Your fearlessness can get you into tight situations, but is a valuable career asset most of the time.

Virgo: You bring diligence and orderly procedures to your creative work, giving it a logical balance. You are capable of being overly critical, and you recognize that quality in others. Your methodical approach solves many problems without undue stress.

Libra: Your sociability contributes to your creative efforts in the work environment. While you desire a position of importance, you are able to work well with others in positions at, above, or beneath yours. Manners are a strong asset.

Scorpio: You have a strong will and you enjoy that quality in others, as long as they don't get in your way. You feel passionately about things and you are fearless in the face of danger and criticism—sometimes even a bit reckless.

Sagittarius: You bring a philosophical attitude to your work and you are able to adapt to rather different circumstances. You thrive in situations that require an open-minded look at the facts.

Capricorn: You can achieve more than most people because of your sheer determination. It is imperative that you have creative outlets in your work environment, so watch out if your responsibilities begin to seem like drudgery.

Aquarius: Your creativity is aided by strong powers of observation and the willingness to participate in a group effort. You understand human nature in general, but may not be quite as clear when it comes to individual differences.

Pisces: Your receptivity puts you in a position of being in on the creative pulse of most situations. You are able to keep a secret, however, and this is a valuable asset in the work environment. You need to maintain a positive outlook, or create one.

Whose Company Do You Enjoy?

Planets in the Fifth House are the most direct indicators of the playmates that you choose. The planets are the actors, and the Fifth House is your stage where creativity is concerned. Where vocation is concerned, these types of people are often the easiest for you to work with, as they tickle your creative fancies.

Creative Expression of Planets in Fifth House

Sun: You enjoy working with powerful, proud people: those in authority, military personnel, royalty, heroic types, cabinet officers, politicians, judges, and public officials. You also may like to be around bankers, stock brokers, biochemists, foremen, jewelers, or public utility workers. You especially work well with men, and anyone in the entertainment industry. Finally, children may be a strong element in your creative entourage.

Moon: You can be creative around a wide range of emotional types, from crazy people to folks who work with children, airline flight attendants to staff members at the gym, from housewives and domestic servants to nurses, midwives, and obstetricians. You enjoy commerce, so exhibitors at fairs, grocers, bakers, shopkeepers, sales people, and the public are likely to stimulate your creativity. Night-workers, watchmen, and bartenders appeal to your nocturnal inclinations. You may even feel creative in an aquatic environment.

Mercury: Details stimulate your mind, so accountants, bookkeepers, educators, engineers, and handwriting experts are all people that you may enjoy. You also can be at your creative best with advisors, agents, announcers, artisans, attorneys, broadcasters, clerks, computer programmers, and others whose work focuses on a multitude of information. Service professions such as gas station employees, nannies, inspectors, and teachers stimulate you to creative achievement as well. Add to the list careers involving finesse, such as locksmiths, jugglers, and ambassadors.

Venus: Clothing manufacturers, art dealers, artists, composers, beauticians, and anyone whose work involves elegance and beauty will appeal to your creative side. Women may be more likely to inspire you. You could provide services for florists, musicians, or even be a bridal consultant. The idea is that you need aesthetics to pervade your work if your creativity is to develop fully. The justice system, particularly judges and juries, could be part of your creative scene.

Mars: Movement is the name of your creative game, and the players will be movers too. You could be around acrobats, athletes, masseurs, firemen, and steelworkers—anyone whose job is physically active. People who use tools and weapons, such as soldiers, gangsters, hunters, and guards may get you going. You could run an army or perhaps supply it. You could work with doctors or pharmaceuticals as well. To be creative you have to be active.

Jupiter: You enjoy being around "true" professionals, so look to attorneys, ambassadors, professors, supreme court justices, or accomplished writers to stimulate your creativity. You could also find that people associated with these professions are just your type, such as journalists, critics, deputies, or registrars. It is the atmosphere of philosophy, learning, and judgment that appeal to you.

Saturn: You are most creative in structured situations, so you will do well around accountants, vocational counselors, chemists, civil engineers, and government workers—anyone whose work depends on organization and structure. You manage responsibility creatively. You can find the creative elements in the work of systems analysts, economists, landlords, and masons. It's the structure of things that attracts and holds your attention.

Uranus: Your unusual approach to the creative makes you comfortable with a wide range of professionals. From astrologers to cartoonists, electricians to gun makers, magicians to promoters, you can fit into the career scene easily. You find that change, even dramatic change, is an integral part of your creative process. You are often able to see into the behavior of others and may work well with psychologists and psychiatrists, researchers of all kinds, sports figures, and even travel agents.

Neptune: Your creative imagination takes you through the veil of reality into another world, populated with artists, movie stars, detectives, and spiritual counselors. You are able to take ideas and manifest them in the material world for others to see. You enjoy being around people who can let their imaginations emerge in their work, like illustrators, writers, and occult practitioners. Hospital and pharmacy employees, opticians, or anyone who changes our perceptions of the world are interesting as well.

Pluto: You enjoy applying your will to creative tasks, and you like to surround yourself with powerful people. This might include the criminal element, but also extends to a wide range of professionals like atomic scientists, chemists, archeologists, and even funeral directors. Water treatment, weather forecasting, and animal control workers may attract your eye in some way, as well as psychics, alchemists, and social welfare advocates.

Peggy Fleming
July 27, 1948
San Jose, CA
03:00:00 PM PDT
ZONE: +07:00
121W54'00"
37N20'00"

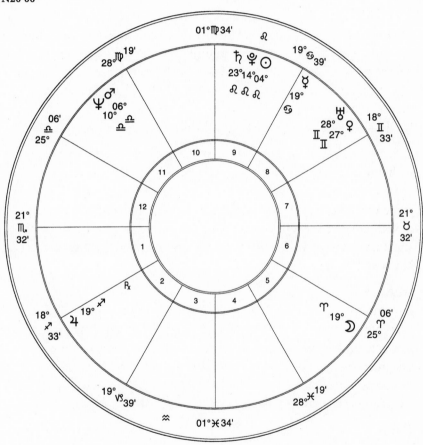

Geocentric
Tropical
Koch Houses

Figure 4. Peggy Fleming's Natal Chart.

Mata Hari
Aug 07, 1876
Leeuwarden, NETH
01:00:00 PM LMT
ZONE: +00:00
005E46'00"
53N12'00"

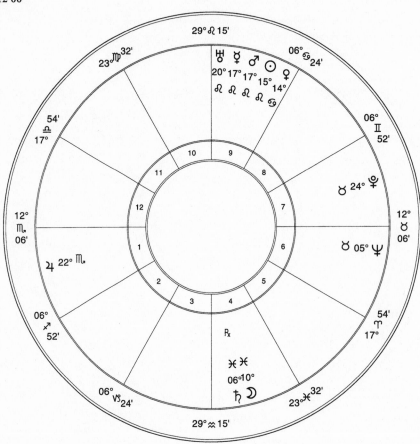

Geocentric
Tropical
Koch Houses

Figure 5. Mata Hari's Natal Chart.

Factors That Influence Creativity

Aspects involving the Fifth House show what factors tend to arise to change your path toward satisfying your inner voice. By their nature they indicate the relative ease with which you can satisfy personal goals. Aspects both to the ruler and to planets in the Fifth indicate how the drama of creativity plays out for you.

Directions, Progressions, and Transits

Over time your awareness of the inner dialogue will shift. You begin to perceive nuances in the process, and tend to seek satisfaction in new or subtler ways. When the Fifth House is aspected by direction or progression, new cycles of feeling enter the picture. Your emotional tone may shift for extended periods of time, and this will be reflected in your willingness to consider different creative activities. Transits tend to focus the cyclical tone by bringing new characters into the drama and giving old players new lines. The challenges change and the results allow you to evaluate progress toward your personal goals. They provide mileposts in your creative life.

Examples from Life

Peggy Fleming and Mata Hari both have Pisces on the Fifth House cusp. In Peggy's case, most of Aries is also in the Fifth. For Mata Hari, Pisces takes up about a third of the house. Both women have a natural focus on inner composure and serenity where pleasure is concerned. They recognize the need for these qualities in others as well, and much of their vocational activity addresses these needs, if in very different ways. Both thrived on the drama of the spotlight and sought to achieve the most perfect expression of their chosen creative talents. For both the fascination had to come from the perception of an inner light that shone in their actions. Mata Hari focused on the sexual drama, both in her espionage career and in her performances, drawing her audience in through sexuality. Peggy Fleming was able to capture the serenity of oneness with the daimon, the composure needed for winning competitions, and the emotional connection to her audiences that made them one with her on the ice.

Both women experienced the need to change career direction. Mata Hari continued to be at the center of action up to her arrest as a spy. Peggy's center shifted from skating to her family, and then to broadcasting and commentary on her sport. In each woman, a natural progression can be seen. Mata Hari met the firing squad at age forty-one. Peggy Fleming has had better luck, perhaps due to her ability to follow the voice of the daimon toward greater serenity and a deepening of unfolding self-awareness.

With no planets in the Fifth, Mata Hari's creative impulses depend on the placement of Neptune in the Sixth House. Neptune is sextile Saturn and the Moon in the Fourth. She made use of opportunities to structure her fantasies and used her imagination to create an exotic dance routine that carried her to Paris and then Berlin. Peggy Fleming has the Moon in the Fifth squaring Mercury and trining Jupiter, Saturn, and Pluto. She has natural grace and power, coupled with the ability to structure her life around practice and school, then around family. Her creativity is instinctive and she has natural self-confidence that is backed up by ambition and responsible behavior. We see again two very different ways for Fifth House energy to manifest.

Chapter Three

How Do You Work Best?

In astrology we are always looking for the abnormal in the chart—the unusual arrangement of planets and aspects. Where we find the normal distribution of any astrological factor, we find the average and the usual. It is in imbalance that we find interesting details about character. Each of us has to learn to work with our abnormal traits and habits. Life is not about changing those habits, at least not most of the time. It is about choosing to emphasize one set of behaviors over another. Out of this character is born. If we constantly changed our behaviors, we would never settle into the strength of character that we need. Generally, when we desire to change ourselves, we aim to change how we understand and work with our inner being, and to accept that being.

The astrological chart reveals how people operate in the world, and thus how they will function in the work environment. This is found by evaluating:

- the element in which the Sun and Moon are found, and the sign in which the Midheaven and Ascendant are located
- the progressed or solar arc positions of these points
- the position of the planets relative to the Midheaven and Ascendant in the zodiac, including the hemisphere and quadrant that the planets occupy and
- the speed of the Moon and the position of Mercury relative to the Sun.

All of these factors are fundamental components of the astrological chart. They are simple to calculate and profound in their significance. Planetary positions and lunar speed do not require an accurate birth time, and thus can be used in the most cursory evaluation of a chart for a particular date. The Midheaven, Ascendant, and quadrant placement of planets contribute to a fuller interpretation of a chart cast for the birth time of an individual.

The Sun

The Sun sign element is indicative of the primary psychological type. Individuals do not necessarily conform to this, especially if they have been encouraged to pursue the preferences of their parents. I resisted the idea of being a water type because my family is full of air and fire types, or they were raised by others who were definitely air types. I had to learn to accept my predisposition to favor the water element. Nevertheless, it is consistent with what we know of the signs that the primary approach to life is through the Sun sign. Hence we can learn a lot from exploring the positive and negative facets of our own Sun sign element.

The Moon

We all have a secondary psychological function that is indicated by the Moon sign. The secondary function offers assistance when the primary function is not complete. Jungian psychology suggests that the functions are each part of an individual's particular approach to the world. These break down into four basic functions of consciousness which are related in pairs: thinking versus feeling, and sensation versus intuition. If a function is dominant, its pair is relatively absent from consciousness. The remaining pair form secondary functions that develop as skill sets that support the dominant function.

In cases where the Sun and Moon are in the same element, the individual will tend toward another prominent planet to develop the secondary function, and may have more than one very strong secondary ability. In cases where the Sun and Moon are in opposite elements (fire and air, or earth and water) the individual has a unique mastery of unconscious material at an early age, a mastery that either takes many years for the rest of us to develop, or is never truly achieved. However, a person born with this combination may lack the adjunct functions that fill in gaps for the rest of us. These people tend to be on a straight and very narrow path so that, like a tightrope walker, they possess an intense focus which they cannot allow to waver.

Elements as Psychological Indicators

Fire: Intuitive

Intuitive types listen to their unconscious sources of information, eschewing normal physical perception. In fact, they are often largely unaware of what is in the immediate environment. These people are the inventors, artists, and visionaries because they can see the possibilities of an idea, often before the means of developing it are apparent. Therefore, they pursue what they know the world is not yet prepared for. Fire types jump to conclusions, but not necessarily without the intermediate steps. They either fly through those steps at the speed of light by sizing up an underlying principle, or simply recognize an inevitable match of an idea's potential with their own desires.

The intuitive fits into the educational system rather well, as many high school and college courses make use of the deductive skills that intuitives share with the thinking type. They respond well to the timed testing that is prevalent today. They master the complexities of mathematics because they can grasp the results without having to ground their learning in linear reasoning.

Intuitives contribute through their inventiveness. They are willing to sacrifice the pleasure of the moment in the hope of greater future achievement. They are often restless and crave inspiration. Because they thrive in situations where getting to the answer is important, they are good at problem-solving and tasks that require ingenuity. Careers in the creative arts, religious inspiration, and scientific discovery all suit the intuitive type. They make inspired leaders and promoters. For them the game is more important than winning, the chase more interesting than the end result.

Mata Hari and Peggy Fleming's Leo Suns cast them both as intuitive types. Mata Hari demonstrated her intuitive ability throughout her extended career as a spy, constantly calculating what to do regarding her less than certain future—she *knew* other people's next moves.

Peggy's success as a skater and broadcaster both reflect her creative intuition. She has been able to intuit what people want and how she can best supply the proper action and tone. Her skating always had the seamless quality that only intuitive certainty can provide—she *knew* what to do next.

If there are no planets in fire signs in a chart, then the career lacks spirit. There is a pessimism that, by doubting a favorable outcome, debilitates the will. Self-confidence may be poor. Such a person will choose a career that provides little challenge or stress. To counteract these less constructive tendencies, the individual can rely on the other elements: planets in earth show the kinds of weightlifting or other physical exercise that will stimulate the physical system and activate the fire that lies deep within the unconscious. Similarly, air planets point to suitable thinking processes and activities, while water planets show where flows of energy can be established.

Earth: Sensation

Sensation types are primarily interested in practical considerations of the world. They will look at the facts first. They depend on their five normal senses for perception. They wish to have experience, not hear about it from others. Sensation types learn by doing, so the learning process may be slower. To be satisfied, they need to go over things carefully. They are not less intelligent because they go slower—they are more careful. When given the time to assimilate information, the sensation type may remember it longer and understand the practical uses in more detail. Studying the theory of engineering may be difficult for the sensation type, but application is their forte.

The earth type demands satisfaction along the way, and will not select occupations that lack positive feedback. They are healthy consumers, loving life and what it has to offer on the material level. They are best in careers that involve real "stuff." They make good real estate people, interior decorators, and chefs. They enjoy working with their hands and can make this a vocation or at least an avocation. They make good doctors and health care professionals. Any career that requires attention to and intimate understanding of details is suited to the sensation type.

A lack of earth in the chart indicates individuals who are not attuned to the practical physical world. They are ungrounded in day-to-day activities and often seem unable to provide for their own physical and security needs. They tend to have unrealistic expectations in the career area and may drift from one job to another without apparent direction. To overcome a lack of earth, they can use planets in air to apply logic to their situation. When logic requires practical action, they will act. They can use fire planets to inspire their thoughts to "imagine" what a practical course would be like. They can use water planets to "pump up" their awareness of the world by focusing on the flow of events, if not the events themselves.

Sigmund Freud had the Sun in Taurus. His psychology was built on the principle that a root cause for a problem could be found, and that the finding itself would produce a cure. The reductionist theory is, at its heart, based on the sensation function. He gave us a framework for understanding mental illness. He used his Gemini

Moon, representing the secondary function of thinking, to bring logic to the experience of psychoanalysis. Using Freud's methods we find the "why" of life in a root cause for our illness.

Carl Jung has the Sun in Leo and Moon in Taurus. The thrust of his analytical psychology was to reach deep into human experience with his intuition, following his heart, as it were, to find the meaningful pieces in a patient's life—pieces that may or may not have been related to childhood events. He then took the practical step of finding the ground on which to build the rest of one's life. His psychology has given us a framework for understanding our humanity and moving into wellness.

Air: Thinking

Thinking types tend to be less personal in their approach to the world. They focus on an objective truth that they hope to find, and not on the people in their path. They choose to be logical. They choose to be truthful. They choose to be argumentative—after all, they have argued with themselves enough times! They are usually able to go through a thought process once and stop, without needing to re-evaluate. Air types benefit from an education that includes logical training, but they remain one-sided if they skip opportunities to appreciate the people and things around them. They judge the world through a logical process that seldom admits consideration of feelings.

Thinking types are good in careers where it is important to organize and assess quantities of information. They tend to be somewhat more businesslike, able to "cut to the chase" in planning as well as performance. They contribute to society through intellectual criticism, through the exposure of wrongdoing, and through scientific research. They perform well in executive positions, partly because such positions are more impersonal. They are willing to tell the truth, even when it is not convenient.

Charles Darwin and Abraham Lincoln had the Sun in Aquarius and the Moon in Capricorn. They were both deep thinkers and applied logical processes to the understanding of their fields. They each had a practical strategy for supporting that logic with concrete action. They both contributed documents to history which radically changed our fundamental thinking (see chapter 13).

A lack of air planets causes individuals to fail to think problems through to solutions. They distrust people who are able to do this and seek career situations where thinking *per se* is not emphasized. They have difficulty adjusting to new ideas and therefore avoid change in the work environment, hence sabotaging their own potential for promotion. Water planets can be used to engender a positive regard for thinkers and their power. Fire planets can focus intuition and lead to the logical implementation of it. Earth planets can provide solid grounding that permits practical application of one's experience to the present.

Water: Feeling

If earth types say, "Just the facts, ma'am," water types say, "How does it feel when that happens?" Water types evaluate situations on the basis of sentiment and disregard logical processes as ineffective with others and unsatisfying to themselves.

Feeling types are successful in careers that call for sensitivity in relating to others. They have the ability to bridge the gap between people, and therefore make good counselors, sales people, heads of families, and members of the clergy—any job where interpersonal relationships are at the core of productive work.

Dr. Charli has the Sun in Cancer (see chapter 8). Her primary function, feeling, comes across strongly in the delineation of a healing career path. With the Moon in a fire sign, she has the intuitive capacity to see into the future needs of clients, and thus she will be able to help them through the difficult present. She can facilitate her clients' discover of their creative energy.

Lack of water can produce all manner of personal psychological and emotional ills. Yet on the surface this element seems less necessary in the work place, without it the smooth functioning of the other elements can be disrupted. There also can be an innate fear or distrust of intuitive types which can be overcome by evaluating their results, not their methods. Earth planets can focus attention on the physical requirements of the body, thereby reducing the potential for illness. Air planets can focus on what is the next requirement in a given situation, placing a logical value on things when the person cannot determine the value of feeling.

The Current Mode of Thinking

As the planets move by progression or direction into new signs, the balance of the elements will change. These shifts allow the individual to experience each of the elements and to develop skills associated with them. Thus, no one goes through life totally lacking an element. The periodic shifts provide for the learning experiences we need to achieve balance within an otherwise lopsided personality, if we take advantage of the learning opportunities as they are presented. By looking at the current progressions or directions, you can see where you can focus your energies differently from your typical (natal) style.

Consider all planets that have changed element by the selected method of progression. A sample delineation of the change might look like this:

> You have Venus in Capricorn, an earth element, in your natal chart. By solar arc direction you have Venus in Aquarius, an air sign. Your natural direction where harmony is concerned is to proceed on a practical basis and to seek immediate material solutions to problems. At this time you have the potential to grow through logical considerations of how factors in the work environment may most likely evolve. By considering the logical outcome, you give yourself another way to evaluate problems and deal with them.

Other Psychological Factors

The organization of the overall chart reflects other psychological tendencies. The hemisphere emphases reveal the tendency toward extraversion (I prefer Jung's usage) or introversion (day and night hemispheres) and also active or responsive styles (left or right hemispheres). These differences influence the career path by steering the native toward particular activities in general, and contribute to the development of specific skills that work better in some careers than others. They also influence the "slice" of a particular career pie that will be most attractive.

These considerations depend on an accurate birth *time*, as time determines the house placement of the planets. Even if you use cosmobiology or another system that does not consider house placement, the above arrangement is still important. The portion of the zodiac between the Ascendant and the Nadir is the first, between the Nadir and Descendant in the second, the space between the Descendant and the Midheaven is the third, and between the Midheaven and the Ascendant is the fourth quadrant.

Introvert or Extravert: Below or Above

When planets fall in the lower half of the chart (the night side), this is one indication that the individual is driven by internal considerations. Planets in the upper half (day side) of the chart indicate that the individual will consider external factors where those planets are concerned. The relative balance of planets above or below the horizon, then, is one indicator of a more introverted or extraverted personality.

In psychological terms, the introvert judges the world in terms of what events mean for him and is not as responsive to others as the extravert. Life's activities tend

Carl Jung
July 26, 1875
Kesswil, SWTZ
07:20:00 PM LMT
ZONE: +00:00
009E20'00"
47N36'00"

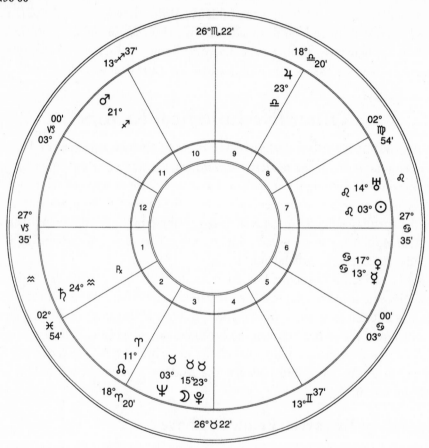

Geocentric
Tropical
Koch Houses

Figure 6. Carl Jung's Natal Chart.

Sigmund Freud
May 06, 1856
Freiberg, GER
06:00:00 PM LMT
ZONE: +00:00
013E20'00"
50N54'00"

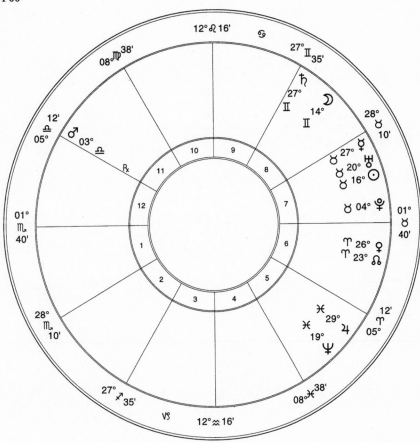

Geocentric
Tropical
Koch Houses

Figure 7. Sigmund Freud's Natal Chart.

Abraham Lincoln
Feb 12, 1809
Hodgenville, KY
02:10:00 AM LMT
ZONE: +00:00
085W44'00"
37N34'00"

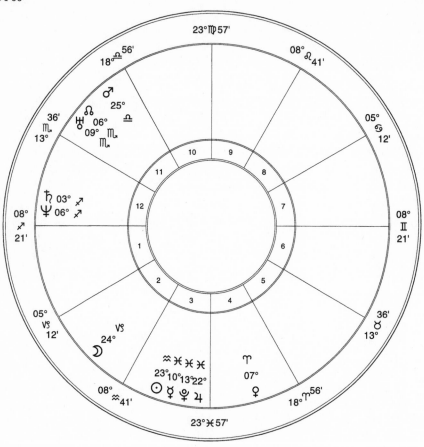

Geocentric
Tropical
Koch Houses

Figure 8. Abraham Lincoln's Natal Chart.

Charles Darwin
Feb 12, 1809
Shrewsbury, ENG
06:00:00 AM LMT
ZONE: +00:00
002W45'00"
52N43'00"

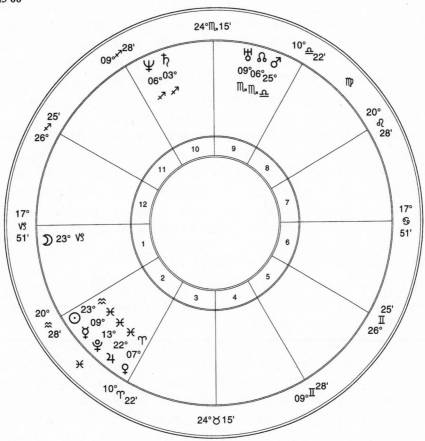

Figure 9. Charles Darwin's Natal Chart.

Geocentric
Tropical
Koch Houses

to be measured on an internal, personally unique basis. In introversion one's thoughts refer more to the self, to what is within the individual. Introverts must understand what life offers before they jump into it. If there is a real world for them, it is the inner world of ideas and subjective understanding. They tend to insulate themselves against the outer world in favor of the inner life.

The extravert evaluates events external to the self. For such an individual the parents, siblings, and other people are the basis for personal decisions. In extraversion the flow of energy is outward; one's thoughts mainly concern external objects. These people live life first and then figure it out afterward. They are usually relaxed and confident, plunging into the water before they know how deep it is. Conduct is essentially governed by external conditions. They tend to unload their emotions as they go along and take an expansive attitude toward everything.

The difference between these two types lies in attitude, not ability. The introvert's attitude is one of self-awareness, while the extravert's attitude is one of awareness of the world around the self. The introvert is more attentive to the inner life, while the extravert is more object-oriented. It is important to remember that no one is all one way or the other. At times we experience movement from the inner life outward and vice versa. The healthy individual learns how to integrate the aims of each attitude.

Active or Responsive: Left or Right

Planets in the east or west sides of the chart are indicative of the continuum of energy from totally self-motivated and self-controlled to totally responsive or reactive to other people and to situations outside the self.

Planets in the eastern hemisphere indicate areas where people have the potential to develop, to increase their skills and awareness. There is movement in the direction of greater personal control where these planets are concerned. The emphasis on planets in the eastern hemisphere indicates that they like to be in command of situations and create their own circumstances. Even if they work for other people, they like to be responsible for their own work. They are able to exercise initiative and find ways to apply will power to projects. They like to see their projects grow and generally will put in the necessary energy for this to happen. They tend to measure success in terms of personal results.

By contrast, planets in the western hemisphere indicate where one experiences a lessening of personal control and an increased tendency to react to outer influences—to respond to the needs and desires of other people. There is the potential to dissolve conditions which are rigid within the personality and to interact with others in a more beneficial manner.

The emphasis of planets in the western hemisphere indicates people who tend to merge their feelings and ideas with other people, caring less for personal ownership and more for cooperative effort. They often make choices that are more beneficial to the people around them, recognizing that they gain more satisfaction from helping others. They make strong facilitators because they are naturally aware of how other people feel and thus are able to provide the motivation and circumstances for them to be successful. They measure your own success in terms of the worldly results.

Each quadrant has two of the four components, and the quadrants speak to the major focus of the personality:

Lower Left: Houses One, Two, and Three form the first quadrant of introverted action. Planets in this quadrant focus one's attention on the self and persona (what we show to the world); the possessions (financial worth) and feelings (self-worth); expression of the self to others; and learning about the immediate environment. This is the area of life over which we have the greatest potential control, as we are the only ones who even know the true content of ourselves. We are also the ones who decide how to act toward others, and we are the source of personal motivation to learn and to communicate.

Lower Right: Houses Four, Five, and Six form the second quadrant of introverted response. This is the area where we respond to others, at home, in personal relationships, and in the work environment. Planets here indicate the ways we choose to relate to the world. Here can be seen the basis for our fundamental beliefs (learned largely through our families in childhood); our attitudes toward all objects of personal love, such as mate, child, or pet, friend; how we choose to respond to the needs of others; our work habits; and our attitudes toward employees.

Upper Right: Houses Seven, Eight, and Nine form the third quadrant of extraverted response. The third quadrant places us as individuals on an equal footing with others. Planets here indicate how we choose to cooperate with people around us and how we choose to grow in that process. We can evaluate how we relate on a one-to-one basis with a partner (or an overt enemy); how the sexual response works; what we receive from others; how we share feelings; and how we engage a higher philosophy and relate to social values.

Upper Left: Houses Ten, Eleven, and Twelve form the quadrant of extraverted action. Planets here indicate the personal roles of leadership—how we exercise authority and earn respect; how we act in nonintimate situations with friends and groups; how we set objectives; how the psychic or inner life develops (the subconscious mind); and how we work in seclusion.

Patterns of Thinking: Moon/Mercury Relationship

The relationship between the Moon and Mercury is indicative of how the mind functions. It is easy to assess, as it does not depend on the birth time. There are four possible combinations:

- Mercury ahead of the Sun and Moon fast
- Mercury behind the Sun and Moon slow
- Mercury ahead of the Sun and Moon slow or
- Mercury behind the Sun and Moon fast.

Moon Fast or Slow

A look at the ephemeris will tell the daily motion of the Moon, which varies between 11 and 14 degrees per day (average about 13 degrees and 10 minutes per day). When the Moon is slow, the individual tends to consider all things carefully and rarely jumps into any situation too quickly. The fast Moon, by contrast is the "eager beaver" type, the person who is always into the next activity ahead of everyone else.

Mercury Ahead of or Behind the Sun

Mercury rises before the Sun when it is in an earlier degree of the zodiac. In this position Mercury acts as the individual's press secretary. Everyone knows you are coming, who you are, and why you are important. Action may precede mental awareness as well. When Mercury is behind the Sun (in a later degree of the zodiac), then action follows consideration. If you have Mercury behind the Sun, you need a human press agent, as you lack the natural one provided by Mercury when it rises first.

It is the unusual which provides the helpful astrological information. The average or normal mental types are those with Mercury ahead of the Sun and a slow Moon or Mercury behind the Sun and a fast Moon. In these cases the two energies balance each other. They move between quickness and deliberation in thought as well as in action. The remaining combinations indicate the unusual and potentially troublesome types of expression.

Mercury Ahead of the Sun and Moon Fast

With Mercury ahead of the Sun and a fast Moon, people tend to be ahead of themselves all of the time. They never take the time to stop and smell the roses, as they are on to the next project already. They will need to cultivate the usual, the normal, and the mundane to be successful in the work environment. They may struggle to learn meditation, since sitting still is actually rather painful. Even if they slow down to a pace they consider deadly, they will still be going faster than most of the people around them. Cell phones and computers were made for them to keep track of details and keep up-to-date as they rush through life. If they are honest about it, they can learn to enjoy life at other people's pace, at least part of the time.

Mercury Behind the Sun and Moon Slow

If Mercury is behind the Sun and the Moon slow, the focus is on another time. Attention to the future leads to good judgment, as they don't jump into things without an idea of what is coming. This is a very convenient trait in the work place. They sometimes seem psychic to others, as they get unexpected results from the careful mental process of the intuitive type. They gain insight suddenly—from the gestalt and not from the details. This is not through inattention to detail, but rather from the ability to step back mentally and see the overall picture. This is a valuable skill for a supervisor or planner. They sometimes are unable to explain their reasons—they simply *know*. This sort of statement does not sit well with the logical rational minds of the so-called norm, any more than the super-fast mentality does. Thus this type has its limitations where work is concerned.

Mercury Retrograde

If Mercury is retrograde at birth, or changes direction by progression, then the relationship between Moon and Mercury changes. You will not experience the opposite of the above delineations, but they will be moderated to a large degree. Even if Mercury is ahead of the Sun, its retrograde motion may withhold or hide the speedy qualities mentioned above. After all, Mercury both rises ahead of the Sun and moves away from the Sun. Even in providing publicity, Mercury is focusing on others instead of on you.

By the same token, with Mercury behind the Sun and retrograde, Mercury moves toward the Sun and toward the Ascendant, but from a position behind you. Thus Mercury represents your best aide and support. This is an internal support, often not visible to others at all. Still, the internal processing is well attuned to your personal needs.

When Mercury changes direction by progression, you experience a shift in your relationship to the world. What used to seem ineffective now works much better or vice versa.

Summary

This chapter has taken a look at factors which can be seen easily in a timed natal chart, as well as some which are evident even when the time is not known. Without extended examination the astrologer can discover a great deal about how an individual's makeup will affect career path. All of life's activities depend on the natural psychological tendencies, and career thrives when the natural direction is followed because it takes advantage of individual strengths, allowing less conscious areas to develop without undo pressure. The result is a well-rounded personality engaged in an appropriate and fulfilling career.

Chapter Four

Aspects: Interactions in Career and Work Environment

The alchemical model suggests that each planet, sign, and aspect of astrology has a positive constructive face and a negative or destructive one. It is the refining process that allows us to draw on the qualities of whichever planets or elements we need most as individuals. Psychologically, we can define the conscious and unconscious extremes of any given energy, the conscious being the more acceptable qualities of the energy, the unconscious the unacceptable. We can conceive of a continuum from the most conscious and positive to the least conscious shadow side of an energy's expression. Such a continuum will be similar for everyone because the archetypal planetary energy is the same for all of us. Differences will make the precise expression of each planet unique because each of us has a personal experience of each planet's archetypal energy.

Astrological aspects show energy patterns in the natal charts. Transiting and progressed aspects reflect moment-to-moment, highly individualized possibilities. Each aspect has its progressive, constructive facet and a less constructive, repressive, or neurotic expression. It is through understanding the interplay between constructive and neurotic expressions of each energy that we can understand how positive intention underlies all human activity, indeed all activity in the universe. Then we can learn how to assist the more positive expression of each energy. Our search for vocational satisfaction is aided by understanding of our personal inclinations and their facilitation.

Conjunction Aspects

The conjunction aspect (0 degrees) defines the beginning and ending point of a circle (360/1). It represents the prominence of a particular point, focusing energy in one sign. Two planetary energies are united, magnified, and emphasized, each by the other. Neurotic focus develops into obsession and leads to compulsive behaviors. Sanity, by contrast, brings poignant emotions into sharp focus.

Life begins as one cell—a cell that houses all the potential for an individual human being. This beginning point is paralleled by the alchemist's *prima materia*—the cell is the physical beginning, the *prima materia* is the psychological beginning.

A new cycle of activity begins at a conjunction; when the cycle has come full circle, as the Sun comes full circle each year, we experience an ending. When two planets come together in conjunction, they remind us of unity. The conjunction reconnects us with fundamental truth, a more basic potential that underlies our daily lives. I have transiting Uranus conjunct my natal Venus in Capricorn in the Eighth House. I experience the intuitive urge to begin new projects with different people; I also experience the death of a teacher. One period of my life ends, signaling a new direction. Both sad and joyful, the unity of the moment is in the intuitive knowing that everything will work out for me and for others.

The conjunction recalls the universal truth of *unity*. When two or more planets are conjunct, their energies are reflected together. This causes them to become prominent in the chart, but not distinct. That is, the planets are evident in the personality, events, and situations of the native, but it may be somewhat difficult to identify the planets individually.

One method of making each influence distinct is to study astrology until you are able identify certain objects in your environment that exemplify the individual planets. For each person this will be somewhat different. A second option is to imagine a story or scene in which representatives of the two planetary energies are interacting, and then identify with the actors individually.

The planetary archetypes are the qualities of the universal self which allow for the comprehension of the individual experience within divine unity. Planetary archetypes can be like the people, or like the tasks mentioned here. They mix together and then can be perceived separately. These are neither positive nor negative in themselves. Movement comes from a balanced position within the conjunction itself. There is a synthesis of two energies. Something similar happens with other aspects, but the desire behind them is different. The desire of the conjunction is to glue the two energies together so that neither is lost. Even though there may be a fear that one of the energies may be lost if the conjunction is dissolved, it is important to experience the two energies as themselves, in order to get the true value of the two energies working together. Fear of loss is the problem. Examination of the energies is essential.

I find that separating the energies of a conjunction in this objective way is helpful because I then can apply what I know of the planets more clearly when working with other people's charts. If I could not separate them, I would not be much help to people who do not share the conjunctions I have. I also find it is helpful to allow the two energies to merge again, as that is how I personally am able to work with them. This process extends itself from the conjunction to include the remaining planets in the stellium.

Solar Conjunctions

Sun conjunct Moon: Throughout your life the beginnings and endings of family relationships are quite clear. When there is disharmony in your relationships, it is a reflection of your inner dissatisfaction. You tend to establish positive relationships and are often successful in working with others. This is because you have an inner sense of personal unity that extends into your relationships with others.

Sun conjunct Mercury: You take a practical, common sense approach to cyclical changes in your life. You can use this approach in business situations by maintaining a sense of your objectives. If you experience a lack of clarity in the midst of changes, you can balance nervousness with physical activity.

Sun conjunct Venus: You feel the beauty of your environment as though it were a living thing. For you, moderation can be difficult yet rewarding.

Sun conjunct Mars: You seem to have limitless amounts of energy; the trick is to learn when to stop for a rest.

Sun conjunct Jupiter: Blessed with good health and generally destined for success, you will gain recognition and accomplish much if you can avoid extravagance.

Sun conjunct Saturn: The constructive qualities of firmness, modesty, and determination develop only after the beginning of a new cycle in which difficult struggles and delicate health are overcome.

Sun conjunct Uranus: Sudden changes bring new circumstances into your life. You have a progressive mind that can manage such changes. It is possible to align your thinking to minimize upsets connected with new conditions.

Sun conjunct Neptune: You are far more sensitive to your environment than most people. Sometimes this comes across as weakness; sometimes it is an indication of increased psychic awareness.

Sun conjunct Pluto: Striving for power is the strongest indicator of transition in your life. You will experience remarkable advancement, as well as dramatic health changes, both for the better and for the worse. You have both the positive and less constructive qualities of leadership at your disposal.

Lunar Conjunctions

Moon conjunct Mercury: Thinking and feeling are aligned for you. You are able to assimilate information and to put it back out; thus you are a good student. Some transitions in your life may be marked with criticism and gossip.

Moon conjunct Venus: You have an intensity in your emotional life that can lead to abrupt endings of relationships. It can also develop into strong emotional bonds with mates and children. Use your innate artistic talent and recognition of beauty to overcome a tendency to dwell on emotional conflicts.

Moon conjunct Mars: Impulsive actions mark the cyclical flow of energy in your life. You tend to begin projects with tremendous energy. Rashness can cause problems that can be overcome through honest self-assessment and personal effort.

Moon conjunct Jupiter: You will be known for the extent of your kindness. You will also form relationships with successful women that affect the major transitions in your life. You need to control expansive gestures to avoid wastefulness.

Moon conjunct Saturn: Your mission in life may center on the development of self-control. There is a difference between thoughtfulness and depression that you will need to define for yourself through clear thinking. Sometimes you feel very isolated from others, especially at life's crossroads.

Moon conjunct Uranus: Cycles in your life end with intensity of emotion. You tend to exaggerate things and to strain your nervous system. Yet you will have sudden successes which come out of these tense periods. You need to balance fear and anxiety with restful periods.

Moon conjunct Neptune: You are often aware of subconscious feelings and thoughts which are not evident to others. This comes through in your awareness of shifting cycles. You seem to have precognitive information about changes.

Moon conjunct Pluto: You have a heightened emotional life that is directed into specific areas of your life. You pursue your goals with almost fanatical zest and must be careful to consider other people in your excitement.

Mercury Conjunctions

Mercury conjunct Venus: You have a sense of design and grace in terms of material objects and in relationships. You tend toward a light-hearted existence and sometimes appear not to care when major events occur in your life.

Mercury conjunct Mars: You use your powerful mind to help you through difficult transitions in your life. A tendency toward rash action can make endings more abrupt than need be. Occasionally you may become involved in legal actions or other controversies. You can develop great skill in argument.

Mercury conjunct Jupiter: Common sense, for you, is grounded in intellect. As long as you take a scrupulously honest approach to life, you will find that you open and close life's episodes positively. Teaching situations bring out your optimism.

Mercury conjunct Saturn: You are logical and thorough in your work and in your personal life. Slow, steady advancement in life is related to your skills of concentration and industry. Endings and beginnings are accompanied by serious thought.

Mercury conjunct Uranus: Your heightened powers of intuition give you greater flexibility in all kinds of situations. Because you know or feel how conditions will change, you are able to maximize the benefits of cyclical movement.

Mercury conjunct Neptune: You have a vivid fantasy life that is connected to some form of psychic activity. While this can produce deceptive currents in your life, it can also develop in you the qualities of compassion and subtle perception. You are seldom surprised by changes, due to your keen foresight.

Mercury conjunct Pluto: Your highly developed powers of persuasion place you in a position to control change in your life. You can be a successful speaker or writer. Your own eagerness can be a detriment to your health unless you support your nervous system with proper nutrition and rest.

Venus Conjunctions

Venus conjunct Mars: You experience passionate relationships because of your ability to moderate between the self and others. You have a warm heart and creative abilities. There can be fluctuating feelings or a lack of tact.

Venus conjunct Jupiter: Love is a hallmark of your life. You have both the possibility of relationship conflicts and the potential for harmonious long-term relationships. The key is in the tactful yet heartfelt communication of your feelings.

Venus conjunct Saturn: Your love life will go through inhibited periods. Your sober, sensible side will emerge at such times. Even temporary separations can cause you pain. Jealousy can be a problem.

Venus conjunct Uranus: You fall in and out of love easily. In fact you enjoy the beginning and ending of relationships because of the excitement. Your actions sometimes appear eccentric to others.

Venus conjunct Neptune: You would prefer to live in a world of illusion and can make this your life work. You idealize love relationships and can be devastated when they end. Know that a new one is just around the corner.

Venus conjunct Pluto: The exertion of power in love relationships can be intensely satisfying. It can also bring about the end of valued relationships. You are artistically gifted.

Mars Conjunctions

Mars conjunct Jupiter: Fortunate decisions mark the major turning points of your life. You have the ability to concentrate on a particular goal and will have successful results professionally.

Mars conjunct Saturn: You experience harmful energy from time to time. Yet your endurance gets you through the difficult times. You are more effective when you throw your energy into tasks without also throwing in your ego.

Mars conjunct Uranus: You will make remarkable achievements during your life, but there is a price. You need to take care to avoid accident or injury because of carelessness. You are brutally honest and sometimes intolerant of others.

Mars conjunct Neptune: You suffer from a periodic lack of energy and are susceptible to infections. You have an innate sense of timing. You are inspired to acts of devotion, but are sometimes moody and subject to feelings of inferiority.

Mars conjunct Pluto: You sometimes appear to have superhuman power. You also seem to solve problems by applying excessive amounts of force. Control cruel urges and you will get further.

Jupiter Conjunctions

Jupiter conjunct Saturn: You are often happiest when you are involved in secluded activities. Your patience, diplomacy, and sense of duty are exemplary. Your life is filled with changes.

Jupiter conjunct Uranus: Fortunate turns in your life are the stuff of legends. Occasionally you miss an opportunity, but generally you seek independence and adventure.

Jupiter conjunct Neptune: The richness of feelings in your life is the result of your close connection to the psychic realm. You are a dreamer and mystic. Sometimes you suffer losses because of unprofitable speculations.

Jupiter conjunct Pluto: You have a pervasive desire for power; this desire focuses, for the most part, on the spiritual or mental sphere. However, you can attain leadership positions. It is possible for you to lose everything.

Saturn Conjunctions

Saturn conjunct Uranus: Inhibited rhythms affect your physical body and your social existence. You are able to overcome difficulties. You are self-willed and gain or suffer because of this.

Saturn conjunct Neptune: You are methodical in your work, planning carefully and working very hard. Do not allow your inner tension or inhibition to create a foundation for illness.

Saturn conjunct Pluto: You have a cruel streak that must be tempered by other factors. You have the potential to grow in spiritual awareness if you can avoid purely egoistic aims.

Uranus, Neptune, and Pluto Conjunctions

Uranus conjunct Neptune: You have the potential for developing your psychic gifts. While you sometimes experience confused psychic states, you can achieve spiritual enlightenment.

Uranus conjunct Pluto: You live for the dare, are constantly active, and sometimes fall precipitously. However, you also have the potential to win big because you are not afraid to take chances.

Neptune conjunct Pluto: You are a highly sensitive person and can develop your psychic gifts steadily throughout your life. You are aware of events before they occur.

No Conjunctions

The lack of conjunctions in your chart indicates that your interests are diverse. In addition, you are able to discern the differences among the energies of the planets clearly. Thus, while you may occasionally be confused about the interactions of energies, you are always able to identify the various energies involved in a situation.

Opposition Aspects

The opposition aspect (180 degrees) defines substance through polarity (360/2). Polarities allow us to see or hear variations, to feel, and to have consciousness. We become aware of the world through perceptions. If no opposition exists within a chart, the astrologer will have to identify alternative approaches to gaining awareness.

The development of a viable physical body depends in the proper splitting of the original cell. Division as a process is required for life as we know it. The dividing process is closely linked to a combining process. The cell must assimilate nutrients to sustain itself and the new cell that will be formed. The two cells grow directly from the one. The act of separation into two is necessary for creation. Unity *is*, but needs to become two in order to manifest itself.

The opposition, when drawn in a mandala, is the only aspect that intersects the center, dividing the circle into equal segments. Many symbols, such as the Tao, are expressions of the profound meaning of polarity, and the opposition is one such representation. The opposition also connects the center with the circumference, symbolizing the connection between inner and outer being.

The oppositions in a chart can be considered to be the most beneficial aspects from a social standpoint, even though they usually carry a less constructive connotation in astrological literature. Value is a quality of this second aspect. We can speak of color values and how we are aware of them; value describes an emotional or feeling evaluation of the world, which follows initial perception. This is one method we use to establish our values and become aware of our inner being. Another method involves projection of our own neurotic tendencies on an object or person. This process can serve to develop awareness and bring about constructive change if we are able to see ourselves in the object of our projection. The opposition defines substance through *polarity* and allows the perception of value.

Solar Oppositions

Sun opposite Moon: You are keenly aware of your inner emotional life and your actions reflect that self-knowledge. You are usually successful in dealings with others because you appreciate the differences among individuals. You face confrontations head on, but with your own personal style, based on the signs in which the Sun and the Moon are found.

Sun opposite Mercury: Your awareness of the nuances of communication places you in an ideal position in business and personal relationships. You know the difference between nervous stress and the joy of a busy career.

Sun opposite Venus: You make social connections easily and have a magnetic attraction. Sometimes you are willing to jump into intense relationships too quickly.

Sun opposite Mars: You advance in life through your own effort, yet your awareness of others makes advancement easy.

Sun opposite Jupiter: Blessed with good health and generally destined for success, you will gain recognition because you are aware of the importance of avoiding arrogance and extravagance in relationships.

Sun opposite Saturn: The constructive qualities of firmness, modesty, and determination develop only after awareness gained through difficult struggles and delicate health.

Sun opposite Uranus: Sudden changes bring new awareness. You have a progressive mind that can manage such changes. You tend to polarize feelings about new relationships.

Sun opposite Neptune: You are far more sensitive to your environment than most people. Sometimes this comes across as weakness; sometimes it is an indication of increased psychic awareness.

Sun opposite Pluto: You have both the positive and less constructive qualities of leadership at your disposal. Dealings with others focus on power issues and make you aware of your own power.

Lunar Oppositions

Moon opposite Mercury: Thinking and feeling form your awareness of the world. You are able to assimilate and use information; you are a good student.

Moon opposite Venus: Intensity in your emotional life can produce conflict. It can also develop strong emotional bonds with mates and children. Use your innate artistic talent and recognition of beauty to overcome a tendency to dwell on emotional conflicts.

Moon opposite Mars: Impulsive actions bring attention to you. You tend to begin projects with tremendous energy. Rashness can cause problems that affect your relationships.

Moon opposite Jupiter: Relationships with powerful women bring you an awareness of the value of kindness in everyday situations. You need to control expansive gestures to avoid wastefulness.

Moon opposite Saturn: Your mission in life may center on the development of self-control. You define the external world through clear thinking. Sometimes you feel very isolated from others.

Moon opposite Uranus: Your relationships are filled with emotional intensity. Nervousness occurs when you are puzzled about how to respond to others. Yet you will have sudden successes which come out of these tense periods. You need to balance fear and anxiety with restful periods.

Moon opposite Neptune: You are often aware of subconscious feelings and thoughts of the people around you. You seem to have precognitive information about the women in your life.

Moon opposite Pluto: You have a heightened emotional life that is directed into specific areas of your life. You pursue your goals with almost fanatical zest and must be careful to consider other people in your excitement.

Mercury Oppositions

Mercury opposite Venus: You have a sense of design and grace which extends both to material objects and to relationships. You tend toward a light-hearted existence and sometimes appear not to care when other people hurt you.

Mercury opposite Mars: You use your powerful mind to help others. Rash action can make endings more abrupt than need be. Occasionally you may become involved in legal actions or other controversies. You can develop great skill in argument.

Mercury opposite Jupiter: Common sense, for you, depends on intellectual awareness. As long as you take a scrupulously honest approach to life, you will find that relationships are positive. Your active mind and optimism are your best teachers.

Mercury opposite Saturn: You are logical and thorough in your work and in your personal life. Slow, steady advancement in life is related to your skills of concentration and industry. You take the world seriously.

Mercury opposite Uranus: Your heightened powers of intuition give you greater flexibility in all kinds of situations. Because you know other people's moods so well, you are able to maximize the benefits of interactions with others.

Mercury opposite Neptune: Your psychic ability makes you aware of hidden traits in others. You are seldom surprised by the decisions of others and you are often one step ahead of them in your thinking.

Mercury opposite Pluto: Your highly developed powers of persuasion place you in a position to control others. You can be a successful speaker or writer. You are known to take a position on issues and stick to it in spite of vigorous opposition.

Venus Oppositions

Venus opposite Mars: You experience passionate relationships because of your ability to moderate between the self and others. Lack of tact can be a problem.

Venus opposite Jupiter: Love is a hallmark of your life. You have both the possibility of relationship conflicts and the potential for harmonious long-term relationships, depending on how freely energy flows between you and your partner.

Venus opposite Saturn: Your love life will go through inhibited periods. Your sober, sensible side will emerge at such times. Even temporary separations can cause you pain. Jealousy can be a problem.

Venus opposite Uranus: You fall in and out of love easily. In fact, you cast yourself as a principal player in love dramas. Your actions sometimes appear eccentric to others.

Venus opposite Neptune: You would prefer to live in a world of illusion and can make this your life work. You idealize love relationships and can be devastated when they end. Know that a new one is just around the corner.

Venus opposite Pluto: Awareness of power is essential in your relationships. Don't be too forceful yourself, but also remember power is a thing to be shared.

Mars Oppositions

Mars opposite Jupiter: Fortunate decisions mark your interactions with people. You have the ability to concentrate on a particular goal and to manifest material results.

Mars opposite Saturn: You experience harmful energy from time to time. Harsh interactions provide vivid experiences. You are more effective when you throw your energy into tasks without also throwing in your ego.

Mars opposite Uranus: You will make remarkable achievements during your life, but there is a price. You need to take care to avoid accident or injury because of carelessness. You are brutally truthful and sometimes intolerant of others.

Mars opposite Neptune: You suffer from a periodic lack of energy and are susceptible to infections. You have an innate sense of timing. You are inspired to acts of devotion, but are sometimes moody and subject to feelings of inferiority.

Mars opposite Pluto: You sometimes appear to have superhuman power. You also seem to solve problems by applying excessive amounts of force. Control cruel urges and you will get further with people.

Jupiter Oppositions

Jupiter opposite Saturn: You are often happiest when you are involved in secluded activities. Your patience, diplomacy, and sense of duty are exemplary. You are a skilled evaluator of people.

Jupiter opposite Uranus: Fortunate turns in your life are the stuff of legends. Occasionally you miss the opportunity, but generally you seek independence and adventure. You form remarkable partnerships.

Jupiter opposite Neptune: The richness of feelings in your life is the result of your close connection to the psychic realm. You are a dreamer and mystic. Sometimes you suffer losses because of your idealistic view of others.

Jupiter opposite Pluto: You have a pervasive desire for power; this desire focuses, for the most part, on the spiritual or mental sphere. However, you can attain leadership positions. It is possible for you to lose everything.

Saturn Oppositions

Saturn opposite Uranus: Inhibited rhythms affect your physical body and your social existence. Yet you are able to overcome difficulties. You are self-willed and gain or suffer because of this.

Saturn opposite Neptune: You are methodical in your work, planning carefully and working very hard. Do not allow your inhibition to cause failure in relationships.

Saturn opposite Pluto: You have a cruel streak that must be tempered by other factors. You have the potential to grow in spiritual awareness if you can avoid purely egoistic aims.

Uranus, Neptune, and Pluto Oppositions

Uranus opposite Neptune: You have the potential for developing your psychic gifts. While you sometimes experience confused psychic states, you can achieve spiritual enlightenment by connecting with like people.

Uranus opposite Pluto: You live for the dare, are constantly active, and sometimes fall precipitously. However, you also have the potential to win big because you are not afraid to take chances.

Neptune opposite Pluto: You are a highly sensitive person and can develop your psychic gifts steadily throughout your life. You are aware of events before they occur.

No Oppositions

Objective awareness can be a problem for you. Confrontations are taken personally. You can develop awareness through careful examination of inner issues and the willingness to consider perspectives different from your own.

Trine Aspects

The trine aspect (120 degrees) represents a division of the 360 degree circle into three equal parts (360/3). The trine aspect is one of ease, because compatible areas of the ego are linked together. In fire signs, creative urges are emphasized. Earth trines are concerned with perceptual issues. Air trines relate to thinking processes, and water trines relate to the feeling components of the mind. As stated previously, the Sun sign indicates the dominant psychological function. Thus, trines in the same element as the Sun sign will be the easiest to manifest in consciousness, while those of the opposite sign will be more difficult to consciously energize and actuate. The remaining two elements fall between these extremes.

This emphasis on elements can explain the uneven expression of trines in a given natal chart. A client can express the energy of the trines of wider orb in certain elements, while other very close trines will be more difficult to bring to awareness. It seems reasonable that Sun sign element trines will be the most available, as they are directly energized by the relationship to the Sun.

One difficult expression of the trine is a certain laziness, as easy conditions often do not call for action. Thus a person may allow a nonconstructive condition to exist through inaction. It is important to work with trines—to take an active role in the expression of the trine's harmony in our lives. The trine reflects the formulation of concepts and emergence of the *ego*.

Solar Trines

Sun trine Moon: There is a harmonious blending of your conscious and unconscious mental activities that allows you to overcome obstacles. You blend activities and energies together smoothly in your life and have a gift for helping others to do the same. People come to you to ask for help with emotionally charged problems.

Sun trine Mercury: You have the ability to blend intellect and common sense harmoniously. You can see past the apparent differences in situations to an integrated understanding of the variables in complex situations.

Sun trine Venus: Conditions exist for you to develop intense relationships.

Sun trine Mars: Life delivers leadership and success to you; take care to develop relaxed relationships and a healthy life style.

Sun trine Jupiter: Blessed with good health and generally destined for success, you gain recognition without effort and accomplish much if you can avoid extravagance.

Sun trine Saturn: The constructive qualities of firmness, modesty, and determination develop and persevere in a climate of inhibition and seriousness.

Sun trine Uranus: Your life is filled with changes but you have a progressive mind that can manage them. You have the ego skills to work with your intuitive ability. You generally have plenty of nervous energy.

Sun trine Neptune: You live in a psychically open state of mind and therefore you experience the world directly and immediately. Sometimes this comes across as weakness. You can be easily influenced by the glamour of a situation.

Sun trine Pluto: You find it easy to wield your tremendous personal power. Conditions arise in which you have volcanic outbursts of feeling, usually connected to a specific cause related to childhood experiences. You can be sentimental as well.

Lunar Trines

Moon trine Mercury: Thinking and feeling are aligned for you. You have the natural ease of mental process that allows you to learn easily and to express what you have learned in turn. You may be a skilled test taker. You are a good teacher.

Moon trine Venus: You have an intensity in your emotional life as well as innate artistic talent. You find yourself at ease with women in nearly all situations. You have a natural beauty and a talent for bringing beauty out in your surroundings.

Moon trine Mars: Impulsive actions reflect the energy in your life. You tend to begin projects with tremendous energy. You find it easy to mobilize your energy when you are interested in a subject. Think things through before you act.

Moon trine Jupiter: You form relationships with successful women that are beneficial to you. You need to control expansive gestures to avoid wastefulness. You tend to fall into lucky circumstances; you also tend to spend very freely.

Moon trine Saturn: It is easy for you to become depressed, sad, or at least very thoughtful. You can use this tendency to focus your mental energies on practical matters. Sometimes you feel very isolated from others.

Moon trine Uranus: Conditions arise in which you exaggerate feelings and become overly nervous. At the same time, you are able to use your intuitive ability to absorb information about unusual situations, thus gaining yourself an advantage.

Moon trine Neptune: You are often aware of subconscious feelings and thoughts. This natural psychic ability leaves you open to the energy flows around you. Because you are hyper-aware, you often have the advantage of knowing what is happening ahead of other people.

Moon trine Pluto: You have a zest for life that can come across as exaggerated emotional reactions. You understand the nature of the birth and death process. You pursue your goals with almost fanatical zest and must be careful to consider other people in your excitement.

Mercury Trines

Mercury trine Venus: You find yourself in situations that appeal to your sense of design and beauty. Generally light-hearted, you are a welcome guest at social gatherings.

Mercury trine Mars: You generally can draw upon the power of your mental resources easily. You can develop great skill in argument, although you are sometimes too quick to speak.

Mercury trine Jupiter: Your intellectual strength provides the ground for apparent luck, but this luck is the result of integrating common sense with intelligence. What is lucky is the ability to use this combination. Your active mind and optimism make you a good teacher.

Mercury trine Saturn: You are able to engage your ego successfully in situations demanding logical, careful approaches. Your life is a series of advancements that are based on this use of mind.

Mercury trine Uranus: Your heightened powers of intuition give you great flexibility in all kinds of situations. It is natural for you to perceive and use intuitive information.

Mercury trine Neptune: You have a vivid fantasy life. Psychic awareness places you in the right place at the right time more often than not. Conditions around you offer information of the subtlest nature. You are seldom surprised by changes, due to your keen foresight.

Mercury trine Pluto: You are at ease in situations where you can speak your mind and be heard. You persuade others by your own convictions, but consistency must be developed to maximize your skills.

Venus Trines

Venus trine Mars: You experience passionate relationships because of your ability to moderate between the self and others. You have a warm heart and creative abilities. There can be a fluctuating desire for independence and intimacy.

Venus trine Jupiter: Love is a hallmark of your life. You have the full range of relationship potential in your life. You find it easy to be popular with others.

Venus trine Saturn: Your love life is inhibited by your serious acceptance of duty. Your sober, sensible side can attract partners who are much younger or older. Even temporary separations can cause you pain. Jealousy can be a problem.

Venus trine Uranus: You fall in and out of love easily. It is easy for you to move from one relationship to another. Your actions sometimes appear eccentric to others.

Venus trine Neptune: You would prefer to live in a world of illusion and can make this your life work. You idealize love relationships. You become known for your good taste.

Venus trine Pluto: When you are in love you are in it all the way. You are willing to engage in unusual sensual pleasures. You are artistically gifted.

Mars Trines

Mars trine Jupiter: Fortunate decisions place you in beneficial circumstances. You find yourself in the position to resolve disagreements. It is easy to expand into new relationships.

Mars trine Saturn: You experience harmful energy from time to time. Yet your endurance gets you through the difficult times. You are more effective when you throw your energy into tasks without also throwing in your ego.

Mars trine Uranus: You will have remarkable achievements during your life, but find you have isolated yourself in the process. You need to take care to avoid accident or injury because of carelessness. You are brutally honest.

Mars trine Neptune: You suffer from periodic lack of energy and are susceptible to infections. You have an innate sense of timing and attract help at just the right moment. You are inspired to acts of devotion.

Mars trine Pluto: You sometimes appear to have superhuman power. You also tend to solve problems by applying excessive amounts of force. Control cruel urges and you will get further.

Jupiter Trines

Jupiter trine Saturn: You are often happiest when you are involved in secluded activities. Your patience, diplomacy, and sense of duty are exemplary. Your honesty is your most effective tool in business.

Jupiter trine Uranus: Conditions frequently exist for you to experience success; you must take some action to manifest beneficial results or they will elude you.

Jupiter trine Neptune: The richness of feelings in your life is the result of your close connection to the psychic realm. You are a dreamer and mystic. Sometimes you suffer losses because of unprofitable speculations.

Jupiter trine Pluto: You have a pervasive desire for power; this desire focuses, for the most part, on the spiritual or mental sphere. However, you can attain leadership positions. It is possible for you to lose everything.

Saturn Trines

Saturn trine Uranus: Inhibited rhythms affect your physical body and your social existence. Your determination overcomes physical limitations. You are self-willed and gain or suffer because of this. Violence can be a part of your experience.

Saturn trine Neptune: You are methodical in your work, planning carefully and working very hard. You experience the struggle between the devil and the angel within yourself.

Saturn trine Pluto: You experience cruelty in your life that must be offset by other factors. You have the potential to grow in spiritual awareness if you can avoid purely egoistic aims.

Uranus, Neptune, and Pluto Trines

Uranus trine Neptune: You have natural psychic gifts that first emerge during sleep or hypnotic states. You can achieve spiritual enlightenment through development of this inner vision.

Uranus trine Pluto: You live for the dare, are constantly active, and sometimes fall precipitously. However, you also have the potential to achieve peak performance if you work with your natural gift to manifest transformation.

Neptune trine Pluto: You are a highly sensitive person and can develop your psychic gifts steadily throughout your life. You are surrounded by mystic energy and can develop it in yourself.

No Trines

For you, energies do not blend easily. Others may find you egocentric in your attitudes, while in actuality you are not aware of your inherent abilities or your presentation of them.

Semi-Sextile and Quincunx Aspects

The semi-sextile (30 degrees) and quincunx (150 degrees) aspects are part of the thirty-degree harmonic as well. The semi-sextile, while called a growth aspect, is not an easy type of energy to control. It might better be billed as energy that leads to "growth through pain," as the growth is often accompanied by some realization about the self which we are not anxious to accept. The semi-sextile, when active, can seem to cause the individual to expend much energy in dealing with the areas of the life which are involved.

The semi-sextile is the complementary aspect of the quincunx (or inconjunct). Both of these aspects have been considered minor factors within the chart; however, this author does not hold such an opinion. The quincunx has a difficult name that is consistent with the difficult nature of the aspect. Expansion is a key word often used for this aspect, and the native definitely feels the effect of expansion into new areas of thought and feeling when the quincunx is activated. Much learning takes place at this time that changes the individual permanently. *Adjustment* is a word that better describes the type of change that the native can experience.

Solar Semi-Sextiles

Sun semi-sextile Moon: There is a harmonious blending of your conscious and unconscious mental activities that allows you to overcome obstacles. You blend activities and energies together smoothly in your life and have a gift for helping others to do the same. People ask for your help with emotionally charged problems.

Sun semi-sextile Mercury: You have the ability to blend intellect and common sense harmoniously. You can see past apparent differences in complex situations to an integrated understanding of the variables.

Sun semi-sextile Venus: Conditions exist for you to develop artistic talents. You find yourself in interesting and intense relationships.

Sun semi-sextile Mars: Life delivers leadership and success to you; take care to develop relaxed relationships and a healthy life style.

Sun semi-sextile Jupiter: Blessed with good health and generally destined for success, you gain recognition without effort and accomplish much if you can avoid extravagance.

Sun semi-sextile Saturn: The constructive qualities of firmness, modesty, and determination develop and persevere in a climate of inhibition and seriousness.

Sun semi-sextile Uranus: Your life is filled with changes but you have a progressive mind that can manage them. You have the ego skills to work with your intuitive ability. You generally have plenty of nervous energy.

Sun semi-sextile Neptune: You live in a psychically open state of mind and therefore you experience the world directly and immediately. Sometimes this comes across as weakness. You can be easily influenced by the glamour of a situation.

Sun semi-sextile Pluto: You find it easy to wield your tremendous personal power. Conditions arise in which you have volcanic outbursts of feeling, usually connected to a specific cause related to childhood experiences. You can be sentimental as well.

Lunar Semi-Sextiles

Moon semi-sextile Mercury: Thinking and feeling are aligned for you. You have the natural ease of mental process that allows you to learn easily and to express what you have learned in turn. You may be a skilled test taker. You are a good teacher.

Moon semi-sextile Venus: You have an intensity in your emotional life as well as innate artistic talent. You find yourself at ease with women in nearly all situations. You have a natural beauty and a talent for bringing beauty out in your surroundings.

Moon semi-sextile Mars: Impulsive actions reflect the energy in your life. You tend to begin projects with tremendous energy. You find it easy to mobilize your energy when you are interested in a subject. Think things through before you act.

Moon semi-sextile Jupiter: You form relationships with successful women that are beneficial to you. You need to control expansive gestures to avoid wastefulness. You tend to fall into lucky circumstances; you also tend to spend very freely.

Moon semi-sextile Saturn: It is easy for you to become depressed, sad, or at least very thoughtful. You can use this tendency to focus your mental energies on practical matters. Sometimes you feel very isolated from others.

Moon semi-sextile Uranus: Conditions arise in which you exaggerate feelings and become overly nervous. At the same time, you are able to use your intuitive ability to absorb information about unusual situations, thus gaining yourself an advantage.

Moon semi-sextile Neptune: You are often aware of subconscious feelings and thoughts. This natural psychic ability leaves you open to the energy flows around you. Because you are hyper-aware, you often have the advantage of knowing what is happening ahead of other people.

Moon semi-sextile Pluto: You have a zest for life that can come across as exaggerated emotional reactions. You understand the nature of the birth and death process. You pursue your goals with almost fanatical zest and must be careful to consider other people in your excitement.

Mercury Semi-Sextiles

Mercury semi-sextile Venus: You find yourself in situations that appeal to your sense of design and beauty. Generally light-hearted, you are a welcome guest at social gatherings.

Mercury semi-sextile Mars: You generally can draw upon the power of your mental resources easily. You can develop great skill in argument, although you are sometimes too quick to speak.

Mercury semi-sextile Jupiter: Your intellectual strength provides the ground for apparent luck, but this luck is the result of integrating common sense with intelligence. What is lucky is the ability to use this combination. Your active mind and optimism make you a good teacher.

Mercury semi-sextile Saturn: You are able to engage your ego successfully in situations that demand logical, careful approaches. Your life is a series of advancements that are based on this use of mind.

Mercury semi-sextile Uranus: Your heightened powers of intuition give you great flexibility in all kinds of situations. It is natural for you to perceive and use intuitive information.

Mercury semi-sextile Neptune: You have a vivid fantasy life. Psychic awareness places you in the right place at the right time more often than not. Conditions around you offer information of the subtlest nature. You are seldom surprised by changes, due to your keen foresight.

Mercury semi-sextile Pluto: You are at ease in situations where you can speak your mind and be heard. You persuade others by your own convictions, but consistency must be developed to maximize your skills.

Venus Semi-Sextiles

Venus semi-sextile Mars: You experience passionate relationships because of your ability to moderate between the self and others. You have a warm heart and creative abilities. There can be a fluctuating desire for independence and intimacy.

Venus semi-sextile Jupiter: Love is a hallmark of your life. You have the full range of relationship potential in your life. You find it easy to be popular with others.

Venus semi-sextile Saturn: Your love life is inhibited by your serious acceptance of duty. Your sober, sensible side can attract partners who are much younger or older. Even temporary separations can cause you pain. Jealousy can be a problem.

Venus semi-sextile Uranus: You fall in and out of love easily. It is easy for you to move from one relationship to another. Your actions sometimes appear eccentric to others.

Venus semi-sextile Neptune: You would prefer to live in a world of illusion and can make this your life work. You idealize love relationships. You become known for your good taste.

Venus semi-sextile Pluto: When you are in love you are in it all the way. You are willing to engage in unusual sensual pleasures. You are artistically gifted.

Mars Semi-Sextiles

Mars semi-sextile Jupiter: Fortunate decisions place you in beneficial circumstances. You find yourself in the position to resolve disagreements. It is easy to expand into new relationships.

Mars semi-sextile Saturn: You experience harmful energy from time to time. Yet your endurance gets you through the difficult times. You are more effective when you throw your energy into tasks without also throwing in your ego.

Mars semi-sextile Uranus: You will have remarkable achievements during your life, but find you have isolated yourself in the process. You need to take care to avoid accident or injury because of carelessness. You are brutally honest.

Mars semi-sextile Neptune: You suffer from periodic lack of energy and are susceptible to infections. You have an innate sense of timing and attract help at just the right moment. You are inspired to acts of devotion.

Mars semi-sextile Pluto: You sometimes appear to have superhuman power. You also tend to solve problems by applying excessive amounts of force. Control cruel urges and you will get further.

Jupiter Semi-Sextiles

Jupiter semi-sextile Saturn: You are often happiest when you are involved in secluded activities. Your patience, diplomacy, and sense of duty are exemplary. Your honesty is your most effective tool in business.

Jupiter semi-sextile Uranus: Conditions frequently exist for you to experience success; you must take some action to manifest beneficial results or they will elude you.

Jupiter semi-sextile Neptune: The richness of feelings in your life is the result of your close connection to the psychic realm. You are a dreamer and mystic. Sometimes you suffer losses because of unprofitable speculations.

Jupiter semi-sextile Pluto: You have a pervasive desire for power; this desire focuses, for the most part, on the spiritual or mental sphere. However, you can attain leadership positions. It is possible for you to lose everything.

Saturn Semi-Sextiles

Saturn semi-sextile Uranus: Inhibited rhythms affect your physical body and your social existence. Your determination overcomes physical limitations. You are self-willed and gain or suffer because of this. Violence can be a part of your experience.

Saturn semi-sextile Neptune: You are methodical in your work, planning carefully and working very hard. You experience the struggle between the devil and the angel within yourself.

Saturn semi-sextile Pluto: You experience cruelty in your life that must be offset by other factors. You have the potential to grow in spiritual awareness if you can avoid purely egoistic aims.

Uranus, Neptune, and Pluto Semi-Sextiles

Uranus semi-sextile Neptune: You have natural psychic gifts that first emerge during sleep or hypnotic states. You can achieve spiritual enlightenment through development of this inner vision.

Uranus semi-sextile Pluto: You live for the dare, are constantly active, and sometimes fall precipitously. However, you also have the potential to achieve peak performance if you work with your natural gift to manifest transformation.

Neptune semi-sextile Pluto: You are a highly sensitive person and can develop your psychic gifts steadily throughout your life. You are surrounded by mystic energy and can develop it in yourself.

No Semi-Sextiles

For you, energies do not blend easily. Others may find you egocentric in your attitudes, while in actuality you are not aware of your inherent abilities or your presentation of them.

Solar Quincunxes

Sun quincunx Moon: At times in your life you will struggle with the need to adjust to situations that arise. These adjustments will affect your relationships with others; more importantly, they will be reflected in your inner sense of well-being. The capacity to adjust to circumstances is a measure of your inner clarity of mind.

Sun quincunx Mercury: By taking a subjective look at situations, you often discover a way to adjust where other people "break."

Sun quincunx Venus: You learn to work with difficult situations by looking for ways to focus your concept of others through a filter of natural beauty and grace.

Sun quincunx Mars: Adapt to your surroundings by engaging in active investigation.

Sun quincunx Jupiter: Blessed with good health and generally destined for success, you mature through experiences with others that reveal the role of arrogance in your personality.

Sun quincunx Saturn: Major changes in your life are the result of difficult struggles and delicate health. You tend to attract serious people into your life.

Sun quincunx Uranus: Sudden changes bring new circumstances into your life. You have a progressive mind that can manage such changes. You must focus on physical demands for the best outcome.

Sun quincunx Neptune: You are far more sensitive to your environment than most people. Thus you need to adjust your activity level to suit conditions that arise.

Sun quincunx Pluto: Striving for power is the strongest indicator of transitions in your life. Remarkable advancements are thrust upon you throughout your life. From these you develop your psychic and your social powers.

Lunar Quincunxes

Moon quincunx Mercury: Thinking and feeling are aligned for you. You are able to assimilate information but acting on it can be a problem. Some transitions in your life demand that you check your attitude and change it.

Moon quincunx Venus: Dealings with women demand that you adjust your impressions to suit their reality. You learn to love by adapting.

Moon quincunx Mars: Impulsive actions mark the cyclical flow of energy in your life. You tend to begin projects with tremendous energy. Rashness can cause problems that can be overcome through honest self-assessment and personal effort.

Moon quincunx Jupiter: Your expansive nature leads you into situations that may later need to be rectified, at some expense to your personal desires. If you take a bit of care, you will achieve happier results.

Moon quincunx Saturn: Your mission in life centers on the development of self-control when change hits you. Cautious thinking may be helpful. Adjustment periods cause you to feel separated from others.

Moon quincunx Uranus: Life demands emotional adjustment from time to time. You tend to exaggerate things and to strain your nervous system. You need to balance fear and anxiety with restful periods, and go with the flow, even if it is not convenient.

Moon quincunx Neptune: You are often aware of subconscious feelings and thoughts that are not evident to others. This comes through in your awareness of shifting cycles. You seem to have precognitive information about changes.

Moon quincunx Pluto: You have a heightened emotional life that is directed into specific areas of your life. You pursue your goals with almost fanatical zest and must be careful to consider other people in your excitement.

Mercury Quincunxes

Mercury quincunx Venus: Relationships demand adjustments in communication. If you can adapt, you will have strong ties with others. By the same token, you can elicit an adaptive response from others through careful choice of words.

Mercury quincunx Mars: Arguing only gets you into more difficulty. Learn to adapt to situations and you will avoid painful confrontations. But have the courage to confront issues when it is truly necessary.

Mercury quincunx Jupiter: Common sense is based on intellect. You learn best from yourself about how to use communication to make needed changes, so listen to your inner teacher.

Mercury quincunx Saturn: You hear what you need to hear throughout your life, from older people. Later you will become the advisor, so make the effort to learn while you are young.

Mercury quincunx Uranus: Intuition tells you when to seek help and when to adapt to situations around you. Less force means better psychic flow.

Mercury quincunx Neptune: Maintain creative flow that matches your breathing pattern. Meditation is a useful tool for self-discovery.

Mercury quincunx Pluto: No amount of force can win some arguments. Adapt when you can't win, and save your energy for the next fight.

Venus Quincunxes

Venus quincunx Mars: You experience irritability or a lack of satisfaction in passionate relationships when you refuse to adapt to your partner. Feelings fluctuate between desire and aloofness.

Venus quincunx Jupiter: Any inclination toward laziness in relationships will force you to adjust, as your partner will not tolerate it. Harmonious long-term partnerships depend on your willingness to remain flexible, even though your beliefs are unchanging.

Venus quincunx Saturn: Your love life undergoes inhibited periods in which you are forced to adjust your attitude. The sober, sensible side of yourself may emerge. Develop the willingness to make sacrifices for others.

Venus quincunx Uranus: You fall in and out of love easily and are constantly making adjustments because of this. Repressed feelings can cause physical pain or illness.

Venus quincunx Neptune: You face adjustment because of your susceptibility to seduction. Each time this happens you learn to trust your psychic senses more completely, until you feel the adjustment coming before you get into the situation, rather than after you have been hurt.

Venus quincunx Pluto: The exertion of power in love relationships requires adjustment on the part of both partners. This is an energy best kept out of the work environment.

Mars Quincunxes

Mars quincunx Jupiter: A tendency to rebel against rules will bring situations that demand that you change your tune. Flexibility is required to resolve disputes. You will benefit from the study of conflict resolution.

Mars quincunx Saturn: You find that your energies are limited when life demands major adjustments. When conditions are especially demanding, rearrange your schedule to include additional rest, exercise, and relaxation.

Mars quincunx Uranus: You will make remarkable achievements during your life, but there is a price. You need to take care to avoid accident or injury because of carelessness. Also seek spiritual freedom while acquiescing in the social sphere, thereby avoiding a build-up of nervous energy.

Mars quincunx Neptune: You suffer from periodic lack of energy and are susceptible to infections. Adequate organized physical exercise can help to channel emotions, and maintain emotional and mental energy levels.

Mars quincunx Pluto: Sooner or later, applying excessive amounts of force leads to situations in which you must adapt or be crushed. Control cruel urges and you will get further.

Jupiter Quincunxes

Jupiter quincunx Saturn: Pessimism can become a problem for you. Situations make you questions your own abilities and annoyances become much bigger issues than necessary. Diplomacy is to be cultivated.

Jupiter quincunx Uranus: Fortunate turns in your life are the stuff of legends. Even apparently negative situations turn out for the best in the long run. Try not to exaggerate in the moment.

Jupiter quincunx Neptune: Your tendency to dream takes you off the track of concrete activity and leads to periods of adjustment because of misunderstandings. The underlying idealism can be channeled into constructive activities by setting goals that match your metaphysical beliefs.

Jupiter quincunx Pluto: You have a pervasive desire for power; this desire focuses, for the most part, on the spiritual or mental sphere. Control of a tendency to fanaticism will reap the greatest rewards.

Saturn Quincunxes

Saturn quincunx Uranus: Inhibited rhythms affect your physical body and your social existence. Emotional stress can lead to physical illness, but can be managed through focused physical exercise and attention to diet.

Saturn quincunx Neptune: Adjustments in your life are accompanied by frequent mood changes. Do not allow your inner tension to create a foundation for illness or for difficulties with others.

Saturn quincunx Pluto: You can be a magician or a cruel, violent sort. If you pursue your own ego urges, you will be forced to adjust to life's demands eventually, so develop your toughness while keeping your principles private.

Uranus, Neptune, and Pluto Quincunxes

Uranus quincunx Neptune: Psychic awareness can be a positive constructive force, particularly when you adapt your thinking to include its consideration. Practice will overcome a tendency toward one-sided psychic interpretations.

Uranus quincunx Pluto: You must work hard to achieve success. You have the tenacity and endurance necessary for the task. Use less force than you think is necessary for best results, and you will have to make fewer repairs along the way.

Neptune quincunx Pluto: You are often aware of events before they occur. Listen to the inner voice that suggests the need to change your direction or your habits. Meditation can forestall a tendency to become obsessed over transitory events.

No Quincunxes

You have no built-in strategy for dealing with adjustments in your life. When they are needed, you will fall back on a strategy that is less suited to the situation and you may feel rather inadequate.

Square Aspects

The square aspect (90 degrees) most directly represents our connection to the material world (360/4). The more substantial and material nature of the square aspect represents energies that are very obvious challenges in three specific areas of psychic energy flow. First, the cardinal squares deal with outgoing energy. They relate to activities that take us out of ourselves and into the world at large. Second, the fixed squares deal with energy of that looks inward, and relate to challenges that we find in our inner processes. In the outer world this type of square is chiefly sustaining in its activity. The mutable square shows where energy of the inner world is linked to the outward-moving expression directly, resulting in a wisdom and harmony which did not exist in the other two cases. This energy, being adaptable and flexible, is the least clear because it is constantly changing, resolving whatever inconsistencies it finds. Each type of square can be seen as a problem; each can also challenge us to greater things. The square connects us to the *material* world directly.

Solar Squares

Sun square Moon: Your relationship to the material world includes your conscious and unconscious mental processes. You manage challenges and problems practically, making concrete changes to handle difficult situations. Because you are uncomfortable with a "wait and see" attitude, you tend toward clear-cut action.

Sun square Mercury: When measurable output is required, you shine. You love to combine the practical demands of the material world with the intellectual challenges of business and personal life.

Sun square Venus: The structure of your life includes intense relationships and occasional overindulgence. You understand some forms of art on a much deeper level than others.

Sun square Mars: You meet life's challenges with energy and activity. You are devoted to accomplishment of your chosen goals.

Sun square Jupiter: Blessed with good health and generally destined for success, you experience challenges that focus your attention on the development of healthy attitudes and good nutritional habits.

Sun square Saturn: The constructive qualities of firmness, modesty, and determination provide concrete situations in which to develop mastery of inhibitions and management of delicate health.

Sun square Uranus: Sudden changes bring new circumstances into your life. You have a curious mind that can respond to people openly. You tend to meet obstacles head-on.

Sun square Neptune: You sense the shape of things psychically before they manifest physically. This sensitivity can become a useful tool in planning and design. You have artistic abilities.

Sun square Pluto: Striving for power is the strongest factor in relationships. You will experience remarkable advancements and decline throughout your life, based on how you exercise control over yourself and others. You test the positive and negative qualities of leadership.

Lunar Squares

Moon square Mercury: Thinking and feeling are compatible factors in your mental process. You are able to assimilate information and to put it back out; your studies should focus on the material "reality."

Moon square Venus: Your intense emotional life can produce conflict. It can also develop into strong emotional understanding. Use your sense of harmony to overcome emotional conflicts, especially with women.

Moon square Mars: Impulsive actions mark your physical body. Rashness can cause problems that can be overcome if you exercise and use control.

Moon square Jupiter: You will be known for the extent of your kindness. You will meet successful women who affect the major transitions in your life. Don't waste your expansive emotions on frivolous activities.

Moon square Saturn: Develop self-control. There is a difference between thoughtfulness and depression. Sometimes you feel very isolated from others. Reckless abandon can cause accidents. Use your mental abilities to think plans through before taking the first step.

Moon square Uranus: Intense emotions can create challenges in your life involving other people. You tend to exaggerate things and to strain your nervous system. Yet you will have sudden successes which come out of these tense periods. You need to balance fear and anxiety with restful periods.

Moon square Neptune: You are often aware of subconscious feelings and thoughts that are not evident to others. This comes through in your awareness of situations that arise in your environment. You often know information about your surroundings and about people which surprises you.

Moon square Pluto: You have a heightened emotional life that is directed into specific areas of your life. You pursue your goals with almost fanatical zest and must be careful to consider other people in your excitement.

Mercury Squares

Mercury square Venus: You have a sense of design and grace in terms of material objects and in relationships. You tend toward a light-hearted existence and sometimes appear not to care about life's details.

Mercury square Mars: You use your powerful mind to help you with difficult challenges. A tendency toward rash action can involve you in controversies. You can develop great skill in argument.

Mercury square Jupiter: Common sense, for you, is grounded in intellect. As long as you take a scrupulously honest approach to life, you will find that life flows in a positive direction. Your active mind and optimism make you a good teacher.

Mercury square Saturn: Clear communication is needed to overcome obstacles in business and family situations. The challenge is to develop a stable base of operation and then stick close to it is spite of pressure.

Mercury square Uranus: Your heightened powers of intuition give you greater flexibility in all kinds of situations. Because you know or feel how conditions will change, you are able to work with the challenges you meet.

Mercury square Neptune: You are challenged to maintain structure when your psychic energy is pulling you off balance. Deceptive currents in your life can also help you develop qualities of compassion and foresight.

Mercury square Pluto: You can be abrasive and coercive, pressing your own values on others to your own detriment. You are persuasive and usually win arguments. Your own eagerness can be a detriment to your health unless you support your nervous system with proper nutrition and rest.

Venus Squares

Venus square Mars: You experience passionate relationships through direct contact between self and others. You have a warm heart and creative abilities. Feelings can run hot and cold at times.

Venus square Jupiter: Love is a hallmark of your life. You meet challenges with concrete facts and the wisdom to work within a caring process. The key is in the tactful yet heartfelt communication of your feelings.

Venus square Saturn: Your love life will go through inhibited periods. Your sober, sensible side will emerge at such times. Your actions reflect the use of intelligence and the attention to factual material.

Venus square Uranus: You fall in and out of love easily. In fact you enjoy the challenge and excitement of the chase.

Venus square Neptune: The world of illusion provides career and personal challenges. You idealize love relationships and can be devastated when they end. You are able to communicate your ideals in some concrete form.

Venus square Pluto: Power issues affect the quality of your relationships adversely if you allow them free rein.

Mars Squares

Mars square Jupiter: Fortunate decisions help you to overcome challenges. You have the ability to concentrate on a particular goal and thus will have successful results professionally.

Mars square Saturn: You experience harmful energy from time to time. Yet your endurance gets you through the difficult times. You are more effective when you throw your energy into tasks without also throwing in your ego.

Mars square Uranus: You will make remarkable achievements during your life, but there is a price. You need to take care to avoid accident or injury because of carelessness. You are brutally honest and sometimes intolerant of others.

Mars square Neptune: You suffer from periodic lack of energy and are susceptible to infections. You have an innate sense of timing. You are inspired to acts of devotion, but are sometimes moody and subject to feelings of inferiority.

Mars square Pluto: You sometimes appear to have superhuman power. You also seem to solve problems by applying excessive amounts of force. Control cruel urges and you will get further.

Jupiter Squares

Jupiter square Saturn: You are often happiest when you are involved in secluded activities. Your patience, diplomacy, and sense of duty are exemplary. Your life is filled with challenges successfully met.

Jupiter square Uranus: Fortunate turns in your life are the stuff of legends. Occasionally you miss the opportunity, but generally you seek independence and adventure, and find them.

Jupiter square Neptune: The richness of feeling in your life is the result of your close connection to the psychic realm. You are a dreamer and mystic. Sometimes you suffer losses because of unprofitable speculations.

Jupiter square Pluto: You have a pervasive desire for power; this desire focuses, for the most part, on the spiritual or mental sphere. However, you can attain leadership positions. It is possible for you to lose everything.

Saturn Squares

Saturn square Uranus: Inhibited rhythms affect your physical body and your social existence. You are able to overcome difficult challenges. You are self-willed and gain or suffer because of this.

Saturn square Neptune: You are methodical in your work, planning carefully and working very hard. Do not allow your inner tension or inhibition to create a foundation for illness.

Saturn square Pluto: You may struggle to attain success and can be proud of your accomplishments. You have the potential to grow in spiritual awareness if you can avoid purely egoistic aims.

Uranus, Neptune, and Pluto Squares

Uranus square Neptune: You have the potential for developing your psychic gifts because you can set aside your "ordinary" consciousness. While you sometimes experience confused psychic states, you can achieve spiritual enlightenment.

Uranus square Pluto: You live for the dare, are constantly active, and sometimes fall precipitously. However, you also have the potential to win big because you are not afraid to take chances.

Neptune square Pluto: You are a highly sensitive person and can develop your psychic gifts steadily throughout your life. You are aware of events before they occur.

No Squares

The lack of squares in your chart can indicate a lack of connection to the physical environment. You will need to make this connection in a conscious manner, using other relationships between planets to establish this type of awareness. You will have to learn how to manage confrontation.

Semi- and Sesqui-Square Aspects

Also within the forty-five degree harmonic, the semi-square (45 degrees) and sesqui-square (135 degrees) are "internal" aspects in the sense that they are shown within the chart as extending from the Ascendant to the middle of the succedent houses, rather than reaching from the Ascendant to one cusp or another. The semi-square and sesqui-square (or sesquiquadrate) indicate tension, insecurity, and irritation, all of which are, for the most part, counterproductive, but signal the creative potential for harmony. *Tension* is inherent in these aspects.

Solar Semi-Squares

Sun semi-square Moon: You have a natural tension between conscious and unconscious activities, which allows you to evaluate situations clearly. Other people are not aware of this tension but they do become aware of your ability to interact creatively with others and to grasp the essentials of any situation.

Sun semi-square Mercury: Tension arises when you cannot reconcile practical observations with logical conclusions. Use this tension to indicate where adjustments need to be made in plans and procedures.

Sun semi-square Venus: Your inner sense of beauty can become a source of tension when you find yourself in excessively indulgent situations. When you are attracted to another individual, use your own physical and mental tension to attract them.

Sun semi-square Mars: Inner tension drains your vitality; find outlets for your emotions, such as exercise.

Sun semi-square Jupiter: Blessed with good health and generally destined for success, tension can cause you to focus too much attention on material circumstances.

Sun semi-square Saturn: The constructive qualities of firmness, modesty, and determination develop when you learn to manage tensions caused by difficult struggles and delicate health.

Sun semi-square Uranus: Sudden changes bring new circumstances into your life. You have a progressive mind that can manage such changes. Your intuition emerges under stress in order to guide you.

Sun semi-square Neptune: You are far more sensitive to your environment than most people. Sometimes this causes nervous weakness; sometimes the inner tension is an indication of increased psychic awareness.

Sun semi-square Pluto: Striving for power can cause stress in your life. You will experience remarkable advancement, as well as dramatic health changes, both for the better and for the worse. Stress can make you difficult to deal with, and power plays can throw you off balance.

Lunar Semi-Squares

Moon semi-square Mercury: Thinking and feeling are internal processes for you. You are able to assimilate information; to put it back out is sometimes stressful for you. Some transitions in your life may be marked by criticism.

Moon semi-square Venus: Intensity in your emotional life is a source of inner conflict. It can also develop into strong emotional bonds, but only if you communicate your feelings clearly.

Moon semi-square Mars: Impulsive actions reflect inner irritation. Rashness can cause problems that can be overcome through honest self-assessment and personal effort. You tend to begin projects with tremendous energy.

Moon semi-square Jupiter: Your kind thoughts require outward expression, as others will often be unaware of your feelings. Relationships with successful women can be stressful. Expansive gestures seem wasteful, but may be the right thing to do.

Moon semi-square Saturn: Your mission in life may center on the development of self-control. Depression caused by your inner thought processes can be a signal to spend time with others, even though you feel like isolating yourself.

Moon semi-square Uranus: Emotional tensions can create strain on your physical body. To avoid this, work with your metaphysical interests and develop an awareness of tension as a signal to refocus subconsciously as well as consciously.

Moon semi-square Neptune: You are often aware of subconscious feelings and thoughts that are not evident to others. This comes through in your awareness of subtle energies and tensions. You have precognitive awareness.

Moon semi-square Pluto: You have a heightened emotional life that can be directed into specific areas of your life. You pursue your goals with almost fanatical zest and must be careful to consider other people in your excitement.

Mercury Semi-Squares

Mercury semi-square Venus: You have a sense of design and grace in terms of material objects and in relationships. You sometimes appear not to care when major events occur in your life, and must verbalize your feelings.

Mercury semi-square Mars: You use your powerful mind to help you through difficult transitions in your life. A tendency toward rash action can create unnecessary tensions. You can use inner tension to guide the direction of persuasive arguments.

Mercury semi-square Jupiter: Common sense, for you, is grounded in intellect. You experience irritation when other are dishonest or negligent by your standards.

Mercury semi-square Saturn: You experienced difficulties in childhood and have had to work hard. Slow, steady advancement in life is related to your skills of concentration and industry.

Mercury semi-square Uranus: Your heightened powers of intuition cause stress and confusion. As you learn to sort out your internal signals, you see increased benefit from your insights.

Mercury semi-square Neptune: You have a vivid fantasy life that can lead nervous stress on the physical plane and confused perception of reality. It can also develop in you the qualities of compassion and subtle perception. You are seldom surprised by changes, due to your keen foresight.

Mercury semi-square Pluto: It is important for you to recognize the inner tensions that sometimes cause you to speak too quickly. Your own eagerness can be a detriment to your health unless you support your nervous system with proper nutrition and rest.

Venus Semi-Squares

Venus semi-square Mars: You experience passionate relationships and you can use the physical tension to moderate between self and others. Irritability is reflected in tactless communication. Your sensuality gets you into relationships; other qualities will sustain them.

Venus semi-square Jupiter: Stress can cause an imbalance in metabolism. This stress can be alleviated through your ability to focus on the proper form of the organs and their processes. Conflict with others goes against your grain.

Venus semi-square Saturn: Difficulty and separation in love relationships causes strain that can impact your health. Even temporary separations can cause you pain. Jealousy can be a problem.

Venus semi-square Uranus: Your tendency to fall in and out of love causes a lot of stress. Spend time learning what you really want in a relationship and then seek it.

Venus semi-square Neptune: You would prefer to live in a world of illusion and this causes stress. You idealize love relationships and can be devastated when infatuations end. Focus on your high ideals.

Venus semi-square Pluto: The exertion of power in love relationships can be intensely satisfying. It can also cause tensions and stress. You are creatively and procreatively fruitful.

Mars Semi-Squares

Mars semi-square Jupiter: Fortunate decisions mark the major turning points of your life. You have the ability to concentrate on particular goals. Manage stress to protect your heart.

Mars semi-square Saturn: You experience harmful energy from time to time, yet your endurance gets you through it. You are more effective when you throw your energy into tasks without also throwing in your ego.

Mars semi-square Uranus: You will make remarkable achievements during your life, but there is a price. You need to take care to avoid accident or injury because of carelessness. You are brutally honest and sometimes intolerant of others.

Mars semi-square Neptune: You suffer from periodic lack of energy and are susceptible to infections. You have an innate sense of timing. You are inspired to acts of devotion. Avoid unnecessary use of drugs.

Mars semi-square Pluto: You sometimes appear to have superhuman power. You also solve problems by applying excessive amounts of force. Control cruel urges and you will get further.

Jupiter Semi-Squares

Jupiter semi-square Saturn: Inner tension can indicate the time to end a relationship. Your patience, diplomacy, and sense of duty are exemplary. Your life is based on steady, patient progress.

Jupiter semi-square Uranus: Fortunate turns in your life are the stuff of legends. You seek independence and adventure, and can build up or release tension through sudden changes in your activities.

Jupiter semi-square Neptune: The richness of feeling in your life is the result of your close connection to the psychic realm. A lack of spiritual rigor can be matched by a lack of physical strength; working with both will help you to avoid instability.

Jupiter semi-square Pluto: You have a pervasive desire for power; this desire can help you to attain leadership positions. It is possible for you to lose everything and then to regenerate your life.

Saturn Semi-Squares

Saturn semi-square Uranus: Inhibited rhythms affect your physical body and your social existence. You are able to overcome difficulties. You are self-willed and gain or suffer because of this.

Saturn semi-square Neptune: You are methodical in your work, planning carefully and working very hard. Do not allow your inner tension or inhibition to create a foundation for illness.

Saturn semi-square Pluto: You have a cruel streak that must be tempered by other factors. You have the potential to grow in spiritual awareness if you can avoid purely egoistic aims.

Uranus, Neptune, and Pluto Semi-Squares

Uranus semi-square Neptune: Stresses in your life can develop into a lack of vitality and energy. While you sometimes experience confused psychic states, you can achieve spiritual enlightenment, perhaps through travel.

Uranus semi-square Pluto: There is a climate of violence or accidents that will affect you, particularly when you allow impatience and other tensions to gain a foothold. You are also able to connect with social reform, exploration, and other positive expressions of your inner restlessness.

Neptune semi-square Pluto: You are a highly sensitive person and can develop your psychic gifts steadily throughout your life. You are aware of events before they occur. Focused attention can steer you away from obsession and confusion. Avoid the misuse of drugs.

No Semi-Squares

It is not that you have no tension in your life. Rather, it is that you have difficulty identifying the tension and dealing with it.

Solar Sesqui-Squares

Sun sesqui-square Moon: When you feel an inner agitation, you will know that some action is needed, even though other people refuse to see the need. Use the agitation as a signal from the unconscious that something is amiss, evaluate the situation, and take action that involves other people directly.

Sun sesqui-square Mercury: A lack of general clarity can lead to agitated feelings and nervousness. Use your awareness of stress to stimulate practical thinking and prudent action. Then tension becomes a mental and emotional ally.

Sun sesqui-square Venus: You tend to eat rich food and to indulge your emotions, causing internal stress. These urges require balance if you wish to maintain inner harmony.

Sun sesqui-square Mars: When you become agitated, you need an outlet for your thoughts and feelings. Direct restless behavior into concentrated meditation and action.

Sun sesqui-square Jupiter: Blessed with good health and generally destined for success, you occasionally allow inner agitation to upset your glandular balance through dietary or emotional excess.

Sun sesqui-square Saturn: The constructive qualities of firmness, modesty, and determination can be derailed by internal turmoil relating to delicate health and pessimistic thoughts.

Sun sesqui-square Uranus: Sudden changes bring new circumstances into your life. Your intuition helps you, but only after some agitation.

Sun sesqui-square Neptune: You are far more sensitive to your environment than most people. However, others will not be aware of this unless you tell them.

Sun sesqui-square Pluto: Strong inner tensions allow you to utilize individuality in your quest for power. You will experience remarkable advancement, as well as dramatic health changes, both for the better and for the worse. You dislike the limitations of working for others, preferring to be the one in charge.

Lunar Sesqui-Squares

Moon sesqui-square Mercury: Thinking and feeling are aligned for you. Mental agitation is a positive process, as it allows you to stir ideas and obtain a synthesis. Your good judgment can prevent unnecessary gossip.

Moon sesqui-square Venus: Emotional agitation places you at a disadvantage with women. Use your innate artistic talent and recognition of beauty to relieve the stress and you will even the balance.

Moon sesqui-square Mars: Agitated thought processes can cause impulsive actions. You tend to begin projects with tremendous energy. Rashness can cause problems that can be overcome through honest self-assessment and personal effort.

Moon sesqui-square Jupiter: You become very upset by conflicts that impinge on your philosophical beliefs. Because this kind of upset affects your entire digestive process, you need to resolve conflict in a businesslike manner.

Moon sesqui-square Saturn: Your mission in life may center on the development of self-control. Clear thinking and careful effort is needed to work through anxiety caused by family. Sometimes you feel very isolated from others.

Moon sesqui-square Uranus: Nervous stress leads to mental agitation and an increased desire for activity. You use your emotional state as a tool to gain success; there is a tendency to overdo the emotional side of life.

Moon sesqui-square Neptune: You are often aware of subconscious feelings and thoughts that are not evident to others, coming through your awareness of shifting cycles. Often you choose to be alone, rather than deal with misunderstandings.

Moon sesqui-square Pluto: Explosive expressions of feeling result from a build-up of internal pressures. These outbursts nearly always relate to a specific cause that has festered for years. There is a complementary sentimental streak.

Mercury Sesqui-Squares

Mercury sesqui-square Venus: Internal tension can be a source of creative energy. You have a sense of design and grace that leads to artistic success and to light-hearted interactions with others. You are overly sensitive at times.

Mercury sesqui-square Mars: If you lack personal control over your feelings, you may develop nervous illnesses. Instead of quarreling and finding fault, you can use your conversational ability to entertain and uplift people.

Mercury sesqui-square Jupiter: Common sense, for you, is grounded in intellect. A scrupulously honest approach to life will make you more successful in your interactions with others. Stress can affect your reflexes.

Mercury sesqui-square Saturn: Tension can cause physical pain. You tend to have many projects going on at once and this can lead to nervousness. You are generally logical and thorough. Slow, steady advancement in life is related to your skills of concentration and industry.

Mercury sesqui-square Uranus: Your heightened powers of intuition give you greater flexibility in all kinds of situations. Because you know or feel how conditions will change, you are able to maximize the benefits of cyclical movement. You may suffer from headaches or facial pain.

Mercury sesqui-square Neptune: You have a vivid fantasy life that is connected to some form of psychic activity. While this can produce deceptive currents in your life, it can also develop in you the qualities of compassion and subtle perception. Tension can cause a loss of sensation.

Mercury sesqui-square Pluto: Your highly developed powers of persuasion can agitate situations. You can be a successful speaker or writer. Your own eagerness can be detrimental to your strong position if you push others too hard. Develop facilitation skills by paying attention to your effect on others.

Venus Sesqui-Squares

Venus sesqui-square Mars: You experience passion in relationships internally and need to express it if you want your partner to be aware of it. Stress causes fluctuating feelings or a lack of tact.

Venus sesqui-square Jupiter: Love is a hallmark of your life. If you become lazy in love relationships, conflict can arise. You have a strong sense of the form that you want relationships to take.

Venus sesqui-square Saturn: Your relationship choices cover the range of possibilities. You may connect with someone much older or younger; you may experience inhibition, jealousy, or faithfulness. The choices are up to you. Relationships may lead you to a more sober view of life.

Venus sesqui-square Uranus: You fall in and out of love easily. In fact you enjoy the beginning and ending of relationships because of the excitement. Tension can have a big impact on your sex life.

Venus sesqui-square Neptune: You would prefer to live in a world of illusion where relationships are concerned. You idealize love relationships and can experience a wide range of interaction with one partner.

Venus sesqui-square Pluto: The exertion of power in love relationships can be intensely satisfying. Relationships can place a great strain on your sexual expression. You sometimes have odd desires.

Mars Sesqui-Squares

Mars sesqui-square Jupiter: Fortunate decisions mark the major turning points of your life. You have the ability to concentrate on particular goals. Manage stress to protect your heart.

Mars sesqui-square Saturn: You experience harmful energy from time to time, yet your endurance gets you through it. You are more effective when you throw your energy into tasks without also throwing in your ego.

Mars sesqui-square Uranus: You will make remarkable achievements during your life, but there is a price. You need to take care to avoid accident or injury because of carelessness. You are brutally honest and sometimes intolerant of others.

Mars sesqui-square Neptune: You suffer from periodic lack of energy and are susceptible to infections. You have an innate sense of timing. You are inspired to acts of devotion. Avoid unnecessary use of drugs.

Mars sesqui-square Pluto: You sometimes appear to have superhuman power. You also solve problems by applying excessive amounts of force. Control cruel urges and you will get further.

Jupiter Sesqui-Squares

Jupiter sesqui-square Saturn: Inner tension can indicate the time to end a relationship. Your patience, diplomacy, and sense of duty are exemplary. Your life is based on steady, patient progress.

Jupiter sesqui-square Uranus: Fortunate turns in your life are the stuff of legends. You seek independence and adventure, and can build up or release tension through sudden changes in your activities.

Jupiter sesqui-square Neptune: The richness of feeling in your life is the result of your close connection to the psychic realm. A lack of spiritual rigor can be matched by a lack of physical strength; working with both will help you to avoid instability.

Jupiter sesqui-square Pluto: You have a pervasive desire for power; this desire can help you to attain leadership positions. It is possible for you to lose everything and then to regenerate your life.

Saturn Sesqui-Squares

Saturn sesqui-square Uranus: Inhibited rhythms affect your physical body and your social existence. You are able to overcome difficulties. You are self-willed and gain or suffer because of this.

Saturn sesqui-square Neptune: You are methodical in your work, planning carefully and working very hard. Do not allow your inner tension or inhibition to create a foundation for illness.

Saturn sesqui-square Pluto: You have a cruel streak that must be tempered by other factors. You have the potential to grow in spiritual awareness if you can avoid purely egoistic aims.

Uranus, Neptune, and Pluto Sesqui-Squares

Uranus sesqui-square Neptune: Stresses in your life can develop into a lack of vitality and energy. While you sometimes experience confused psychic states, you can achieve spiritual enlightenment, perhaps through travel.

Uranus sesqui-square Pluto: There is a climate of violence or accidents that will affect you, particularly when you allow impatience and other tensions to gain a foothold. You are also able to connect with social reform, exploration, and other positive expressions of your inner restlessness.

Neptune sesqui-square Pluto: You are a highly sensitive person and can develop your psychic gifts steadily throughout your life. You are aware of events before they occur. Focused attention can steer you away from obsession and confusion. Avoid the misuse of drugs.

No Sesqui-Squares

It is not that you have no tension in your life. Rather, it is that you have difficulty identifying the tension and dealing with it.

Quintile and Biquintile Aspects

The quintile (72 degrees) and biquintile (144 degrees) aspects are indicative of a level of human function beyond the material and scientific. Here we find the quality of organization between individuals. Organization occurs at the conceptual level of the trine, but it is not limited to the experience of the budding ego. This level of expression is fully invested with the energy of scientific knowledge and understanding. The individual brings all emotion, all information, and all experience to bear in the creative solution of problems and the creative generation of new works.

Quintiles represent latent talent and creative potential. This potential can be seen in the quintile aspects themselves *and* in the quintile-type movement through the five-pointed star. This movement is depicted in the Chinese five-element system, moving both forward and backward, as well as through the star, as when we draw a star in one pen stroke.

Creativity at this level demands a nonattachment to ego. We need to be able to act as independently as possible, not making personal considerations our primary thought. The expression of artists is often at its best when it transcends personal limitations and contacts the group or better, the larger mind of the solar system or the universe. I believe humanity is moving in the direction of this kind of creativity, becoming less attached to form and the limitations of science and more capable of inspired choice of behavior. The quintile, at the same conceptual level as the trine, adds experience to the formula, joining intellect, emotion and experience in the *creative* process.

Solar Quintile

> *Sun quintile Moon:* Your creative talents draw on the close connection between your conscious awareness and your inner, spiritual nature. You feel better when you are actively using your natural abilities to bring about creative change.

> *Sun quintile Mercury:* The combination of practical thinking and organizational ability complements your creative efforts.

> *Sun quintile Venus:* One of your strongest talents lies in knowing how to attract people to your point of view.

Sun quintile Mars: You have creative abilities that can further your ambition. Direct any stubbornness into creative channels by relaxing your hold on others.

Sun quintile Jupiter: Blessed with good health and generally destined for success, your talents bring you both material and spiritual gains.

Sun quintile Saturn: The constructive qualities of firmness, modesty, and determination develop your talents. You learn to deal with health issues and modest circumstances creatively.

Sun quintile Uranus: Sudden changes bring new circumstances into your life. You have a creative response to the most difficult situations.

Sun quintile Neptune: You are far more sensitive to your environment than most people. Increased psychic awareness can add to your creativity.

Sun quintile Pluto: Creative power places you in positions of leadership and advances you in the minds of others. They see your creative regeneration of situations as innovative and fresh.

Lunar Quintiles

Moon quintile Mercury: Thinking and feeling are aligned for you, allowing the creative assimilation of information as well as its expression.

Moon quintile Venus: Intensity in your emotional life can be a source of tremendous creative energy. You can also develop strong emotional bonds with others. Use your innate artistic talent and recognition of beauty to direct your emotional energies into material form.

Moon quintile Mars: Your creative impulse can lead to excited periods of productivity. The unconscious mind is a valuable source of inspiration.

Moon quintile Jupiter: You enjoy creative activities that involve women. You are a social success when you allow your talents to flow without wastefulness or negligence.

Moon quintile Saturn: The creative process for you lies in the careful gathering of resources and conscientious application of effort. Sensitive health issues deserve the same creative attention.

Moon quintile Uranus: You grasp creative moments with ease, especially when you let your intuition run free. Sudden success comes out of these moments of clarity.

Moon quintile Neptune: You are often aware of subconscious feelings and thoughts that are not evident to others. This comes through your awareness of shifting cycles. You seem to have precognitive information about change.

Moon quintile Pluto: You have a heightened emotional life that feeds your creative process. You pursue your goals with zest and attract interest in your artistic output.

Mercury Quintiles

Mercury quintile Venus: You are creative with words and forge solid relationships based on clear communication. Your light-heartedness is sometimes mistaken for a devil-may-care attitude.

Mercury quintile Mars: You use your powerful mind to create positive outcomes in every area of your life. You are a creative, forceful debater.

Mercury quintile Jupiter: Common sense is the foundation of your creativity. You focus on process and take an optimistic view of life.

Mercury quintile Saturn: Your innate understanding of structure is evident in your work and play. Serious thought accompanies all decisions, but you add a creative twist that gains respect.

Mercury quintile Uranus: Creative activity arises from intuitive insight. You know just the right thing to say and how to get the best results from your efforts.

Mercury quintile Neptune: Fantasy is your creative source. You speak from a well of compassion and grasp the subtleties in most situations.

Mercury quintile Pluto: You manipulate discussions to achieve maximum creative gain, for yourself and for others. You are the consummate deal maker.

Venus Quintiles

Venus quintile Mars: You are able to set your ego aside in love relationships, thereby inspiring the creative focus between you and your partner. You have a warm heart, although feelings may fluctuate.

Venus quintile Jupiter: Love is a hallmark of your life. You transcend personal limitations to emphasize harmony in relationships. Marriage and family life are an expression of your creativity.

Venus quintile Saturn: Your love life will go through inhibited periods. You manage difficult periods by using your talent for making sacrifice look easy and natural.

Venus quintile Uranus: You use your artistic talent to enhance relationships. You express your love in varied ways and never bore your partner. Your actions sometimes appear eccentric to others.

Venus quintile Neptune: You would prefer to live in a world of illusion and use your creative abilities to maintain ideal relationships. There is a mystical thread in your organizational work.

Venus quintile Pluto: While you pour your creative energies into love relationships, you may not particularly connect the recreational qualities of sex with procreation. The exertion of power in love relationships can be intensely satisfying.

Mars Quintiles

Mars quintile Jupiter: People may recognize your ability to cope with difficult circumstances as your best organizational skill. Your creative ability to concentrate on a particular goal is actually the source of successful professional results.

Mars quintile Saturn: You experience harmful energy from time to time. Your endurance gets you through the difficult stages of the creative process where others often fail.

Mars quintile Uranus: You will make remarkable achievements during your life, but there is a price. You need to take care to avoid accident or injury because of carelessness. You are brutally honest and sometimes intolerant of others.

Mars quintile Neptune: You suffer from periodic lack of energy and are susceptible to infections. You have an innate sense of timing. You are inspired to acts of devotion, but are sometimes moody and subject to feelings of inferiority.

Mars quintile Pluto: You sometimes appear to have superhuman power. You also seem to solve problems by applying excessive amounts of force. Control cruel urges and you will get further.

Jupiter Quintiles

Jupiter quintile Saturn: You are often happiest when you are involved in secluded activities. Your patience, diplomacy, and sense of duty are exemplary. Your life is filled with changes.

Jupiter quintile Uranus: Fortunate turns in your life are the stuff of legends. Occasionally you miss the opportunity, but generally you seek independence and adventure.

Jupiter quintile Neptune: The richness of feeling in your life is the result of your close connection to the psychic realm. You are a dreamer and mystic. Sometimes you suffer losses because of unprofitable speculations.

Jupiter quintile Pluto: You have a pervasive desire for power; this desire focuses, for the most part, on the spiritual or mental sphere. However, you can attain leadership positions. It is possible for you to lose everything.

Saturn Quintiles

Saturn quintile Uranus: Inhibited rhythms affect your physical body and your social existence. You are able to overcome difficulties. You are self-willed and gain or suffer because of this.

Saturn quintile Neptune: You are methodical in your work, planning carefully and working very hard. Do not allow your inner tension or inhibition to create a foundation for illness.

Saturn quintile Pluto: You have a cruel streak that must be tempered by other factors. You have the potential to grow in spiritual awareness if you can avoid purely egoistic aims.

Uranus, Neptune, and Pluto Quintiles

Uranus quintile Neptune: You have the potential for developing your psychic gifts. While you sometimes experience confused psychic states, you can achieve spiritual enlightenment.

Uranus quintile Pluto: You live for the dare, are constantly active, and sometimes fall precipitously. However, you also have the potential to win big because you are not afraid to take chances.

Neptune quintile Pluto: You are a highly sensitive person and can develop your psychic gifts steadily throughout your life. You are aware of events before they occur.

No Quintiles

Your creativity comes out through other aspect relationships in the chart, particularly sextiles and squares. You access to internal information will be through sesqui-squares and quincunxes, both of which are harder to manage.

Solar Biquintile

Sun biquintile Moon: When you observe a situation, you allow the direct perception to run through your inner mind, thus making connections that are not evident to others. Your talent lies in the use of this ability to suggest dynamic solutions for interpersonal problems. You are willing to use your own personality to produce positive change.

Sun biquintile Mercury: Because you are able to run your intellectual decisions through a practical preview, you are able to avoid common pitfalls in business and relationships.

Sun biquintile Venus: Creative expression takes a path through the inner recesses of your mind. Thus, you take an object, pull up subconscious material, and transform it.

Sun biquintile Mars: Your energetic approach to creative process includes a sweep of subconscious ideas and feelings.

Sun biquintile Jupiter: Blessed with good health and generally destined for success, you use your talents best when you maintain a healthy attitude toward life, free of inner conflicts.

Sun biquintile Saturn: The constructive qualities of firmness, modesty, and determination develop through an inner examination of difficult struggles and delicate health. You find creative solutions for inherited problems.

Sun biquintile Uranus: Sudden changes bring new circumstances into your life. You have the creative mind for handling such changes. You draw ideas from a deep inner well.

Sun biquintile Neptune: You are far more sensitive to your environment than most people. Sometimes this comes across as weakness of creative energy; sometimes it is an indication of increased psychic awareness.

Sun biquintile Pluto: Your creative and even transformative efforts are strongest when you connect personal drive for power with awareness of your environment and other people.

Lunar Biquintiles

Moon biquintile Mercury: Thinking and feeling are creative sources of understanding concerning the world. Working with women can be a valuable source of ideas.

Moon biquintile Venus: The creative flow of ideas and activities in your life is subject to inner processes of a cyclical nature.

Moon biquintile Mars: Impulsive actions mark your creative connection with the world. You tend to begin projects with tremendous energy. Honest self-assessment and personal effort can overcome your tendency to judge yourself harshly.

Moon biquintile Jupiter: You are optimistic about the creative possibilities in your life. Connection between your personal philosophical beliefs and your experience of the world will result in positive social outcomes.

Moon biquintile Saturn: Your creative activities build upon a tradition of inherited ideas. Channel you energies into conservative lines of work in which other people play a strong role.

Moon biquintile Uranus: You become excited about creative ideas that emerge from subconscious dreams. You then strive toward an objective that emphasizes the metaphysical quality of your creative process.

Moon biquintile Neptune: Subconscious feelings connect your inner world with the creative process of the social sphere. Your awareness of shifting energy patterns places you in the right spot to avoid being exploited.

Moon biquintile Pluto: You can use your deeply rooted feelings to interact creatively with others. Rather than stifling emotional outbursts, use that energy to pursue conceptual links between your talents and outer reality.

Mercury Biquintiles

Mercury biquintile Venus: You have a sense of design of material objects and grace in relationships. You take a light-hearted approach to your creative endeavors.

Mercury biquintile Mars: You use your powerful mind to fuel your creative activities. Determination is the key to success. You use speaking skills to bring people together in organizations.

Mercury biquintile Jupiter: Expansive ideas, an active mind, and a gift for speech make you a creative performer. You have remarkable physical reflexes. A failure at dishonesty, you can be successful in many careers.

Mercury biquintile Saturn: Thorough planning and logical thinking lay behind all of your organizational successes. Slow, steady advancement in life is related to your skills of concentration and industry.

Mercury biquintile Uranus: Your revolutionary thinking and inventiveness, along with the ability to suddenly achieve higher awareness, give you a dynamic edge over others. Because you know or feel how conditions will change, you have powerful influence in group activities.

Mercury biquintile Neptune: You have a vivid fantasy life that is connected to psychic activity. While this can produce deceptive currents in your life, it can also develop in you the qualities of compassion and subtle perception. You would make an excellent creative writer.

Mercury biquintile Pluto: Your highly developed powers of persuasion place you in a position to organize group activities successfully. You can be a successful speaker or writer. Your own eagerness can be a detriment to your health.

Venus Biquintiles

Venus biquintile Mars: You are able to set your ego aside in love relationships, thereby inspiring the creative focus between you and your partner. You have a warm heart, although feelings may fluctuate.

Venus biquintile Jupiter: Love is a hallmark of your life. You transcend personal limitations to emphasize harmony in relationships. Marriage and family life are an expression of your creativity.

Venus biquintile Saturn: Your love life will go through inhibited periods. You manage difficult periods by using your talent for making sacrifice look easy and natural.

Venus biquintile Uranus: You use your artistic talent to enhance relationships. You express your love in varied ways and never bore your partner. Your actions sometimes appear eccentric to others.

Venus biquintile Neptune: You would prefer to live in a world of illusion and use your creative abilities to maintain ideal relationships. There is a mystical thread in your organizational work.

Venus biquintile Pluto: While you pour your creative energies into love relationships, you may not particularly connect the recreational qualities of sex with procreation. The exertion of power in love relationships can be intensely satisfying.

Mars Biquintiles

Mars biquintile Jupiter: People may recognize your ability to cope with difficult circumstances as your best organizational skill. Your creative ability to concentrate on a particular goal is actually the source of successful professional results.

Mars biquintile Saturn: You experience harmful energy from time to time. Your endurance gets you through the difficult stages of the creative process where others often fail.

Mars biquintile Uranus: You will make remarkable achievements during your life, but there is a price. You need to take care to avoid accident or injury because of carelessness. You are brutally honest and sometimes intolerant of others.

Mars biquintile Neptune: You suffer from periodic lack of energy and are susceptible to infections. You have an innate sense of timing. You are inspired to acts of devotion, but are sometimes moody and subject to feelings of inferiority.

Mars biquintile Pluto: You sometimes appear to have superhuman power. You also seem to solve problems by applying excessive amounts of force. Control cruel urges and you will get further.

Jupiter Biquintiles

Jupiter biquintile Saturn: You are often happiest when you are involved in secluded activities. Your patience, diplomacy, and sense of duty are exemplary. Your life is filled with change.

Jupiter biquintile Uranus: Fortunate turns in your life are the stuff of legends. Occasionally you miss the opportunity, but generally you seek independence and adventure.

Jupiter biquintile Neptune: The richness of feeling in your life is the result of your close connection to the psychic realm. You are a dreamer and mystic. Sometimes you suffer losses because of unprofitable speculations.

Jupiter biquintile Pluto: You have a pervasive desire for power; this desire focuses, for the most part, on the spiritual or mental sphere. However, you can attain leadership positions. It is possible for you to lose everything.

Saturn Biquintiles

Saturn biquintile Uranus: Inhibited rhythms affect your physical body and your social existence. You are able to overcome difficulties. You are self-willed and gain or suffer because of this.

Saturn biquintile Neptune: You are methodical in your work, planning carefully and working very hard. Do not allow your inner tension or inhibition to create a foundation for illness.

Saturn biquintile Pluto: You have a cruel streak that must be tempered by other factors. You have the potential to grow in spiritual awareness if you can avoid purely egoistic aims.

Uranus, Neptune, and Pluto Biquintiles

Uranus biquintile Neptune: You have the potential for developing your psychic gifts. While you sometimes experience confused psychic states, you can achieve spiritual enlightenment.

Uranus biquintile Pluto: You live for the dare, are constantly active, and sometimes fall precipitously. However, you also have the potential to win big because you are not afraid to take chances.

Neptune biquintile Pluto: You are a highly sensitive person and can develop your psychic gifts steadily throughout your life. You are aware of events before they occur.

No Biquintiles

Your creativity comes out through other aspect relationships in the chart, particularly sextiles and squares. You access to internal information will be through sesqui-squares and quincunxes, both of which are harder to manage.

Sextile Aspects

The sextile aspect (60 degrees) relates elements to each other that are considered compatible in the western astrological system (360/5). Fire and air work well together; earth and water are necessary to each other. We are able to create things for their value, manifesting in the world through our knowledge of material means.

The fully empowered human being, using the energy of the sextile, can simply think of things and make them manifest. Jesus did this with the loaves and fishes. He decided there were enough for everyone, and there were enough. He didn't have to actively plant seed, make flour, and bake. He didn't need to cast a net to catch more fish. He only had to make this decision. Sextile aspects contain what is necessary. All we need to do is notice the opportunity that exists in things, and make use of it without depending on ego.

Growth does not come without some effort; the individual must recognize his opportunities and act upon them in a timely manner. The sextile, more than any other aspect (except perhaps the trine) allows the individual to maintain control over the course of events. While squares represent energies that act upon us, the sextile needs guidance from us in order to produce a significant effect. Thus, we can achieve growth by using the energies made available to us and indicated by the sextile aspects. The sextile brings healing by *decision*, without effort.

Solar Sextiles

Sun sextile Moon: You often are able to make something of opportunities that involve you personally because you can see the constructive value of situations. However, you must take action to get productive results. You measure an opportunity in terms of the outer potential as well as the inner feeling qualities that are presented to you.

Sun sextile Mercury: You instinctively link learned practical skills with clarity of mind to take advantage of opportunities as they arise.

Sun sextile Venus: Your intense feeling nature gets you into situations where powerful relationships can develop. You periodically find opportunities to development an artistic talent.

Sun sextile Mars: You find that you have the energy to work with diverse situations and take whatever opportunities come your way.

Sun sextile Jupiter: Blessed with good health and generally destined for success, you are able to control expansion in your life by choosing your direction consciously.

Sun sextile Saturn: The constructive qualities of firmness, modesty, and determination develop in the context of opportunities to consciously create structure in your life.

Sun sextile Uranus: Sudden changes provide the animation of your intuitive self-guidance. It is possible to align your thinking to minimize upsets as you see golden opportunities where others see only defeat and disaster.

Sun sextile Neptune: You are far more sensitive to your environment than most people. Without careful attention to your choices, you make emphasize weaknesses in your physical body. Increased psychic awareness that helps you to make the most of your possibilities.

Sun sextile Pluto: Striving for power is the most evident quality in your value system. You will experience remarkable advancement, as well as dramatic health changes, based in the opportunities you pursue.

Lunar Sextiles

Moon sextile Mercury: Thinking and feeling are aligned for you. You are able to assimilate and use information; you are a good student. You can use your mental capabilities to promote healing.

Moon sextile Venus: Emotional intensity in your life produces conflict. Opportunities arise to work with women. Use your innate artistic talent and recognition of beauty to overcome a tendency to dwell on emotional conflicts.

Moon sextile Mars: You tend to begin projects with tremendous energy, and then let opportunities slip away. Rashness can cause problems that can be overcome through honest self-assessment and personal effort.

Moon sextile Jupiter: You will have chances to form relationships with successful women. You need to control expansive gestures to avoid wastefulness.

Moon sextile Saturn: Your mission in life may center on the development of self-control. You control the movement in your life by examining opportunities carefully. When emotional openings allow depression to creep in, you need to define yourself through clear thinking. Sometimes you feel very isolated from others.

Moon sextile Uranus: Your mind's eye has a camera that is animated by opportunities. You will have amazing successes that come out of these personal "movies." You tend to exaggerate things and to strain your nervous system.

Moon sextile Neptune: You are often aware of subconscious feelings and thoughts that are not evident to others. You seem to have precognitive information about changes, and create healing environments using that information.

Moon sextile Pluto: You have a heightened emotional life that is directed into specific areas of your life. You pursue opportunities with almost fanatical zest and must be careful to consider other people in your excitement.

Mercury Sextiles

Mercury sextile Venus: You have a sense of design and grace that you apply to life's offerings. You tend toward a light-hearted existence that belies the growth that emerges from choices you make.

Mercury sextile Mars: You use your powerful mind to help you take advantage of opportunities. You are sometimes quick to argue and find fault.

Mercury sextile Jupiter: Common sense, for you, provides intellectual opportunity. Your scrupulously honest approach to life positions you for positive career development. Your active mind and optimism make you a good supervisor or manager.

Mercury sextile Saturn: You find opportunities to be logical and thorough in your work and in your personal life. Slow, steady advancement in life is founded on clear thought and communication. Opportunities arise through careful planning.

Mercury sextile Uranus: Your heightened powers of intuition give you greater flexibility in all kinds of situations. Because you know or feel how conditions will change, you are able to grasp opportunities and run with them.

Mercury sextile Neptune: You have a vivid fantasy life that is connected to some form of psychic activity. You are seldom surprised by changes and see them as openings for further insight.

Mercury sextile Pluto: You relish opportunities to influence others and are a strong speaker and leader. For you the pen truly is mightier than the sword.

Venus Sextiles

Venus sextile Mars: You experience passionate relationships because of your ability to moderate between self and others. You have a warm heart and creative abilities. There can be fluctuating feelings or a lack of tact.

Venus sextile Jupiter: Love is a hallmark of your life. You have both the possibility of relationship conflicts and the potential for harmonious long-term relationships. The key is in the tactful yet heartfelt communication of your feelings.

Venus sextile Saturn: Your love life will go through inhibited periods. Your sober, sensible side will emerge at such times. Even temporary separations can cause you pain. Jealousy can be a problem.

Venus sextile Uranus: You fall in and out of love easily. In fact you enjoy the beginning and ending of relationships because of the excitement. Your actions sometimes appear eccentric to others.

Venus sextile Neptune: You would prefer to live in a world of illusion and can make this your life work. You idealize love relationships and can be devastated when they end. Know that a new one is just around the corner.

Venus sextile Pluto: The exertion of power in love relationships can be intensely satisfying. It can also bring about the end of valued relationships. You are artistically gifted.

Mars Sextiles

Mars sextile Jupiter: Fortunate decisions mark the major turning points of your life. You have the ability to concentrate on a particular goal and thus will have successful results professionally.

Mars sextile Saturn: You experience harmful energy from time to time. Yet your endurance gets you through the difficult times. You are more effective when you throw your energy into tasks without also throwing in your ego.

Mars sextile Uranus: You will make remarkable achievements during your life, but there is a price. You need to take care to avoid accident or injury because of carelessness. You are brutally honest and sometimes intolerant of others.

Mars sextile Neptune: You suffer from periodic lack of energy and are susceptible to infections. You have an innate sense of timing. You are inspired to acts of devotion, but are sometimes moody and subject to feelings of inferiority.

Mars sextile Pluto: You sometimes appear to have superhuman power. You also seem to solve problems by applying excessive amounts of force. Control cruel urges and you will get further.

Jupiter Sextiles

Jupiter sextile Saturn: You are often happiest when you are involved in secluded activities. Your patience, diplomacy, and sense of duty are exemplary. Your life is filled with change.

Jupiter sextile Uranus: Fortunate turns in your life are the stuff of legends. Occasionally you miss the opportunity, but generally you seek independence and adventure.

Jupiter sextile Neptune: The richness of feeling in your life is the result of your close connection to the psychic realm. You are a dreamer and mystic. Sometimes you suffer losses because of unprofitable speculations.

Jupiter sextile Pluto: You have a pervasive desire for power; this desire focuses, for the most part, on the spiritual or mental sphere. However, you can attain leadership positions. It is possible for you to lose everything.

Saturn Sextiles

Saturn sextile Uranus: Inhibited rhythms affect your physical body and your social existence. You are able to overcome difficulties. You are self-willed and gain or suffer because of this.

Saturn sextile Neptune: You are methodical in your work, planning carefully and working very hard. Do not allow your inner tension or inhibition to create a foundation for illness.

Saturn sextile Pluto: You have a cruel streak that must be tempered by other factors. You have the potential to grow in spiritual awareness if you can avoid purely egoistic aims.

Uranus, Neptune, and Pluto Sextiles

Uranus sextile Neptune: You have the potential for developing your psychic gifts. While you sometimes experience confused psychic states, you can achieve spiritual enlightenment.

Uranus sextile Pluto: You live for the dare, are constantly active, and sometimes fall precipitously. However, you also have the potential to win big because you are not afraid to take chances.

Neptune sextile Pluto: You are a highly sensitive person and can develop your psychic gifts steadily throughout your life. You are aware of events before they occur.

No Sextiles

Unlike many people, you make your own opportunities through hard work and awareness of conditions around you. Growth and development are relatively conscious processes for you.

Summary

The aspects, then, demonstrate stages of development in a logical harmonic progression. While they are indicators of other energies as well, this model of process is useful to the individual who is directing attention toward creative development. Used with any chart, such an approach to aspect delineation defines energy flows on a larger scale and brings them into conscious awareness more fully.

Chapter Five

Saturn and Mars as Vocational Indicators

Astrologer Grant Lewi blamed the disastrous vocational situation of the 1930s on the fact that there were not enough jobs to go around. This seems obvious enough until we realize "jobs" are not a form of organic life that human beings must live off as a kind of parasite. Nor is their shortage analogous to the potato famine. Work is a human activity that does not diminish when survival is threatened. To the contrary, in an emergency everyone should be employed. It is a tribute to the primitive nature of our economies that full-time employment is only insured when war demands that everyone make an active contribution to the annihilation of the species, whereas jobs are certain to be scarce in times of dearth when many are required to make a passive contribution to their own starvation.

As we approach the millennium the number of jobs is not the problem. The difficulty comes from the fact that there are so many vocations, and that the vocational possibilities are rapidly changing. Many of us are considering our second or even third career because our original choice is becoming obsolete, makes demands upon us that we could not have anticipated, is losing prestige, no longer pays as well, or has become so mechanized as to bore us to automated tears, among other reasons.

Lewi went on to say: "The jobs now available will go to those men and women who know what they want; aim at a type of job which they are preeminently fitted, by nature, to do; and approach the getting and keeping of a job with the maximum of self-knowledge" (Lewi, "Your Job and Astrology," *American Astrology Magazine* 3, no. 5 (1935): 19).

These points form the foundation for career counseling, whether it be through astrological or psychological methods. The additional problems faced in today's world are these: How do you keep up with the rapidly changing job market? How do you become informed about new career fields that will suit your personal qualifications?

One's skills and talents can be assessed from an astrological perspective so that qualifications can be matched to the career marketplace. While jobs are ever-changing, personality is founded on a solid base. Understanding this will supply physical, emotional, mental, and spiritual clues to your best line of work. Then you can determine how to apply your best to the career field you find most attractive.

This chapter on Saturn will come as a refreshing change from older astrology books that described Saturn as the Greater Malefic—a sort of teacher/devil that called you to task for your shortcomings and restricted your every move. Career is one area where Saturn can reflect the best of our abilities and interests. Careful consideration of Saturn and its place in the horoscope provides the foundation for career success.

Once Saturn has been delineated, we will then turn to the relationship between Saturn and Mars in the horoscope. While Saturn provides the mold or container for career aptitude, Mars provides the energy for its fulfillment. How they work together is reflected by their relationship in the natal chart.

Saturn

Saturn stands at the boundary between the personal inner planets and the more recently discovered outer planets. As such it represents the pivotal balance of intelligence. By intelligence I mean the full use of human faculties, including the intuitive and nonlinear aspects of creativity. Western science has tended to define intelligence as exclusively rational and logical, as if the principle of reason could operate isolated from our subjective motivations, or as if the appearance of matters were all upon which we can base our decisions, a viewpoint which constitutes a limitation of the potential of the mind. Saturn's influence in the chart suffers from no such limitation, even though Saturn represents structure. The apparent durability of form is due to its structural limit. But the mutability of form and its inevitable dissolution are also aspects of the universal cyclical structure of nature. The imposition of limits is constant, but the form of any particular limit is temporary. Saturn, like structure, is neither good nor bad. Rigid, inflexible adherence to structure can be painful, but we could not manage without the structure of bones and skin to hold the physical body together. Nor could we manage without mental, emotional, and even spiritual structures to guide our lives. In all areas of human experience rigidity is the source of limitation. A clearer understanding of Saturn can provide a more flexible base for all functions, vocation included.

Saturn also provides the function of shattering old forms that are worn out and no longer useful. However, we tend to hold on to the old form, even if it no longer serves us. "Better the devil you know" is itself a timeworn maxim. Traditional astrology states that Saturn is dignified in Libra, the sign of the scales. When we reach the balance point and go beyond, we experience the pull of the familiar while also yearning for something new, something different. Vocational questions reflect this desire for change. But it is not merely change that we seek. We are truly seeking that vocational path which fulfills our basic needs and speaks to our other needs as well.

The fundamental qualities of Saturn that bear on the vocational question are considered in the following sections. I consider the emotional bias first because that sets the tone for action. If something is attractive emotionally, it is easier to pursue. If an activity is emotionally repugnant, then even if it is good for you, it will not be a likely choice. The nature of Saturn's sign placement shows the personality factors that limit career success. By understanding these factors, you can select the perfect job within the career field to keep personal inclinations from impeding your progress.

Saturn in the Signs: Emotional Biases

Aries: *obstinacy.*

You will do better in a career where personal responsibility and authority are maximized. Working for someone else can aggravate the tendency to demand your own way. Working for yourself, or at least in an area where you direct your own activities, is preferable because you can use your creativity without limitations.

Taurus: *inertia.*

Without outside stimulation you can tend to slow down almost to a halt. You are better suited for a position in your career field where you work closely with others or have a boss who gives you specific assignments with realistic deadlines. Your perseverance is then supported by exterior milestones of achievement.

Gemini: decreased adaptability.

You are best suited for a position that has change and flow to it, but that does not demand on-the-spot decision-making. You thrive in situations where you can think through and plan changes, as this draws on your problem-solving ability. You don't thrive under severe time constraints.

Cancer: hypersensitivity.

Your best work is done in an encouraging, positive environment. You don't appreciate criticism that misses the performance mark and instead focuses on personal traits. You work best in a team environment where the eye is on the goal and not the inevitable missteps along the path.

Leo: caution.

Caution in itself is a good thing, but it can inhibit job performance in careers where the keynote is on-the-spot action. You have the greatest career success in areas where a conservative attitude is well placed, such as financial management. You may be the person who seems to throw cold water on ideas that will drain personnel or financial resources too completely.

Virgo: overly critical nature.

You are hard on yourself. You don't need a boss who magnifies your mistakes and seems incapable of seeing your strengths. Because of your desire to be understood by others, you do best in a job where you have the freedom to communicate clearly, and the responsibility to do so. Your capacity for detail makes a good work focus.

Libra: discontent.

You are rarely willing to settle for less than the whole banana where work is concerned. You dislike being held back by superiors when you see where you want to go. You do best with a partner or colleagues who create the initial plan with you and then let you run with the ball. This maximizes your reliability while maintaining interest.

Scorpio: *melancholy or emotional struggle.*

You fret over your work, much as you fret over other areas of your life. Your best work is done in a serious environment, and you may not participate in office pranks or silliness. While you are off working, you are also working with your emotions in the back of your mind. Avoid job situations where your feelings are put on display.

Sagittarius: *self-doubt.*

Because you tend to doubt yourself, your best career direction is one that allows you to study the theory and philosophy carefully before you put them into practice. The legal and religious professions provide strong possibilities because they are based on an established body of information. Such careers draw on your prudence and intuitive judgment.

Capricorn: *self-will and egocentricity.*

You tend to believe you know the "only" right way to do things. As such, you are best placed in an independent career situation that maximizes your ability to work hard. Your advancement may not be as fast as you would like, but you will benefit from knowing that you are responsible for your personal success.

Aquarius: *eccentric ideas and expectations.*

You thrive on the unusual, even the bizarre. You belong in a career that focuses on the unusual while emphasizing your ability to plan and to follow through to completion. You can tolerate being on the cutting edge of your career field.

Pisces: *timidity and depression.*

Saturn is not strong in Pisces when it comes to emotion. You will work best in an environment that is respectful of your reserved attitude and that removes you from unnecessary personality struggles with others. You like challenging problems, but need a quiet space in which to solve them.

Concentration and Perseverance

Staying power is not only mental focus but also a distilled concentration of mental, emotional, and spiritual values. The sign placement of Saturn indicates the nature of the distillation or the direction of the focus. Without staying power we flounder in career, just as we do in all areas of our lives. Saturn shows where perseverance can be found, what our particular brand of perseverance looks like, and the kind of results we can expect.

Saturn in the Signs: Concentration and Perseverance

> *Aries:* ambition and endurance.
>
> *Taurus:* steadfastness and methodical pursuit of goals.
>
> *Gemini:* studiousness and mental thoroughness.
>
> *Cancer:* family considerations and controlled action.
>
> *Leo:* reliability and loyalty.
>
> *Virgo:* meticulous accuracy and thoroughness.
>
> *Libra:* conscientiousness and sense of responsibility.
>
> *Scorpio:* research capability and emotional endurance.
>
> *Sagittarius:* sense of justice and logical follow-through.
>
> *Capricorn:* self-restraint and steady advancement.
>
> *Aquarius:* capacity to plan and reliability.
>
> *Pisces:* ability to work alone and spiritual stamina.

Personal Strengths to Be Developed

The house placement of Saturn indicates the personal assets you will need to achieve career success. Saturn mirrors the lessons you will learn along the vocational path, and thereby indicates the specific strengths you need to develop. You may have experienced a situation in which your typical personality strengths did not serve you the way they usually do. This is certainly true of career. What works well with your friends, for example, may not work in your career.

Saturn in the Houses: Personal Strengths

First House: independence, courage, modesty, self-restraint, and self-confidence.

Second House: understanding both the value of money and one's own value.

Third House: solid study habits and training of the mind, either through formal education or through personal effort.

Fourth House: the ability to establish a personal base of operations, both in terms of a home and in terms of independent feelings and beliefs.

Fifth House: understanding of your self-worth without an associated obsession about independence.

Sixth House: cheerful attitude toward the humdrum details of work, and perseverance.

Seventh House: cooperative attitude and tactful demeanor.

Eighth House: appreciation for the help others can—and do—offer.

Ninth House: philosophical and logical education, either through college or other continuing education.

Tenth House: restraint—ability to moderate talents, skills, desires, and arrogance.

Eleventh House: independence from family and friends.

Twelfth House: personal reserve, executive capacity, and ability to exercise authority.

Career Development

Saturn shows by house placement the area of life where you can work hard and achieve results. Because of Saturn's balancing position between the personal and the transpersonal realms, he often steers us in a direction that we cannot easily perceive from within the confines of past experience. We have to look into the larger context of our lives to find the best place for our efforts. We also think that our career should provide status, or money, or some other satisfaction, while the exercise of our capabilities in what we think of as an avocation delivers far more satisfaction. So the type of work indicated by house may seem odd, but deserves consideration nonetheless.

Saturn in the Houses: Career Development Opportunities

First House: You need to begin with a job that forces you to think for yourself, to stand on your own two feet, to make your own decisions, and to the use or develop your supervisory skills.

Second House: The best job for you to start with has a salary or at least a contract that demands accountability on both sides; your career should not involve speculation.

Third House: Begin with a job that requires mental accuracy—work of an intellectual or logical nature. Later your quick wits can be brought into the picture.

Fourth House: You thrive with a job where you start at the bottom and work up. The focus is on the management of emotional and mental faculties, not individual people.

Fifth House: You can start to work for a friend or family member, and move to a position with a social or political dynamic where you get a broad perspective of the career field.

Sixth House: Your first job may require very hard work, but you build character for later, more prestigious positions.

Seventh House: Your first job needs partnership qualities, even if you are not an equal partner. There should be an executive quality to the work that will help you to build conscientious work habits and a track record for reliability.

Eighth House: Take financial support that is offered to you and use it to begin a business. You should handle the money personally for best effect.

Ninth House: Begin with a job that requires mental accuracy—work of an intellectual or logical nature. Later your quick wits can be brought into the picture.

Tenth House: You can start just about anywhere and rise quickly. Executive positions are good from the get go.

Eleventh House: The first job can be in a large organization. You can establish interpersonal connections while earning the respect of the people around you.

Twelfth House: Break away from personal ties for that first job, even if it means some loss in status or financial level. The idea is to develop personal responsibility and to assert yourself, independent of your elders.

Vocational Path

The vocational path outlined by Saturn has strictures, which, if followed carefully, will inevitably lead to greater career success. The guidelines provide a map for a cautious yet progressive approach to vocation. This map reflects a developmental process that is well suited to individual needs, aside from the considerations of other people in one's environment.

Saturn in the Houses: Career Goals

First House: The best long-term goal is to control your own business or to be the top executive in someone else's. You may end up in a career that allows you to influence others directly.

Second House: The focus should be on making and handling money and material assets. There should be meticulous adherence to honest practice and you should avoid speculation of any kind.

Third House: After strong basic training and education, you will thrive in a business or profession that demands your quick perception. You are not a natural executive and may want to avoid such positions until later in your career, as you need to produce in your own right.

Fourth House: Because your end goals include security and a peaceful existence, your career direction will resist the temptation of power for its own sake and will focus instead on a personal sense of success.

Fifth House: Your strong personality will demand recognition. A solid start will lead you to such a position in your career, provided you follow your personal ambition closely. Diplomacy will gain you the help you need along the way.

Sixth House: After a hard working beginning, you can go in just about any direction, as you have the ability to work and study hard in a profession or business.

Seventh House: You are a natural partner, so cooperation continues to be a big part of your work life. Together you gain the attention and success that you deserve.

Eighth House: You can rise to the directorship of a company through your financial acumen. Cooperative efforts will result in the best gains.

Ninth House: If you have had the benefit of a strong higher education, coupled with an internship or training, you can pursue a career that focuses on you and your ability to produce results.

Tenth House: You will need to take stock from time to time and consolidate your position before you make any big moves. Your natural understanding of the way things work leads you to withdraw or retire while you are at the height of your power, instead of waiting until you have already lost ground.

Eleventh House: No goal is too high for you. From a solid start you can achieve greatness, either as an executive, or through connections to other powerful people.

Twelfth House: You end up in an independent career of some stature, one that affords you the security you so strongly desire. Professions and the arts are promising avenues for you to follow, and you may attain executive stature.

How You Learn Best

All of the above Saturn considerations come together into a package of skills, decisions, and goals. The sum total is a description of your ability to learn from experience. If you are well placed in a career field, emotionally suited to the demands of the actual job, and oriented clearly to your goals, you will be successful. The sign Saturn occupies indicates how you tend to learn best, so keep this in mind in every area of endeavor, not just vocation.

Saturn in the Signs: How You Learn Best

Aries: diligent, serious application of effort.

Taurus: methodical processes over time.

Gemini: thorough study and logical thought.

Cancer: *family, tradition, and history.*

Leo: *informal yet diplomatic situations.*

Virgo: *discriminating examination of details.*

Libra: *close associates and team effort.*

Scorpio: *deep research and metaphysical experiences.*

Sagittarius: *serious study of theory.*

Capricorn: *focused studies.*

Aquarius: *creative application of ideas and information.*

Pisces: *mystical means and empathic channels.*

Mars: How to Apply Your Energies

Having looked at how a solid foundation may be established through Saturn, we now turn to the application of your personal energy to the goal of fulfilling your dreams. Saturn suggests the form or structure of your career, while Mars shows how you pursue it. How do you apply yourself? What drives you? How far can you go? These questions are all answered by examining Mars and its relationship to Saturn.

Traditional astrology has named Saturn the Greater Malefic and Mars the Lesser. The combination is often considered to be among the worst, astrologically speaking. Reinhold Ebertin began by saying that Mars and Saturn combine to produce "harmful or destructive energy, inhibited or destroyed vitality," and ends by saying this combination occurs in "cases of death." Yet he also states that a strong interaction between them results in "endurance, the power of resistance, indefatigability" (Ebertin, *Combination of Stellar Influences*). It is clear that we must consider the relationship of these two planets carefully if we are to avoid the worst of possibilities and maximize the constructive potential of Saturn and Mars—structure and energy.

To resolve the dilemma of working with these planets, let us begin by asking, "What dies or ends?" Obviously we do not die whenever there is a Mars/Saturn combination. We survive many such transits. But the question is a good one. When we have a Mars/Saturn transit, or even a difficult combination in a birth chart, we can expect changes, and we can be on the lookout for danger. The application of attention to such conditions is necessary to avoid harm and to extract whatever gain is possible. The death of one idea gives rise to another, the death of one cycle begins the next.

By understanding the astrological combination of Mars and Saturn, you begin to understand how your energy is contained in the mold—the structure—of Saturn, and you learn how to reshape the structure of your life to suit your energies. The goal is to develop a détente between these two planets that allows you to use your energy fully and creatively while remaining true to the structural demands of your personality. Three astrological considerations combine to form your knowledge of Mars and Saturn acting together. First, are they forming an aspect to each other, and how does that aspect work? Second, what are the relative house positions of Mars and Saturn, and how do they complement each other? The third has to do with the cycles of these two planets as they move forward by transit.

Mars Aspects to Saturn

Conjunct: This combination depends a great deal on the other aspects Mars and Saturn form, as it may tend toward accident and injury unless carefully managed. Because of its intense difficulty, it can form a serious impediment to career unless carefully controlled. The conjunction favors service-oriented careers in which aggression is not a large factor, where tact is an advantage, and where the persistent application of energy is desirable. Generally if the influence of Saturn takes the lead and Mars energy is applied in the appropriate direction, this achieves the best results.

Opposition: The tendency is for Mars and Saturn to struggle. Mars fights against the structure that Saturn imposes and seeks to take the vocation in a different direction from the optimum. The exuberance of Mars is likely to resist the steady development that Saturn demands, taking an easier path and failing to develop the staying power the long run requires. The individual is responsible for the end result and has to exercise control. Self-discipline must be cultivated in order to restrain your energy and to pursue a steady sort of career development. Awareness is as important here as with any opposition.

Square: The Mars/Saturn square presents the challenge of restraint in that Saturn's demands must be met, lest an outside agency represented by Mars' sign and house come into the picture later to interfere with the career. With proper attention to Saturn's demands, there will be no opening for an outsider to cause problems. The square, then, will be an indication of accidents of circumstance that cause the career to flounder; however, proper attention to structure and form early on will ameliorate the negative tendency of this aspect.

Sextile/Trine: The career can flourish through the cooperative efforts of energy and structure, as conditions exists which make this path easy to follow. On the one hand, the structure of the best career path is enhanced by the application of energy, while on the other hand, one's energy is easily directed to fill the requirements of the career's structure. In this way the detrimental and stressful tendencies toward harmful action or weakness are decreased, while one's energy is skillfully applied in the most fruitful direction.

Semi-Square/Sesqui-Square: Dramatic internal stresses are caused by career headings which are off mark. If attention is directed toward stable and steady career growth, one may feel held back and resentful. If the energy is allowed to take its own direction, then one feels overly responsible for any and all failures. This can result in an apparent "no win" situation. However, as the life progresses, the native learns to interpret the early signs of stress and to make adjustments accordingly. Thus later in the career the individual has far greater control because the barometer of change has been calibrated and refined.

Quintile/Biquintile: These aspects provide a creative possibility to an otherwise problematic combination. You may focus on medical, conflict resolution or other careers where you can use your talents to repair damage or resolve difficulties. The work itself can deal with creative thought processes and planning; it may also involve actual production.

Semi-Sextile: You may get the cart before the horse in terms of career development because you can always see the future clearly and you want it now. You need to learn to be careful when you reach for the brass ring, at least early on, to avoid falling off your horse in the process.

Quincunx: Adjustments will be required in terms of career, but the circumstances may have little to do with work. They have more to do with your physical capacity to continue at your usual pace. Personal health can be the issue. If such a situation arises, you have a built-in ability to adapt as needed, although you may not want to do so.

House Positions of Mars

Whether Mars and Saturn form an aspect or not, the house relationship between them shows the most suitable career path. The nature of the aspect shows how (and with what difficulty) the career path is to unfold. The houses involved show the types of career that are best. By considering the house placement of each planet, you can determine the best form for the career, as well as the best direction for your energy to take. By combining these, you get a sense of the principal qualities of career fields that are good for you. Saturn in the houses has been discussed above; now we turn to Mars in the houses.

The placement of Mars in the houses indicates how you tend to use your energies. Early in life, energy almost seems to use you, as you have little control over desires. Throughout childhood and adult development, you learn to moderate desires of the moment with longer term plans, and you adapt to the environment of parental control, school requirements, peer pressure, marriage or relationship responsibilities, etc. Mars becomes, instead of its own director, an agent for your use, guided by the Sun in its actions. The descriptions of Mars in each house include uses of energy that may occur early or late in the career, depending on your personal developmental path and how you respond to life. Some uses may seem out of reach in youth and commonplace in middle age, or vice versa.

Effect of Mars in the Houses

First House: This placement may indicate recklessness in the beginning, and a tendency toward injury. There is an independent spirit that can work alone easily. Such a person can be in charge of others, but only after independence becomes a skill rather than a goal. Early impatience can develop into ambition suited to the career chosen. Early argumentative tendencies can become skilled negotiation. While energy may be wasted in the beginning, a more directed strategy may develop later.

Second House: Early in life, stubbornness can present a fierce obstacle to career progress. The tenacity reflected in this quality can develop into the staying power one needs for the long haul, so that endurance becomes a trademark. A tendency toward vindictiveness must be overcome. Rather, a relaxed attitude of "what-goes-around-comes-around" will serve you better. The desire for material things can be all-consuming at first, but practical skills in acquisition become career assets.

Third House: Early restlessness can keep you moving from one job situation to the next, seemingly without direction. You also tend to scatter your energies into projects that appear to be a waste of time. The qualities underlying these feeling, the readiness for action, mobility, and versatility, are qualities that carry the later career development to its highest point. You also have a sense of humor that grows out of your richness and variety of experience, and a sense of humor is a career asset for you.

Fourth House: You are able to draw on instinct and even psychic powers throughout your life. Early in life you "know" what is happening in your job situation but may not know skillful ways to use the information. Later you develop a talent for knowing what is coming and for utilizing that information to further your own career development. You tend to be somewhat moody and must learn to contain your feelings, or to channel them into your work. You may be suited to working at home, as that is where you are most comfortable.

Fifth House: You have abundant energy that in early life may be directed to gambling and speculation, selfish activities, and undirected passion. The vocational direction will suffer from these unless or until redirection of energy is achieved. You develop an enterprising spirit from the gambling urge, along with a certain fearlessness. The selfish quality becomes self-confidence and self-possession. Your passion is channeled into zeal for your work (at least while you are at work). You develop a sense of responsibility in the process that can make you a good supervisor and leader.

Sixth House: Early in your career you may be critical, even though you barely know what you are talking about. You can also be irritable for no apparent reason, and somewhat nervous. As you gain experience, these seeming limitations develop into job skills. You organize your work environment neatly and efficiently. You develop work methods and skills that allow you to be on top of every situation. You learn from your nervousness how to adapt to situations before they cause you discomfort. Your skills take you in the direction of detailed work or scientific investigation (even if your field is not science).

Seventh House: In your youth you tend to depend over much on your feelings to guide you through life's situations. You also are truthful to a fault, and this often leads to argument instead of resolution. As you develop work skills, you turn the dependence on feeling into skillful assessment of coworkers and an enthusiasm for team work. You will always be a truth teller, but you learn to balance truth with tact, and can be cordial and diplomatic without becoming false.

Eighth House: Early in life you want to be in control and impose your power on others. You can be ruthless and critical in your manner. You may even be willfully destructive in your approach. These intense qualities can become your allies in the work place if you learn to reserve your ruthlessness for the clinches. You can be in a position of power without stomping on others, even though you may never be a diplomat. You learn to destroy only that which you are certain you will never need again. What you learn most from these qualities is to become conscious of your goals and to find skillful means of attaining them without burning bridges unnecessarily.

Ninth House: You can be rash and adventuresome, and early extravagance can cause problems in the work place if you don't learn control. Later, however, you find you have developed an infectious enthusiasm for your work. You also find you have a talent for saying what needs to be said without overdoing the point. Your sense of adventure keeps your work interesting and alive, for you and for those around you.

Tenth House: In the beginning you tend to over-estimate your talents and skills. You can be single-minded in pursuit of your objectives, even though they are not well conceived. Egotism can be a problem. However, you turn these seeming limitations into strengths as you pursue the development of your career. Ambition is a trait that carries you to career heights. You have the will to achieve success, and the self-confidence to keep you going. Throughout you have a sense of reality that serves you in the work environment.

Eleventh House: Without development, you tend to be somewhat superficial. You enjoy contradiction that has no purpose and you can be inconsistent or fickle. You manage to overcome these limited expressions of your energy so that you pursue career goals deliberately. You love to try new things and are in the forefront where computer tools are involved. Instead of being contradictory, you are able to see several sides of a question and you can get your team to pull together to achieve their goals.

Twelfth House: Early on you experience a lack of self-control that can lead to secrecy and even addictive behaviors. You may also be somewhat unreliable in your work. Yet you develop, from these less auspicious beginnings, the ability to hold back and plan skillfully, a capacity to accomplish tasks with little supervision, and a talent for understanding the undercurrents of office politics. You enjoy the social activities at work, as they provide an opportunity to "read" your associates.

Summary

You may find that Mars and Saturn seem to be at terrible odds and that resolution will never be possible. Life experience, however, draws these two planets together, allowing them to work together for your best interests. The key here is that Saturn, in the long run, indicates what is needed for career to develop to its fullest capacity. Mars shows how to use your energies best in service of that career.

Chapter Six

The Tenth House: Career

Examination of the Tenth House reveals the astrological indicators of career and career success. It is helpful to think of career success separately from the money earned, as success is not limited to material gain. A person could be held in very high esteem in his career field and not be the biggest financial success. Also, the particular focus will often determine the earning potential. Of the three houses involved with vocation, the Tenth House is the most public. Here is where reputation is built, and here is where one gains authority in one's field. Ambition is also reflected in the sign on the Tenth House. This chapter will first consider ambition, how one responds to authority, the most suitable career fields, and places where the career may flourish. Then we will look specifically at the Midheaven as an indicator of what you know about yourself. Delineation of the Tenth House will consider:

- sign on the Tenth House cusp
- Tenth House ruler—house and sign placement
- aspects of the Tenth House ruler to the Tenth House cusp and planets in the Tenth House
- closest aspect of the Tenth House ruler to another planet
- planets in the Tenth House and their aspects and
- progressions, directions, and transits to the above planets and cusps.

Ambition and Authority

Examination of the sign on the Tenth House cusp reveals how the client responds to authority and how ambition affects career decisions. Read the following chapter on the Midheaven for detailed information about each sign as it relates to personality. The following list includes brief statements focusing on the employee/employer relationship and what to expect from each sign, as well as how each sign relates to ambition.

Sign on the Tenth House Cusp

Aries: The focus is on the individual and his or her aims in life. Ambition, confidence, and optimism combine to make this individual a potentially strong leader, and conversely, a not-so-successful follower. However, here as elsewhere, this one consideration cannot be used to assess the total career package, or the whole person.

Taurus: This individual is persistent and has much endurance. There is a slow but sure evolution toward security and, at the same time, a development of tolerance for others. This individual can be entrusted with projects that require steady attention to bring them to fruition. This person can be happy as an employee only when his or her personality is given elbow room.

Gemini: The Gemini Midheaven signals a person with multiple talents and skills, as well as the energy to apply them. However, this is not necessarily the stuff of a long-term career in one place. The tendency to scatter one's energy can actually develop into a package of skills that make for the successful manager, as this individual can keep track of many projects and guide employees well. Give this employee the right mix of responsibility and people contact and he or she will thrive.

Cancer: The desire for independence comes out strongly with Cancer at the Midheaven. This individual also is considerate of the other people in the work environment. Just don't try to push him or her too far. This individual can work well alone, establishing an independent business, or can work with others if his or her sensibilities are kept in mind.

Leo: Leadership is a word designed for the Leo Midheaven. From childhood this individual wants to be in charge of things. Not a person who enjoys being the target of your humor, this individual wants the spotlight to show off only the best, most socially attractive side of the personality. This person needs to move up from the bottom rung of the employment ladder at the earliest possible moment in order to find that spotlight.

Virgo: Virgo at the Midheaven signals a desire for secure livelihood, and therefore makes a loyal employee who wants nothing more than a permanent position and the opportunity to advance without flamboyance. An orderly attitude makes this person ideal for positions requiring a careful approach to the details of the job. In leadership positions be careful to avoid petty criticism, as there is a tendency toward hypersensitivity.

Libra: The Libra Midheaven advances through the cooperation of others and through the use of social contacts. There is some tendency to exploit others, and this could be a problem if carried to extremes. Since no one is always nice, after a while we may come to suspect the Libra Midheaven of insincerity.

Scorpio: Here is a Midheaven that is not afraid of the hard work—a person who can get in the trenches with coworkers when necessary. Ambition leads to striving to come out on top of every situation. This attitude can make for overextension of one's energy as well as the appearance of ruthlessness. Actually there is usually an accurate grasp of the situation in nearly every case, accompanied by surprising sympathy toward others.

Sagittarius: Sagittarius at the Midheaven marks the born strategist. Here is a person who can seemingly see into the future and figure out just the right direction to take. At the same time this individual wants to be held up as a shining example for his or her peers, so being stuck in an office alone is not good. Expect a mix of conservative attitudes with spiritual leanings.

Capricorn: Endurance is a trait that advances the ambitions of the Capricorn Midheaven. There is such a strong focus on the career and its demands that this individual may become more lonely over time because other people are not included in his or her plans. There is the ability to lead if the tendency to concentrate over much is curbed. This individual makes an employee who can be turned loose on projects with good results.

Aquarius: The Aquarius Midheaven is fully capable of cooperation with others—under his or her leadership, of course. They tend to grasp the possibilities early in the game and thus come out pretty well in the end. They tend to plan too much and thus scatter their energy. Creative energy flows in periodic waves, and they have to develop the patience to wait for the next wave.

Pisces: Simplicity is sought by the Pisces Midheaven. This may work well in the career environment, but it can lead to a lack of clarity because of over simplification. The Pisces Midheaven needs time alone to reflect, and therefore is not well placed in a position under constant fire. They can see the global picture and feel it deeply as well.

Career Field

The career field itself is indicated by the sign on the cusp of the Tenth House. In reading the following lists, bear in mind that it is the quality or tone of the career as much as the actual work itself that is significant. Hence, not all Aries Midheavens will be butchers, or even work with knives, yet the incisive quality of these careers carries through to all career activities. The Tenth House usually contains all or part of another sign as well. This sign presents a second set of possibilities, and often indicates a second career started somewhat later in life.

Career Fields Indicated by Sign on Tenth House Cusp

Aries: adventurer, diamond cutter or dealer, fireman, hairdresser, hat maker, high-rise construction worker, iron worker, meat packing, metallurgical engineer, metal worker, military in general, optometrist, physical therapist, police work in general, and service station owner or attendant.

Taurus: actor, art dealer, artist, banking in general, cabinetmaker, candy maker, cashier, commercial artist, convention planner, dancer, fashion designer, finance in general, geologist, hospitality industries in general, hotel or restaurant manager, moneylender, musician, psychometrist, sculptor, singer, and surveyor.

Gemini: accountant, advertising in general, bookseller, book binder, bookkeeper, broadcasting in general, bus driver, cab driver, clerical worker, computer operator, railroad employee, court reporter, editor, handwriting expert, informant, information manager, journalist, letter carrier, librarian, linguist, literary critic, mechanic, messenger, merchandiser, news reporter, novelist, office worker, photo engraver, photographer, proofreader, radio and television in general, repairman, secretary, translator, and travel agent.

Cancer: agricultural worker, baker, boat builder, caterer, child care worker, clothes cleaner, community activist, cook, early childhood education in general, farmer, fisherman, gardener, grocer, hotel manager, housekeeper, laundry worker, marketing in general, merchant, milkman, miner, mushroom grower, nurse, plumber, real estate agent, restaurant manager, sailor, shepherd, silversmith, social worker, tavern keeper, and water management worker.

Leo: broker, cartoonist, chairman, dealer and manufacturer of sporting goods, director, entertainer, film star, foreman, forester, gambler, goldsmith, government official, heart specialist, investment banker, manager, money lender, motion picture producer, organizer, politician, prime minister, royalty, speculator, and theater manager or owner.

Virgo: administrator, animal trainer, cheese maker, chemist, civil servant, craftsman, critic, crop grower, dental hygienist and technician, dietitian, doctor, domestic servant, draftsman, editor, food purveyor, healer, illustrator, inspector, masseuse, mathematician, merchant, military in general, nanny, nerve specialist, nurse, office worker, poultry raiser, relief worker, secretary, service professions in general, statistician, stenographer, textile worker, teacher, veterinarian, and workmen in general.

Libra: actor, arbitrator, beautician, business partner, candy maker, clothing design, courthouse employee, decorator, dressmaker, florist, intermediary, jeweler, juggler, lawyer, milliner, negotiator, salesmen in general, singer, sociologist, and wig maker.

Scorpio: bail bondsman, brewer, bill and tax collector, chemotherapist, dentist, demolitionist, detective, distiller, druggist, doctor, executioner, insurance salesman, junk dealer, laboratory technician, lumberjack, magician, meat packing, mortician, nuclear scientist, pharmacist, paleontologist, psychiatrist, psychic, radiobiologist, radiotherapist, researcher, sorcerer, surgeon, traffic manager, and vice squad agent.

Sagittarius: advertising agent, airline employee, attorney, bookseller, book publisher, broadcasting technician, churchman, clergyman, counselor, explorer, flight engineer, foreign policy in general, higher education in general, hunter, jockey, judge, lecturer, military in general, missile engineer, pilot, professor, publicity director, publishing in general, radio and television announcer, theologian, travel agent, traveling salesman, and writer.

Capricorn: administrator, ambassador, architect, buyer, carpenter, cemetery worker, chiropractor, civil engineer, contractor, efficiency expert, gardener, government official, governor, industrial engineer, landlord, land owner, leather clothing designer, mathematician, miner, orthopedic surgeon, philanthropist, rancher, real estate agent, and vocational counselor.

Aquarius: airplane mechanic, astrologer, astronaut, auto mechanic, aviator, chiropractor, congressman, furniture manufacturer, instrument manufacturer, legislator, motion picture producer, photographer, psychologist, psychotherapist, radiologist, reformer, researcher, scientist, social worker, space physicist, telephone and telegraph operator, television technician, translator, venture capitalist, and x-ray technician.

Pisces: artist, astrologer, aquatic occupations in general, boat maker, character actor, chemist, dancer, detective, distiller, chemical engineer, fisherman, hospital worker, ice skater, monk, mystic, nun, oceanographer, photographer, psychic, priest, prison guard, secret service agent, service station owner or attendant, occult writer, and weaver.

Tenth House Ruler: House and Sign Placement

The house and sign placement of the ruler of the Tenth indicates an area of life which affects the career directly. If there are no planets in the Tenth, the ruler's placement becomes a major factor in the unfolding of career. It can indicate skills which can be directly applied to the career and may influence the choices one makes in where and how to pursue the career field. A natal chart of a lawyer, Christine Cuddy, featured in Lois Rodden's *Profiles of Women* provides a good example. Sagittarius is on both the Ninth and Tenth House cusps, so the legal profession is a strong possibility. With no planets in the Tenth House, we look to Jupiter in the Twelfth for an indication of what part of the legal field she might pursue, and it reflects the reality that she is not a courtroom lawyer—she works in a more private area of law—specifically, contract negotiations for the entertainment business.

Aspects of the Tenth House ruler to the cusp or planets in the Tenth House indicate the natural direction of the career. Cuddy's Jupiter does not aspect the Tenth House. This is another indication that the career is not focused on the public side of the career.

The closest aspect of the ruler of the Tenth indicates the strongest pull in a particular career direction, particularly if there are no planets in the Tenth. Cuddy's Jupiter opposes Pluto with a ten minute orb, and trines Neptune with an eleven minute orb. Even though Jupiter is in the Twelfth, indicating a less public posture, the aspects to Pluto and Neptune indicate awareness of the power and fame in her Hollywood work environment (Pluto in Leo) and the glamorous clientele (Neptune in the Seventh House).

Career Focus

Planets in the Tenth House and the placement of the ruler of the Tenth reveal the players one will encounter in the career, as well as the direction one's attention will follow. While the sign on or in the Tenth describes the general career area, the ruler and planets in the Tenth describe the exact area of the career field that is best. Suppose the client has Sagittarius on the Tenth. You think of law as a potential career field, but your client is not suited to the years of study that would be required. This does not mean that law is out, it simply means that your client will pursue some facet of the legal profession other than lawyer. If the skills exist or can be developed, possibilities include police work, clerical work in the sheriff's department, food service in a prison or jail setting, paralegal work, detective work, as well as many others.

This is where the synthesis of information is essential. Once potential career areas and individual personality traits have been determined (by examining the Midheaven and Tenth House), the aspects to the Tenth and its planets, as well as other factors can be considered.

Christine Cuddy
Feb 14, 1950
Bethesda, MD
08:11:00 AM EST
ZONE: +05:00:00
77W06'00"
38N59'00"

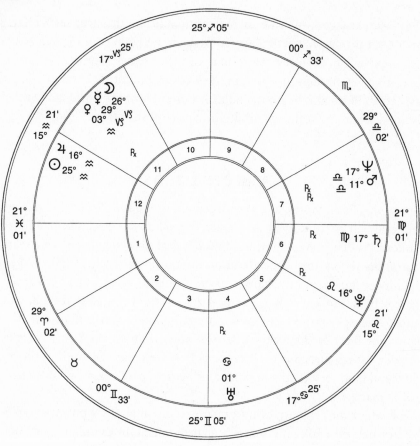

Geocentric
Tropical
Koch Houses

Figure 10. Christine Cuddy's Natal Chart.

Abilities and Career Indications of Planets in the Tenth House

Sun: *conscience, authority, dignity, illumination, leadership, loyalty, zeal, and self-sufficiency.*

Acting, animation, army officers, athletics, celebrity, eyes, fame, gambling, government, the heart, large animal veterinarians, leadership roles, oranges, overseas jobs, prana, prominent positions, stock market, and public utilities.

Moon: *adaptability, change, curiosity, illumination, receptivity, and osmosis.*

Allergists, babies, baking, boats, candles, chefs, common people, crops, diet, fresh water, fertility, furniture, health fields, hotel management, meteorology, nursing, optics, plumbing, real estate, and vintners.

Mercury: *humor, ambidexterity, coordination, craftsmanship, cleverness, and mental ability.*

Advising, agents, advertising, atlases and maps, bicycles, biographers, books, the brain, cartography, education, libraries, linguistics, office machine repair, post offices, service industries, and writing.

Venus: *humor, aptitude, joy, kindness, tact, refinement, poise, and persuasiveness.*

Art, bedrooms, beauticians, brides, clothing design, cosmetics, hair, hotel management, manicurists, music, poetry, and theatrical agents.

Mars: *one's working ability, assertiveness, bravery, mechanical ability, participation, stamina, ferocity, and haste.*

Ceramics, defense, fire departments, gymnastics, manufacturing, metallurgy, performance, police or sheriff departments, rock music, and the steel industry.

Jupiter: *politeness, reverence, serenity, mirth, piety, spontaneity, honesty, trustworthiness, and the nature of one's achievement.*

Brokers, counselors, horse breeders, travel, lending, passports, podiatry, rehabilitation, religious orders, shoes, and textbook publishers.

Saturn: *diligence, patience, persistence, desire for solitude, and the ability to see the basics.*

Archeology, boots, cattle, chiropractors, civil engineers, locksmiths, mathematicians, nightclub employees, orthopedists, prison employees, real estate, and shoes.

Uranus: *mechanical ability, assertiveness, clairaudience, determination, and quickness.*

Adoption agents, air planes, broadcasting, car manufacturing and racing, chiropractors, crisis management, drivers, nuclear physics, psychology, recording, repairs, and spiritual healers.

Neptune: *captivation, clairvoyance, credibility, pliancy, resilience, rhythm, sympathy, osmosis, and imagination.*

Alcohol, angel products, charitable work, coffee, deep sea, drugs, hypnotherapists, market research, missionaries, narcotics, photography, poetry, sailing ships, smuggling, wine, and witchcraft.

Pluto: *cooperation, collaboration, passion, forcefulness, and subconscious connections.*

Alchemy, archeology, astrophysics, atomic energy, chain store employees, coroners, demolition, espionage, insurance, magic, pirates, plastics, psychoanalysis, reptile experts, surgery, violence, welfare, and wetlands developers.

Chapter Seven

Aspects and Transits to the Midheaven

Now that the nature of the Tenth House has been established for each zodiacal sign, we turn to consideration of aspects between the Midheaven and the planets. In the natal chart the Midheaven is the fastest moving point, with the possible exception of the Ascendant. In the Northern Hemisphere, the Ascendant moves faster than the Midheaven in the signs of Capricorn through Gemini, while in the Southern Hemisphere the Ascendant is faster in the signs of Cancer through Sagittarius. The point here is that the Midheaven applies and separates to aspects to all the planets in the natal chart.

In terms of direction and progression the Midheaven moves at the same speed as the Sun when it is calculated according to solar arc. In solar arc directions every object moves at the same speed. In secondary progressions each planet moves at the rate of one day per year; the Midheaven moves at the speed of the Sun, and the Ascendant is calculated from the progressed Midheaven at the new location of the individual. Thus the progressed Ascendant will reflect long and short ascension in the same way as described above for the natal chart.

Daily transits must consider the dual motions of transits forward through the zodiac (counterclockwise motion) and the diurnal movement of heavenly bodies through the sky (clockwise motion). The Sun will move forward one degree through the zodiac each day; it moves 360 degrees around the chart according to the time of day.

The Midheaven is subject to the diurnal consideration only. In the natal chart the time of day *determines* the Midheaven. If we think of the Midheaven as a fixed point in the southern sky, the zodiac transits clockwise across that point at the rate of one degree every four minutes. If we think of the Midheaven as a moving point, it transits through the zodiac at the same rate. The result in either case is that the Midheaven changes at the fastest rate of any object in the chart (again with the exception of the Ascendant in signs of short ascension). Therefore, the Midheaven applies and separates from aspects to all the planets and is mutually applying or separating if the planet is retrograde. The transiting Midheaven is not often used in natal astrology, but diurnal motion becomes very significant in such applications as business and gambling, to name only two.

Natal Aspects Involving the Midheaven

The zodiacal sign of the Midheaven is the first consideration. We get a benchmark understanding an individual's self-awareness from the degree at the Midheaven. The previous chapter elaborated on the meaning of the Midheaven (Tenth House cusp) in each of the signs. To expand this understanding we integrate the Midheaven with the rest of the chart through aspects to the planets. The following section defines the nature of Midheaven aspects to each planet, focusing closely on the nature of ego-consciousness. This section draws heavily on Reinhold Ebertin's work, *The Combination of Stellar Influences.*

Midheaven/Sun

In terms of consciousness this combination addresses the very goals of life. Individuals with the Sun and Midheaven in aspect may be more in touch with their own consciousness *because* what they are and what they know about that are directly related. With no aspect between Sun and Midheaven, the connection is less direct. The constructive expression of a Midheaven/Sun aspect is through advancement toward success. One knows oneself well enough to recognize direction or mission. The nature of the aspect reveals the developmental focus of individuality in terms of ego-consciousness.

Aspects of the Midheaven to the Sun

Conjunction: The beginning of a new cycle, emerging from the end of the previous cycle, involves the self, self-awareness, and goals in life.

Semi-Sextile: You experience growth in knowledge of your personal attributes, sometimes through painful realization.

Semi-square: Internal stress is an indicator that self-awareness is emerging.

Sextile: You have opportunities to gain self-awareness through openness to the world and to other people.

Quintile: You find you have a talent for self-discovery that is more refined than in other people.

Square: Situations impel you to become self-aware.

Trine: Conditions exist in which you may gain self-awareness.

Sesqui-Square: Agitation caused by events or internal struggle lead you to ego-consciousness.

Biquintile: Talents and abilities play a part in emerging ego-consciousness by providing for concrete expression.

Quincunx: Life adjustments bring self-awareness.

Opposition: Awareness of self comes through others.

Midheaven/Moon

When the Midheaven applies to an aspect with the Moon, there is a direct connection between ego-consciousness and the soul. The emphasis on inner spiritual meaning, and values become a catalyst for self-understanding. The focus is less on individual expression, and more on a flexible life path that asserts the desire to nurture others in terms of what one knows about oneself. This flexibility does not encourage the focused approach of the Midheaven/Sun aspect; rather it allows for diffuse interests based upon deeply rooted, spiritual values. The nature of the Moon is to allow preconscious or unconscious motives to emerge into awareness; the nature of Midheaven/Moon aspects is to make these motives part of what one knows about oneself. When there is no Midheaven/Moon aspect, the individual becomes aware of spiritual motives separately from ego-consciousness. These motives are no less potent, only less integrated with one's knowledge of self.

Aspects of the Midheaven to the Moon

Conjunction: The new cycle here involves the soul, relationships, and changing objectives.

Semi-Sextile: Growth in self-knowledge comes through the unconscious.

Semi-Square: Internal stress indicates the process of coming to self-awareness concerning unconscious drives.

Sextile: Opportunities to gain self-awareness about deep internal issues are available.

Quintile: There is a talent for self-discovery through dreams and visions.

Square: Situations impel the individual into ego-consciousness by forcing one to look at unconscious material.

Trine: Conditions exist in which the individual may gain self-awareness about the soul.

Sesqui-Square: Agitation caused by events or internal struggle lead the individual to ego-consciousness, based upon feelings.

Biquintile: Unconscious talents and abilities play a part in emerging ego-consciousness.

Quincunx: Life adjustments bring self-awareness concerning deeper feelings and the moods they can cause.

Opposition: Awareness of self comes through contact with others, particularly the opposite sex.

Midheaven/Mercury

An aspect between Midheaven and Mercury addresses self-knowledge through the same avenues that one would address any kind of knowledge. The thought processes are readily available for self-examination. To the extent that thought processes have been cultivated, this individual is well-equipped to plan and pursue objectives on the mental level. Thus, it is essential for the individual with strong Midheaven/Mercury aspects to train the mind. Sloppy thinking will only lead to sloppy pursuit of objectives. One quality of Mercury is its changeability; Midheaven/Mercury aspects can lose focus if the mind is not well trained and practiced. Another quality is the capacity to resolve conflict; a Midheaven/Mercury aspect allows the individual to come to resolution directly through self-awareness, or ego-consciousness, whereas other Mercury aspects would indicate other means. When there is no Midheaven/Mercury aspect, the easiest path to self-awareness is *not* through thinking; rather it is through other energies indicated by Midheaven aspects to other planets.

Aspects of the Midheaven to Mercury

Conjunction: A new cycle focuses on clear thinking, ego-conscious action, and vocational change.

Semi-Sextile: Growth in self-knowledge is gained through thought processes.

Semi-Square: Internal stress indicates the process of coming to self-awareness through clarifying objectives.

Sextile: Opportunities are available to gain self-awareness through mental relaxation and meditation.

Quintile: The talent of self-discovery is based in trained mental processes.

Square: Situations impel the individual into ego-consciousness through expression of opinions.

Trine: Conditions exist in which the individual may gain self-awareness through consciousness-training activities, such as meditation.

Sesqui-Square: Agitation caused by events or internal struggle lead the individual to ego-consciousness concerning personal thought patterns and their effects.

Biquintile: Unconscious talents and abilities play a part in emerging ego-consciousness about one's own mind.

Quincunx: Life adjustments bring self-awareness concerning the need for both mental control and mental flexibility.

Opposition: Awareness of self comes through reflection on interactions with others.

Midheaven/Venus

According to Ebertin, the Midheaven/Venus aspect addresses the quality of individual love. According to esoteric astrology, Venus relates to concrete knowledge. The essence, it seems to me, of this combination is the profound awareness that all concrete knowledge is rooted in the love principle. Another expression of the Midheaven/Venus aspect is through artistic expression. The close connection between beauty and ego-consciousness allows expression to embody harmony and balance in concrete form. This can include plastic arts, writing, and any activity whose aim is to achieve a higher level of harmony in the physical world as well as in interpersonal and social relations.

When there is no Midheaven/Venus aspect, love is experienced indirectly or less consciously. It will have the force of archetypal drive for the individual and may never be clearly understood.

Aspects of the Midheaven to Venus

Conjunction: The capacity to love undergoes change as a new cycle begins. There can be new attachments or falling in love.

Semi-Sextile: Growth in knowledge of inner beauty, sometimes through the discovery of painful awareness of one's personal limitations.

Semi-Square: Internal stress indicates the process of coming to self-awareness concerning one's true disposition.

Sextile: There are opportunities to gain self-awareness about the capacity to love.

Quintile: The talent of self-discovery is found through artistic endeavor.

Square: Situations impel the individual into ego-consciousness through whatever feelings of love are engendered.

Trine: Conditions exist in which the individual may gain self-awareness through interpersonal relationships.

Sesqui-Square: Agitation caused by events or internal struggle lead the individual to conscious awareness of feelings toward the self.

Biquintile: Unconscious talents and abilities play a part in emerging ego-consciousness about inner beauty.

Quincunx: Life adjustments bring self-awareness concerning interpersonal relationships.

Opposition: Awareness of self comes through love of others, both given and received.

Midheaven/Mars

Mars is energy and action. Midheaven/Mars aspects indicate ego-conscious action. The ability to decide what to do and the action itself is closely connected to the awareness of self. This connection between self and action leads to organizational ability, independence, and determination. It also is indicative of prudence, a quality not normally associated with Mars, because the individual is bringing self-awareness to his or her activities. The integration of ego-consciousness with action results, then, in more orderly activities and fewer missteps—that is the constructive side. Less constructive expression can result in careless action, due largely to the lack of cultivation of thinking processes. As usual with Mars, control results in improved results.

When there is no Midheaven/Mars aspect, energy often is expressed outside of self-awareness—hence the fluid action of the athlete who is *not* thinking about each movement, but rather allowing a trained movement to occur.

Aspects of the Midheaven to Mars

Conjunction: Here a new cycle of success begins, with the potential achievement of goals, change in occupation, and ego-conscious action.

Semi-Sextile: Growth is found in knowledge of personal energy and its sources.

Semi-Square: Internal stress indicates the process of coming to self-awareness concerning expenditure of energy in any activities.

Sextile: Opportunity to gain self-awareness about the effects of energy on ego-consciousness is present.

Quintile: The talent of self-discovery is based on personal energy.

Square: Situations impel the individual into ego-consciousness through energetic, sometimes angry interactions.

Trine: Conditions exist in which the individual may gain self-awareness about personal energy flow and energetic style.

Sesqui-Square: Agitation caused by events or internal struggle lead the individual to ego-consciousness concerning the impact of unconscious energy use.

Biquintile: Unconscious talents and abilities play a part in emerging ego-consciousness through their energetic emergence into awareness.

Quincunx: Life adjustments bring self-awareness concerning the flow of energy in the body and mind.

Opposition: Awareness of self comes through energetic interaction with others; the drive for independence is based on ego-consciousness.

Midheaven/Jupiter

Jupiter indicates expansion, optimism, and religious or spiritual interests. Aspects of the Midheaven to Jupiter emphasize the nobler facets of human expression as a result of consciousness. The urge to expand is joined with self-awareness to produce direction and optimism. This combination often signals success throughout life because the higher, more comprehensive awareness of cosmic law is so closely linked to ego-consciousness. It is as though the two are one expression for the individual. The desire to accomplish something important can be a powerful motivation; it can also lead to a sense of self-importance, depending on the aspect of the Midheaven to Jupiter.

When there is no Midheaven/Jupiter aspect, the individual has a less conscious, but no less potent, relationship to spiritual experience. Expansion is experienced rather than pondered.

Aspects of the Midheaven to Jupiter

Conjunction: Now is a time to look for the achievement of success, fulfillment of conscious objectives, and the experience of optimism in general.

Semi-Sextile: Growth is found in knowledge of one's own consciousness, sometimes through changes in life style and circumstances.

Semi-Square: Internal stress indicates the process of coming to self-awareness concerning one's objectives in life.

Sextile: Opportunities are present to gain self-awareness in the areas of physical and mental health, and for achieving success in the outer world based upon self-awareness.

Quintile: The talent of self-discovery serves to awaken contentment and optimism.

Square: Situations impel the individual into ego-consciousness through the generosity expressed to and from others; changes in occupation and status affect ego-consciousness.

Trine: Conditions exist in which the individual may gain consciousness of personal goals; desire and effort are necessary.

Sesqui-Square: Agitation caused by events or internal struggle lead the individual to ego-consciousness concerning achievement of personal and career objectives.

Biquintile: Unconscious talents and abilities play a part in emerging awareness of aims, as well as self-understanding.

Quincunx: Life adjustments bring self-awareness concerning occupation and status; major life changes have direct impact on the ego.

Opposition: Awareness of self comes through understanding the successes and failures of others.

Midheaven/Saturn

This combination relates structure to ego-consciousness and can lead to rigid ideas about the world. There will be far less movement with this combination, as it is less about awareness of change and more about the limitations we find in the physical environment. There is a focus on the structure of one's own personality rather than on things outside the self. Because the individual does not develop a strong sense of the structure of social systems, there is a tendency to be self-critical, sometimes leading to an actual loss of ego-consciousness. Ego-consciousness is not placed within the framework of the world, and thus has not solid ground on which to develop. The result is a difficulty in career and relationships that can only be overcome through steadfast adherence to one's goals. Once again, the need for sufficient practice in thinking is apparent; clear thought processes will negate the tendency toward depression and mental disorder.

Aspects of the Midheaven to Saturn

Conjunction: This is not a time for unrestrained change. It is a good time to learn from experience and engage in self-examination.

Semi-Sextile: Growth in knowledge of the structure of one's own mind and how that structure serves or limits personal development.

Semi-Square: Internal stress indicates the process of coming to self-awareness concerning rigid patterns that need to be modified.

Sextile: Opportunities are available to gain self-awareness about one's inner "map" of consciousness.

Quintile: The talent of self-discovery permits self-awareness.

Square: Situations impel the individual into ego-consciousness through fear of the loss of self or awareness. The square is indicative of major changes in career and goals.

Trine: Conditions exist in which the individual may gain self-awareness through experience.

Sesqui-Square: Agitation caused by events or internal struggle leads the individual to ego-consciousness because rigid structures are being "shaken down" to reveal new goals.

Biquintile: Unconscious talents and abilities play a part in emerging ego-consciousness in which limitations are seen as challenges rather than obstacles.

Quincunx: Life adjustments bring self-awareness concerning old structures and inhibitions that now must give way to new forms.

Opposition: Awareness of self comes through observation of the structures in other people's lives.

Midheaven/Uranus

Ebertin, when discussing Uranus, emphasizes the qualities of suddenness and change as well as rhythm, independence, and even rebellion. I feel that all of this is true, but it is true because most people cannot understand the true role of Uranus as the provider of equilibrium. Midheaven aspects to Uranus indicate the state of being ready to take action, coupled with a strong intuitive sense of what direction to take with one's life. When these aspects are controlled by a well-trained mind, they do indeed provide equilibrium in one's life, as the individual can foresee conditions and events clearly. When they are out of control, emotional imbalances result and change controls you, instead of the other way around. The more out of balance Midheaven/Uranus aspects seem, the more they are an indication that one's ego-consciousness is ignoring some significant portion of the psyche and its messages. When there is no Midheaven/Uranus aspect, equilibrium is not a conscious consideration. Balance is therefore achieved through instinctual adjustment to circumstances.

Aspects of the Midheaven to Uranus

Conjunction: Originality is on the rise as the new cycle begins. There is potential for assertive action, with the probability of career advancement. There may be sudden changes in circumstances.

Semi-Sextile: Growth in knowledge of assertiveness is indicated, sometimes through the pain of misdirected aggression.

Semi-Square: Internal stress indicates the process of coming to self-awareness concerning equilibrium and how it is achieved and maintained.

Sextile: Opportunities are available to gain self-awareness through fortunate or sudden changes in life.

Quintile: The talent of self-discovery focuses on rhythmic processes such as music and dance.

Square: Situations impel the individual into ego-consciousness through intense expenditure of energy.

Trine: Conditions exist in which the individual may gain self-awareness about ego-conscious control of the breath and other bodily processes.

Sesqui-Square: Agitation caused by events or internal struggle leads the individual to ego-consciousness concerning the value of internal equilibrium.

Biquintile: Unconscious talents and abilities play a part in emerging ego-consciousness about emotional balance, goals, and the interaction of the two.

Quincunx: Life adjustments bring self-awareness concerning how to regain balance when it is upset by sudden changes in circumstances.

Opposition: Awareness of self comes through interaction with others. Typically urges toward independence must be balanced with the desire for relationship.

Midheaven/Neptune

Uncertainty is the keyword for this combination. Ego-consciousness is frequently not available, or only after great effort. The individual with this combination must work hard to manifest the higher qualities of psychic awareness. The strength gained from contemplative practice of meditation can balance this aspect with a consistent mental focus which compensates for the dreaminess and aimlessness of Midheaven/Neptune aspects. As people move into the twenty-first century, they will find better ways to work with Neptune energy, thereby relieving the depression and mental disturbance which this planet can bring. Midheaven aspects to Neptune, balanced with other aspects, become a source of depth and strength. The prerequisites are the trained capacity for mental focus and a grounded connection to the material world. Definition in the physical realm balances the lack of definition coming from Neptune combinations.

When there is no Midheaven/Neptune aspect, the power of psychic awareness is felt more in the body and less in the mind. It may be difficult to gain clarity about moods and other mental irregularities.

Aspects of the Midheaven to Neptune

Conjunction: There may be uncertainty as a new cycle begins. There is intense devotion to objectives, and there may be strange ideas or the possibility of deception.

Semi-Sextile: There is growth through the knowledge that insecurity is a sign that more information is needed in a situation.

Semi-Square: Internal stress indicates the process of coming to self-awareness concerning one's response to uncertainty.

Sextile: Opportunity to gain self-awareness and self-confidence through application of trained cognitive processes.

Quintile: The talent of self-discovery focuses on the investigation of the unconscious realm.

Square: Situations impel the individual into ego-consciousness by demanding the ability to tolerate a lack of clarity. Dreamy objectives create susceptibility to strange influences.

Trine: Conditions exist in which the individual may gain self-awareness through devious pathways; an example is the drug trip which reveals "universal truths," or a meditation practice which opens the mind to the One.

Sesqui-Square: Agitation caused by events or internal struggle produces new levels of ego-consciousness by bringing the wandering thought practice back to physical realities.

Biquintile: Unconscious talents and abilities play a part in emerging ego-consciousness because they provide landmarks for otherwise undefined objectives.

Quincunx: Life adjustments bring self-awareness concerning the existence or lack of mental clarity.

Opposition: Awareness of self comes through experiencing the lack of direction in others.

Midheaven/Pluto

The power of Pluto manifests directly in Midheaven aspects as a force to shape one's individuality. Through sheer force of will, this combination inclines one to seek a mission in life and to fulfill it. No longer simply thought, the mission becomes a guiding force for transformation. As the ego-consciousness is focused on life's mission, personal power is mobilized to attain success, to organize one's life, and to express personal authority. Any misuse or misdirection of personal power can lead to disaster. Power out of control is like a race car without a conscious driver, dangerous in the extreme. Stories about the sorcerer's apprentice address the fact that power without the knowledge to control it can lead to ruin. Here, as with the other planets, one must train the mind and open one's consciousness to broader vistas as well as to refined focus. Then the power of will inherent in Midheaven/Pluto aspects is based on informed ego-consciousness.

When there is no Midheaven/Pluto aspect, power is outside conscious control to a large degree. Will is governed by unconscious drives, as indicated by Pluto aspects from other planets.

Aspects of the Midheaven to Pluto

Conjunction: Power is part of the picture as a new cycle begins. Authority and fame are part of the dramatic changes, along with potential attainment and recognition.

Semi-Sextile: Growth in knowledge of personal power is expressed through sometimes painful experiences of coercion or resistance.

Semi-Square: Internal stress indicates the process of coming to self-awareness concerning how to manage one's will in a self-aware manner.

Sextile: Opportunity to gain self-awareness is found through public exposure and its ramifications.

Quintile: The talent of self-discovery reveals one's personal mission and its transformative power.

Square: Situations impel the individual into ego-consciousness through the application of power and the consequent development of individual will.

Trine: Conditions exist in which the individual may gain self-awareness through allowing the misuse of power. Undirected power can result in crises; directed power and will can prevent them.

Sesqui-Square: Agitation caused by events or internal struggle lead the individual to ego-consciousness concerning the proper application of will in the pursuit of solutions to problems.

Biquintile: Unconscious talents and abilities play a part in emerging ego-consciousness about the ultimate sources of personal power and will, as well as their appropriate uses.

Quincunx: Life adjustments bring self-awareness through application of therapeutic processes. Therapy can come from within as well as from another person.

Opposition: Awareness of self comes through the experience of coercion from others. One's own authority only develops when it is tested by others.

Progressions, Directions, and Transits to the Midheaven

Directions and transits to the Midheaven signal change as no other aspect combinations can. The Midheaven is the most prominent and public point in the chart; at the same time it indicates the path toward awareness of the deepest psychological mysteries of one's being. Ego-consciousness involves the knowledge of where the basis for personal change is to be found.

Solar Arc Midheaven/Planets

When the Midheaven forms aspects to the planets, major shifts in one's approach to life occur, according to the nature of the planet and the aspect that is formed. The emphasis in on mind: mental capabilities and tendencies are brought to bear on specific areas of life indicated by the position of the planet being aspected. It is the mind that is bringing about change in one's life. Ego-consciousness is the active factor and therefore directions or progressions of the Midheaven to natal planets signify life changes that are a result of self-awareness.

By contrast, the energy of each planet as it aspects the natal Midheaven by direction and transit speaks to the nature of changing self-awareness at that particular time. Because the Midheaven is the most elevated point in a chart, it has a public position. Planetary aspects to the Midheaven often accompany events that bring us publicity, sometimes when we don't want it. Changes in status, such as marriage, death, career change, and the like are usually not private. Yet there is often profound personal change related to such events, change that demands that we shift our self-awareness.

When a planet aspects the Midheaven (the Tenth House cusp), it also aspects the Nadir (the Fourth House cusp). This coaspect reveals the internal unconscious source of energy that often drives the outer-directed activities of the Midheaven. For example, a sextile to the Midheaven indicates opportunities of the sort indicated by the planet. At the same time there is a trine to the Nadir, indicating that conditions exist for the release of information from the unconscious, again indicated by the particular planet. Thus the energy applied to developing ego-consciousness is accompanied and sometimes even driven by one's deepest unconscious connections to self and to the collective mind.

Progressed aspects are indicative of major shifts in energy currents. As such they point to trends and events in our lives, as well as psychological conditions which accompany and sometimes cause change. Transits are the triggers for events. The timing of an event indicated by solar arc directions depends on a transit, often the Moon or Mars. For example, solar arc Neptune may make a sextile to the Midheaven for an entire year, but the opportunities indicated by that aspect will manifest only when Mars or the Moon forms an aspect to Neptune. There will be several transiting aspect that may activate the progressed aspects of the Midheaven, thereby mirroring more than one event.

Transits also signal the moment when one feels the psychological impact of situations and events indicated by direction or progression. In the above example, Neptune sextile the Midheaven can signal opportunities for intensified self-awareness. Transits from Venus or Uranus will coincide with the entrance of individuals into one's life who have profound emotional impact. Venus alone might involve a chance meeting which is not connected to the rest of one's affairs; Uranus could signal a meeting which has continuing effects over many years. Remembering the coaspects to the Nadir, these events trigger recall of forgotten things or the upwelling of new material that may affect ego-consciousness.

The kinds of events indicated by directions and transits involving the Midheaven fall into three general categories:

- changes in status
- stresses to the ego that demand change and
- changes which are motivated by shifts in ego-consciousness.

Changes in status includes events that happen around us that profoundly affect us. The death of a parent is a good example. The death does not happen to us; it is the impact of that event which changes our status. A promotion at work may involve little change in the actual work we are doing, yet it changes our status, perhaps from employee to supervisor. A marriage or divorce of a parent changes a child's relationship to authority, regardless of the child's age.

The above events all include some outside agency that brings change into our lives. Events that we choose also have the effect of increasing self-awareness. Contrast the promotion with a personal decision to change careers. One depends on the boss' decision; the other depends only on the self. Compare death of a parent to the decision to leave home and go to college or to work. Death we cannot control; we *can* decide when to move out into the world. We cannot control what our parents do but we do control our own marriages, divorces, and other major life-changing events. Even though we have more control, however, we still feel the impact of our decisions on self-awareness.

Some of the above events cause intense stress. Death of a parent engenders grief and other emotions; a promotion can cause stress in one's daily life; marriage or divorce bring with them the strain of revising our intimate relationships.

Personal decisions cause stress that can lead to greater self-awareness. When we decide to undertake something new in our lives, there is resistance because we have to move some old thinking out of the way to make a place for the new. Although the limitless quality of spirit does not require removing one idea to make room for another, actual experience tells us that we feel as if we must let go of one thing to grasp another. The stress of this mental process is called resistance.

After we have experienced changes, either because of events outside ourselves or because of personal decisions, we undergo changes in ego-consciousness. Those changes, in turn, create an atmosphere in which we are motivated to additional changes.

Self-motivated growth and development contrast sharply with change that is forced upon us. We often feel the guidance of a higher spiritual connection when this kind of choice occurs. We are responding to a larger consciousness as we develop clearer self-awareness. We identify a new sense of mission, a role in the universal plan, and we act upon that awareness. When we are acting on this level of consciousness, we often experience far less stress. The changes we consider seem so natural, so right, that we don't worry as much. We are "in the flow" of our own energy.

These changes are often easier to read through the coaspect to the Nadir. This is because the inner motivations are coming from the deep well of unconscious knowledge—the foundation of personality indicated by the Nadir. For example, a semi-sextile of the progressed Moon to the Midheaven indicates emotional growth, perhaps because of painful experiences. The coaspect is a quincunx to the Nadir. This suggests that an adjustment to unconscious contents is occurring. Personal awareness is adjusting to this new material, allowing growth in awareness of self. Without consideration of this less conscious, less obvious mental activity, the conscious growth may seem to be happening in a void. That is rarely the case. The impulse from the collective mind comes through the personal unconscious, guided by Spirit. The resulting ego-consciousness is not an isolated occurrence.

Aspects to Midheaven by Transit and Direction

Sun to Midheaven: The Sun/Midheaven aspect by direction or transit signals change which is based on personal effort. When the Sun forms the aspect, we find that authority is invoked. This can be the inner personal authority that has been cultivated, or it can involve outside authority figures, such as the father. In either case personal expenditure of energy is required. We feel exposed to the scrutiny of others; we are available to ourselves for self-examination. Often Sun/Midheaven aspects coincide with career or social advancement.

Moon to Midheaven: The Moon/Midheaven aspect by direction or transit signals change based upon feeling and upon the soul's direction. There are often spiritual (karmic) relationships which become apparent through lunar aspects. These aspects make emotional awareness possible. Signs on the Midheaven and Nadir indicate the nature of the polarity that is being illuminated. Those signs also indicate the quality of emotional flow that can occur. Moon/Midheaven aspects may have the feeling of fate acting in our lives, as the changes seem inevitable.

Mercury to Midheaven: The Mercury/Midheaven aspect by direction or transit indicates change based on self-knowledge. Such change is often caused by communication, and can involve changes in vocation as well. The communication may come from outside the personality, or it may come from an inner voice that makes itself heard through dreams and imagination. Again the signs on the Midheaven and Nadir indicate the conflicting thoughts that may arise; they also indicate the processes through which resolution can occur.

Venus to Midheaven: Change when Venus aspects the Midheaven is based in social interaction. This can involve love relationships and often does; it can also involve self-love or vanity. This combination can coincide with the projection of unconscious material onto persons in the social sphere as well. To become aware of such projections requires a great deal of self-awareness. The Midheaven/Nadir zodiacal signs show whether these changes tend to be grounded and nurturing, or whether they tend to be fiery, exciting changes. Either way ego-consciousness undergoes profound changes when interpersonal contacts are involved.

Mars to Midheaven: Action is always the nature of Mars aspects to the Midheaven by direction or transit. Changes in occupation often occur on this transit. With Mars, emerging unconscious material can be intense and vivid, and may be accompanied by anger or other emotions that demand action. There is little doubt that something momentous is occurring; the only doubt is whether the ego can manage the energy effectively. The older we are, the better we seem to be able to manage. This is because we have had several Mars transits through the same aspect, and therefore can draw on similar experiences.

Jupiter to Midheaven: One often achieves goals when Jupiter aspects the Midheaven by direction or transit. Directions may set the stage for change, while following aspects from Mars or the Moon bring the changes to fruition. Jupiter/Midheaven aspects bring optimism as well. The Midheaven/Nadir signs show the reasons for optimism. They indicate areas of the inner life which are coming to our attention to benefit our personal growth as well as our public status.

Saturn to Midheaven: Saturn requires remarkable changes when it aspects the Midheaven because the nature of Saturn is to define structure. There can be inhibition and difficulties in manifesting change. There can be separation from people and things which have been mainstays of an individual's structure. The restructuring of ego-consciousness is a difficult process precisely because its structure has been the main defense of the psyche against emotional pain. We resist changes in ego-structure with all the tenacity we can muster; the Nadir aspect can show both why change is so difficult and what the unconscious motivation toward change is.

Uranus to Midheaven: The changes indicated by Uranus directions and transits to the Midheaven occur through emotional tension. There is often a sense of originality in the ideas which emerge—they are indeed fresh from the perspective of the ego. However, the ideas are actually emerging from the deepest point of personal equilibrium—the intuition. Regulated breathing can lead to insight concerning one's destiny because it helps us to connect with the deep inner resources indicated by the sign on the Nadir. Circumstances provide unusual and unplanned opportunities for changes in ego-consciousness, and force us to find an inner gyroscopic balance.

Neptune to Midheaven: At the time of Neptune transits to the Midheaven, there is a decided lack of ego-consciousness. There can be an opening to larger mystical and intuitive understanding which is indeed not grounded in personal ego, but rather is indicative of awareness which transcends the present. Profound realizations can emerge from the collective unconscious at such times, or from contact with spiritual sources outside ourselves. These unusual mental states include indecision, self-deception, wrong ideas, and aimlessness. Supernatural or psychic awarenesses can emerge, as indicated by the esoteric expression of the Nadir sign.

Pluto to Midheaven: The desire for power inherent in Pluto directs the ego-consciousness to action. Inner changes will result from whatever outer events occur. The empowerment of self-awareness can have a dramatic effect on the pursuit of one's mission. Coercion from outside can also have its effect. The Midheaven sign reveals much about one's contact with the "other," the outside world, while the Nadir sign provides a door into the depths of one's unconscious connection to the universe.

Chapter Eight

Client Consultation: Dr. Charli

Dr. Charli: I am a Cancerian, born on July 1, 1947. I have been feeling a mental, emotional, physical, and psychic pull over the past year toward a new vocation. Is this a midlife crisis or a real leap of faith?

S. C.: I'd like some more information: what have you been doing so far, career-wise, and what career are you changing to?

Dr. Charli: I am currently a gerontological nurse practitioner (care of folks over sixty). I plan to take about three months off to investigate other avenues of health delivery . . . you notice I said *health*, not illness! Since Congress gave the insurance companies more power in determining medical care for their clients, it has been getting harder to get my patients what they need. They are hospitalized more frequently, etc.

I am very interested in alternative health care systems, such as acupuncture, herbs, and diet. I have been using them in my practice for years. I have also been invited to become an expert witness for civil medical suit trials. I am interested if they are suing the insurance companies.

I am also a solitary wiccan and have been for about twenty-five years. I use energy work in my practice and may go into that exclusively. I also make healing and power shields for my friends—they say I should sell them.

So, lots of options. Whatever it is, it must be full of *positive* energy so that I can maintain my own wellness—hard to do in an illness environment.

S. C.: You have outlined your situation very thoroughly, and I see you have a wealth of interests and experience. What I want to do first is to outline some of the basic career indicators in your chart. Then I will begin to address the specific questions you have raised.

The Planets

Pluto is the best planet, with Neptune and Saturn running a close second. It is imperative that you don't fall into traditional traps of thinking about these planets. They have tremendous power, and while power can be misused, it can also be wielded for good. Taking Pluto first: you have a natural tendency to develop your personal power, and probably to resist coercion from others. Whatever your principles, you stand on them and rarely deny them. This is not always a comfortable position to take, but you have the good fortune of having the strength to take a position and mean it. So from the very first interpretation, I can see that you would be a powerful expert witness. You are able to look at the situation and measure it against your principles, then inject your personal power. I would recommend that you take the offer to be an expert witness—*without limitations*. There may be very few cases that do not involve the insurance companies—cases where individuals could benefit through your ability to take a strong position. Since being a witness is probably not a full-time career, we need to look further. Besides, you probably don't want to do that all the time.

Neptune provides strong vision of what can be accomplished and how to motivate others. You combine a psychic sense of how things are with a sympathetic understanding of what people need. You are responsive to those needs. You may feel the desire to be in a glamorous position in your career field, or at least to attain the spotlight through your efforts.

Progressive healing methods are certainly right up your alley career-wise. You are willing to experiment with new ideas and evaluate the results. You will want to avoid any fraudulent activities or connections that give such an appearance.

Saturn is a runner-up for best planet. Saturn provides the structure in our lives. It also has to do with the aging process, hence your interest in gerontology. In fact, wicca and many of the things you mentioned are built on a structure of knowledge and practice. Your stability comes in part from the groundedness of Saturn's energy. Saturn is also the teacher. At this time you may want to consider a teaching role of some kind as part of your work.

Dr. Charli
July 01, 1947

MIDDLE RING
Directed Chart
July 28, 1997

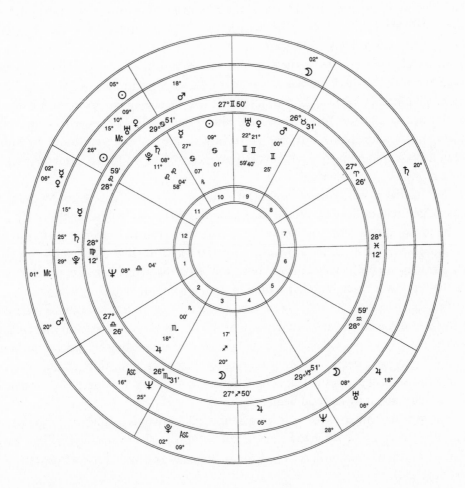

OUTER RING
Transit Chart
July 28, 1997

Geocentric
Tropical
Koch Houses

Figure 11. Dr. Charli's Directed and Transit Chart.

Saturn and Pluto are conjunct in Leo in your birth chart in the Eleventh House. I will say more about this later, but now I just want to suggest that the two energies *are* together and need to work smoothly together. As a solitary you have had time to work with your personal power and develop it without interference from others. You have developed a structure that can be the base from which you move forward. You have established yourself as an authority in the health care field. These are all potential components of your next career.

In any chart Saturn shows the best foundation for career success. It describes the type of career, the staging or development of the career, and the possible long-term outcome. Charli, where career is concerned, there are strong factors in your favor.

Caution is a factor. You do not rush into things without proper thought. The conservative path is certainly needed in health care, as you wish to do no more than necessary to help your patients achieve health. And you wish to take the right action for each individual.

Your ability to concentrate your efforts and your perseverance through changes has helped you to develop reliability and loyalty as strong character traits. By the same token, if you feel you cannot deliver—either you no longer feel loyal to an employer, or your loyalties are with the patient and not the employer—you will choose to move on, as you will not compromise on the principles. If your employer wanted you to act in an unreliable manner, you would not be willing to do so.

Personal assets that you bring to your career include independence from family and friends. You are not restricted in where you can live by ties that limit movement. Where you can work hard and achieve the most is an interesting consideration. Your first job may have been working for a relatively large organization. In that atmosphere you were able to establish connections and to earn the respect of your peers. That environment was a good beginning.

The expected outcome of following Saturn's directives is not limited. No goal is too high for you. The offer to be an expert witness is one indicator that you have followed Saturn's guidance, paid your dues (so to speak), and prepared yourself for the next level.

Your ability to learn from experience focuses on informal situations that retain a somewhat diplomatic quality. This could mean that you learn easily from on the job training, for example. Also, this is an indication of your ability to teach, I feel.

Whereas Saturn tells a lot about what will work best in terms of career, Mars reveals how you apply your energy to that work. This is another planet that has gotten a bad name from some traditional astrologers. Mars represents your energy, and as such, it is neither good nor bad. Here is a way to describe your endurance, your powers of resistance, and where your energy can be placed to get the maximum benefit from moderate expenditure. Because you mentioned that you want a career that is rich in "positive" energy so that you can maintain your own wellness, Mars should be considered carefully as it relates to Saturn. These planets form a very wide sextile aspect. In fact it approaches the quintile, so I will discuss both. First, you may find that cooperative efforts are easy for you. There can be an easy flow of energy in two ways: you are able to apply your energy well to the situations which arise; in addition your career is enhanced by the energy you put into it. Thus harmful actions are less likely for you, and you receive the maximum benefit from what you do. Secondly, there are creative possibilities for you to use your energy. You may focus on medicine, conflict resolution, or other careers where you can use your talents to repair damage or resolve difficulties.

You may find that Mars encourages you to rash action from time to time. At this stage of your career, you may have learned not to give in to such urges, yet you bring enthusiasm to your work that can rub off on the people around you. You also have the ability to say what needs to be said without going too far—an excellent quality for an expert witness.

The Tenth House

Activity in the Tenth House provides information about the career itself, and since the question relates to changing the career, this is where I am concentrating my response. With Gemini on the Tenth House cusp (the Midheaven) and with Sun and Mercury in the Tenth, there is a lot of information about career and the potential for successful change in this area.

The Gemini cusp suggests that you have multiple talents and skills, and the energy to work with them all. You seem to have managed not to scatter your energy too much (a potential problem with this sign), and you mention the desire not to do so in the future. You are the type of person who needs a good mix of responsibilities to be happy—no one track-mind here! Potential career fields for Gemini include, but are not limited to, accounting, book selling, clerical and office work, editing, information management, mechanics, and repair work. There are some elements of these careers in what you have been doing, but no strong focus.

You have most of the sign Cancer in the Tenth House, and this suggests a second set of career possibilities, including agriculture, gardening, nursing, restaurant or hotel management, sailing, social work, and silversmithing. These seem a more likely group, considering your stated interests. Some of the Gemini careers may be adjunct, such as doing your own bookkeeping and office work, or the paper work of your nursing job.

Mercury is the planet associated with the Tenth House. Abilities you bring to career include a good sense of humor, ambidexterity or good body/mind coordination, craftsmanship, cleverness, and strong mental abilities. Possible career directions include advising, advertising, books, brains, education, writing, and the post office.

The Moon is the planet associated with Cancer, the second sign in the Tenth. Abilities suggested by this sign include adaptability, curiosity, illumination of a situation, receptivity, and absorption of information by osmosis. Possible career directions include babies, candles, fresh water, baking, crops, diet, fertility, furniture, fermentation, health, nursing, plumbing, and allergies.

With the ruler of the Tenth House in the Tenth, you develop your capabilities and strength steadily and will rarely make a serious misstep. You give personal attention to your career and tend not to depend on others for decisions. With the ruler in Cancer, nurturing is a significant part of your career. Even if you are not in a career focused on nurturing, you are able to unselfishly facilitate others to make use of their talents and strengths, as well as doing this for yourself.

The Moon, ruler of the second sign in the Tenth, is in Sagittarius in the Third House. You find that you inspire loyalty in every area of your life, and this is particularly true of your career. Because you are generally tolerant and honest, they will permit a bit of dogmatism from time to time, as they understand you have good reasons for your strong position. You are able to show many faces in your career, and you may indeed have more than one career at any given time, or more than one set of responsibilities in your job. Your versatility makes you a natural in working with people.

Aspects of the Midheaven

The Midheaven makes several aspects in your chart, indicating that you may be more in touch with your own consciousness than most people because what you are and what you know about yourself are directly related. If there were no aspect between Sun and Midheaven, the connection would be less direct. You constructively express your energy by focusing on advancement toward success. You know yourself well enough to recognize your direction or mission early in the game.

You use your thought processes to develop self-awareness. To the extent that thinking has been cultivated, you are well equipped to plan and pursue objectives on the mental level. It is essential for you to train the mind. Sloppy thinking will only lead to sloppy pursuit of objectives. One quality of your mind is its changeability; you can lose focus if your mind is not well trained and practiced. Another quality is the capacity to resolve conflict; you come to resolutions directly through self-awareness, or ego-consciousness, whereas other people may use different means. Growth in knowledge of self occurs through thought processes. When you apply yourself to problem solving in your career, you discover inner strength and focus your thinking ability.

You are capable of a profound awareness that all concrete knowledge is rooted in the love principle. The close connection between beauty and ego-consciousness allows expression to embody harmony and balance in concrete form. This can include plastic arts, writing, and any activity whose aim is to achieve a higher level of harmony in the physical world as well as in interpersonal and social relations.

You feel an emphasis on the suddenness and change in your life as well as rhythm, independence, and even rebellion. You are usually in a state of being ready to take action, coupled with a strong intuitive sense of what direction to take with your life. Controlled by a well-trained mind, intuition can indeed provide equilibrium in your life, as you can foresee conditions and events clearly. When you are out of control, emotional imbalances result and change runs your life, instead of the other way around. The more out of balance you seem, the more your ego-consciousness is ignoring some significant portion of the psyche and its messages. A new cycle of originality emerges from time to time in your life, providing the capacity for assertive action to advance in your career and to manage sudden changes in circumstances.

Through sheer force of will you seek a mission in life and to fulfill it. No longer simply thought, the mission becomes a guiding force for transformation. As ego-consciousness is focused on life's mission, personal power is mobilized to attain success, to organize your life, and to express personal authority. Any misuse or misdirection of personal power can lead to disaster. Power out of control is like a race car without a conscious driver—dangerous in the extreme. Stories about the sorcerer's apprentice address the fact that power without the knowledge to control it can lead to ruin. You must train your mind and open your consciousness to broader vistas. Then power of will comes to be based on informed ego-consciousness. You learn to manage your willfulness in a more self-aware manner by paying attention to your own internal feelings. Use stress as an early warning system for the build up of coercive energy within you.

Planetary Aspects

Mercury also makes several aspects, indicating that thinking and feeling are creative sources of understanding concerning the world. Working with women can be a valuable source of ideas. Fantasy is your creative source. You speak from a well of compassion and grasp the subtlest inmost situations. You are logical and thorough in your work and in your personal life. Slow, steady advancement in life is related to your skills of concentration and industry. Endings and beginnings are accompanied by serious thought.

The Moon is active in your chart as well, suggesting that intensity in your emotional life can produce conflict. You can also develop strong emotional bonds with mates and children. Use your innate artistic talent and recognition of beauty to overcome a tendency to dwell on emotional conflicts. Yet, your relationships are filled with emotional intensity. Nervousness occurs when you are puzzled about how to respond to others. Yet you will have sudden successes which come out of these tense periods. You need to balance fear and anxiety with restful periods.

You are often aware of subconscious feelings and thoughts that are not evident to others. This comes through in your awareness of shifting cycles. You seem to have precognitive information about changes. Your kindness, especially toward women, affects the major transitions of your life. Expansive gestures of kindness lead to spiritual growth.

Progressions and Transits

At the time of this reading, there is likelihood that you can re-create your current income source into something you like better, or find creative sources of income to replace your present one. Your mission in life may center on the development of self-control. You define the external world through clear thinking. Sometimes you feel very isolated from others.

You are often aware of subconscious feelings and thoughts. This natural psychic ability leaves you open to the energy flows around you. Because you are hyper-aware, you often have the advantage of knowing what is happening ahead of other people.

At times in your life you will struggle with the need to adjust to situations which arise. These adjustments will affect your relationships with others; more importantly, they will be reflected in your inner sense of well being. The capacity to adjust to circumstances is a measure of your inner clarity of mind.

You can use your deeply rooted feelings to interact creatively with others. Rather than stifling emotional outbursts, use that energy to pursue conceptual links between your talents and the outer reality. Common sense sometimes seems to short-circuit good ideas. Upon reflection, however, you often find that you have experienced a minor setback and avoided a major disaster. Your psychic ability makes you aware of hidden traits in others. You are seldom surprised by the decisions of others and you are often one step ahead of them in your thinking. Emotional tensions can create strain on your physical body. To avoid this, work with your metaphysical interest and develop an awareness of tension as a signal to refocus subconsciously as well as consciously.

It is easy for you to become depressed, sad, or at least very thoughtful. You can use this tendency to focus your mental energies on practical matters. Sometimes you feel very isolated from others. You have opportunities to gain self-awareness through openness to the world and to other people. You also will see career opportunities, and need to take action if you want them to materialize.

In about two years you will find that situations impel you into ego-consciousness through fear of the loss of self or awareness. There may be of major changes in career and goals during your life, and you need a flexible interior structure to manage outer developments. Mental clarity becomes essential when you encounter periods of adjustment. Don't fall into the temptation to put on a act to get through a difficult situation.

Because these two conditions are coming up, you want to prepare for them in every way possible. Thus, if you are to make changes, do it now so that a stable base is there in one and one-half to two years. Also, maintain a meditation or other practice that will help you to stay more up beat as well as keep your mind clear. Third, exercise like weightlifting, walking, jogging, or aerobics can help you to focus your attention and get the blood moving, thus combating any fear or depression that might arise. Be prepared and these will not be big factors.

Chapter Nine

The Sixth House

The best vocation is one that permits the expression of your highest ability amid the surroundings ruled by the most auspicious planet in your birth chart. However, raw ability may lead to discordant circumstances in the work environment. In addition, new abilities can be learned and old ones improved upon. There is no substitute for adequate education and training. Still, planetary patterns show where the latent abilities lie, thereby guiding you to the appropriate studies.

Sign on the Sixth House Cusp

Where the work environment and the securing of employment are concerned, the Sixth House tells the story. It also deals with the actual work that is undertaken. The sign on the cusp of the Sixth indicates how you react to work, to your work associates, and to the work environment itself. Thus, regardless of the actual title you hold, the place where you do the work and the people around you make a tremendous difference in the attitudes you develop in the work place. The Sixth House shows how you go about obtaining the job as well. Thus a chart devoid of any progressed or transiting aspect to the Sixth would make it difficult to be hired, or even to find a suitable place to work.

It is useful to consider the things ruled by the sign on the cusp, as these are attractive to you. Given a choice, you would naturally gravitate toward a kind of employment that suits these indications. In addition, consider the kinds of places ruled by the sign. This includes the type of building, the site on which the building is placed, and even the city or country ruled by either the sign or the planet.

One advantage of knowing about your own chart is that you can choose between job possibilities based on just this sort of thing. You may not have ever considered this on a conscious level, but you certainly have done so on an unconscious level. You are probably aware of how your home is different from any place you have worked. In fact, you know that certain things that are indispensable at home would be inappropriate in the work place, and vice versa. This is because you want to evoke certain feelings and attitudes in one place that you don't wish to focus on in the other. Once you understand the nature of the Sixth House in your chart, you can select a work environment that maximizes your potential more effectively.

Suppose you are offered two jobs with essentially the same pay, benefits, and responsibilities. The people you will work with seem about the same. How do you choose? Well, if one place is across the street from the fire department and one is on a hill overlooking a valley in the wine country, your impressions of the two places will be different. And don't discount either as a possibility. Some people enjoy being in each kind of place.

The Ruler of the Sixth House

Next, consider the ruler of the Sixth. What does this planet rule—what kinds of places, objects, and feelings? A sign and its ruler govern similar kinds of things. However, the sign indicates a filter through which you can work, while the planet indicates the kinds of actions taken and the players involved.

Planets in the Sixth House

A planet in the Sixth House is an indicator of the type of people you will gravitate toward in the work environment. They indicate what those people look like, their emotional tone, their intellectual capacities, how they apply themselves to their work and to relationships with fellow workers. Aspects to these planets reveal the quality of your interaction to coworkers. If there are no planets in the Sixth, this does not mean you have no coworkers. Rather, it indicates that your relationships to these people depend on or are secondary to other considerations.

Aspects to the Sixth House

Aspects of the planetary ruler of the Sixth to the cusp of the Sixth House or to planets in the Sixth reveal more about the nature of the work and the work environment. In particular the aspects show how the energies involved will work out in terms of employment as it relates to other areas of your life.

In judging the importance of aspects, we consider the nature of the aspect, its orb, and whether it is applying or separating. The orb of an aspect is the number of degrees from perfect. Thus a planet at 10 degrees of Aries forms a square to a planet at 8 degrees of Cancer. The square is a 90-degree aspect, and the orb is 2 degrees because the two planets are actually 88 degrees apart. Some astrologers allow orbs of over 10 degrees for the Sun and the Moon. Some would limit the orb of each aspect to lower amounts. The point here is that the closer to a 0 degree difference, the more powerful the aspect, and thus the more consideration it should be given.

The most important aspect to the ruler of the Sixth, in terms of employment, is the aspect with the closest orb. This is because the closer the orb, the more easily the energies will manifest. This is true for both constructive and less constructive aspects. Because this aspect relationship is so significant to your employment, it is most helpful to know that it is. Then, if the aspect is a constructive one, you can maximize its effect. If it is a less constructive, more stressful aspect, you can work with the energies of the two planets to resolve the difficulty. Astrologers recognize that some of our greatest successes come from the necessity of working with our less positive qualities.

The concept of applying and separating aspects is a bit more complicated. A planet applies to aspect a slower moving planet. Thus if the Mars is at 10 degrees of Aries and the Moon at 8 degrees of Cancer, then the Moon applies to the square. If the Moon is at 10 degrees of Aries and Mars at 8 degrees of Cancer, then the Moon separates—it has already past the closest point of the aspect. This is significant because the aspect is stronger when it is coming to exactness, and weakens as it moves away. It's like tuning a radio—you get a better signal as you approach the exact station on the radio, and the signal weakens when you are past that exact point.

Sixth House Aspects

Conjunction: Gives power and illuminates the situation. It also represents an understanding of beginnings and endings.

Sextile: Shows where opportunities lie.

Square: Demonstrates challenges—where apparent obstacles can be turned to more constructive expression.

Opposition: Exposes factors in the work environment and those incidental to it and how they relate to each other.

Semi-Square and Sesqui-Square: Indicate where internal (bodily or emotional) sensations provide cues about how to proceed.

Trine: Indicates naturally easy conditions where no effort is required, but also where attention is needed to guide conditions into the proper direction. Trines can lull you into a sense of well-being so that you ignore obvious problems when they first arise.

Quincunx (inconjunct): Shows where overall adjustments in the work situation may be needed.

Quintile and Biquintile: Indicate areas where talents lie, and ways to develop them into specific skills. (Quintiles and Biquintiles are discussed in Chapter One.)

Septile: Indicates where you are fated to apply your energies. By fate I mean that you are so drawn to a thing that you cannot resist it without painful consequences. These aspects are so subtle that many people never experience them. Many astrologers don't compute them at all. They reflect the nature of the daimon or mission.

Progressions to the Sixth House

Progressed aspects to the ruler of the Sixth House indicate changes in the type of labor performed, whereas aspects to the Midheaven or ruler of the Tenth House indicate honor accrued or changes in the level of responsibility (promotions). At different times in your work career you will be seeking different energies, different goals. The transition from one kind of work to another is often marked by progressed aspects to the Sixth House ruler. Saturn will bring thoughts of Saturnian things, while Venus will bring very different considerations.

Real Life Examples

So you always thought you wanted to be a championship level ice skater? Or maybe you wanted to be an international spy? Tough call? Okay, here are two charts with certain similarities, but the two individuals had very different careers. The skater is Peggy Fleming and the spy is Mata Hari. Both have the Sun in the Ninth House and Scorpio Ascendants. The progressions, solar arc directions, and transits are calculated for climactic events in each life: for Peggy Fleming the year of her first skating title (June 1, 1960), for Mata Hari the date of her trial and conviction as a spy (July 25, 1917).

Peggy Fleming:

- Aries on the Sixth House cusp
- Mars in Libra in the Eleventh House
- Mars Quincunx the North Node in the Sixth House
- Mars sextile the Sun, septile Pluto, quintile Jupiter, semi-square Saturn, and conjunct Neptune
- Mars septile Pluto
- North Node in the Sixth square the Sun and Pluto and
- progressed Moon conjunct natal Mars, solar arc Mars sextile natal Pluto, solar arc Moon to 0 degrees Taurus in the Sixth, solar arc North Node sesqui-square natal Mars, solar arc Uranus sextile natal North Node, transiting Neptune semi-sextile natal Mars, transiting Saturn square solar arc Mars, and solar arc Venus sextile natal North Node.

Mata Hari:

- Aries on the Sixth House cusp
- Mars in Leo in the Ninth House
- Mars trine the Sixth House cusp
- Mars trine the Sixth House cusp, conjunct Mercury, conjunct the Sun, and conjunct Uranus
- Mercury conjunct Mars
- Neptune in the Sixth septile the Moon, sextile Saturn, and semi-square the North Node and
- progressed Mars sextile natal Venus and biquintile the Sixth cusp, solar arc Jupiter sesqui-square natal Mars, solar arc and transiting Pluto sextile natal Neptune, transiting Neptune square natal Neptune, and progressed Moon sesqui-square natal Neptune.

Peggy Fleming
July 27, 1948
San Jose, CA
03:00:00 PM PDT
ZONE: +07:00
121W54'00"
37N20'00"

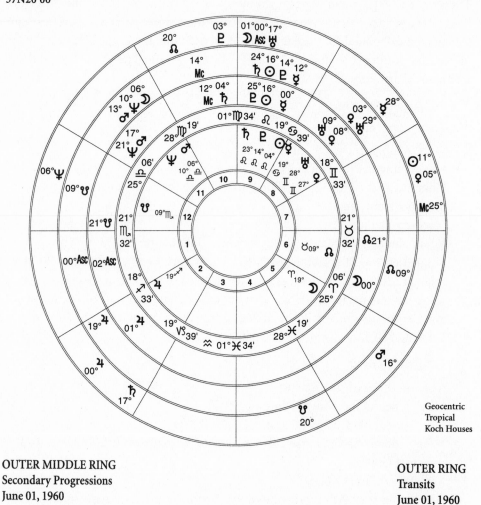

OUTER MIDDLE RING
Secondary Progressions
June 01, 1960

OUTER RING
Transits
June 01, 1960

Geocentric
Tropical
Koch Houses

Figure 12. Peggy Fleming's Directed, Transit, and Progressed Chart.

Mata Hari
Aug 07, 1876
Leeuwarden, NETH
01:00:00 PM LMT
ZONE: +00:00
005E46'00"
53N12'00"

INNER MIDDLE RING
Solar Arc Directions
July 25, 1917

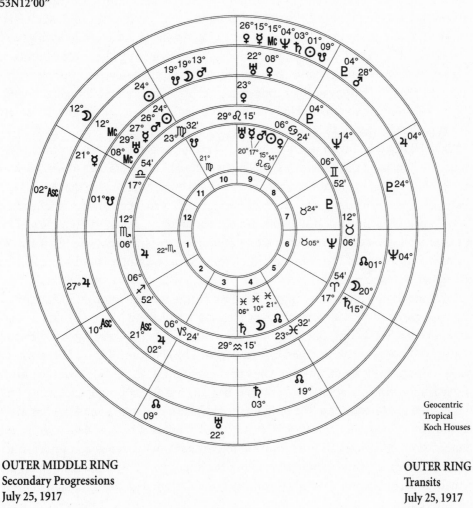

OUTER MIDDLE RING
Secondary Progressions
July 25, 1917

OUTER RING
Transits
July 25, 1917

Geocentric
Tropical
Koch Houses

Figure 13. Mata Hari's Directed, Transit, and Progressed Chart.

The Sixth House and Its Ruler

As you can see from the charts, both have Aries on the Sixth House cusp, with one point in the Sixth in Taurus. Fleming has the North Node in the Sixth, while Mata Hari has Neptune there. Fleming has Mars in the Eleventh conjunct Neptune, while Mata Hari has Mars in the Ninth conjunct the Sun, Mercury, and Uranus. Aries indicates an actual work location on the higher floors of buildings or on high ground. Mata Hari worked at many geographical locations. Peggy Fleming lived in Colorado Springs and practiced at the rink at the Broadmoor Hotel, on the slopes of Cheyenne Mountain. With Aries on the cusp, the nature of work for both is creative, fiery, pioneering, with a "me first" quality. However, the expression of those qualities is strikingly different. Peggy Fleming, with the North Node in the Sixth, depends on associations with others to a large degree (steady Taurean types).

Mata Hari worked with the illusion and glamour of Neptune (which rules espionage) in Taurus in the Sixth, always using her physical allure as part of her stock in trade. This is not to say that Fleming does not have those qualities, or that Mata Hari had no Taurean work associates. Rather, the idea here is to locate the focus of energy in the work environment. Both women's careers focus on Mars, as Fleming's Mars quincunxes the Node in the Sixth, while Mata Hari's Mars trines the Sixth House cusp. The influence of the quincunx in Fleming's chart is not as significant, due to the rather wide orb.

With the Sixth House ruler in the Eleventh House we find another indication of the importance of associations for Peggy Fleming's work. And Mars is conjunct Neptune, which rules skating. She depended on coaches and choreographers to develop skating programs to suit her personal strengths. The glamour of the whole package came, in part, from them. She has Mars in the midpoint of the Node and the Midheaven, indicating her ability to work with her coaches and colleagues, a quality that has carried her forward into the broadcasting of skating events. Mata Hari has Mars in the Ninth, conjunct the Sun, Mercury, and Uranus. She traveled widely and depended on communication of information for her work. Uranus accounts for her unusual line of communication. Mars is in the midpoint of the Sun/Mercury and the Sun/Uranus, indicating the ability to think critically, but also the tendency to hasty or rash action.

Aspects of the Sixth House ruler indicate how the work will proceed. In fact, the closest aspect is a key factor. For Peggy the closest aspect is a septile to Pluto in the Ninth. She is virtually fated to travel and to put her energy into her work. This combination also speaks to the effort required to become a champion of her caliber.

Other aspects include a quintile to Jupiter, indicating the creative success she enjoyed; Sun sextile Mars, indicating the opportunity to advance through her own efforts; Mars semi-square Saturn, indicating the physical stresses involved in sports. Mata Hari's closest Mars aspect is a conjunction with Mercury. Career focuses on the power of thought and the sense of determination to become successful. She loved the communication factor and was skilled in this area. The risk factor is seen here (Ebertin mentions rashness and the potential for lawsuits in connection with Mercury/Mars). Other Mars aspects include the Sun conjunct, indicative of her vitality and stamina, vocational success, and overcoming obstacles; Mars conjunct Uranus, showing the danger she entertained as a spy, and indeed throughout her varied careers. The risk of danger expressed itself in her relationships; she had a violent marriage which allegedly was the cause of death of one of her children.

Each woman has aspects from the Sixth House. Fleming's Node squares the Sun and Pluto, and in fact is in the exact midpoint. This indicates the importance, once again, of the associations she forms with others, and that they share in the responsibility for her rise to success. Mata Hari's Neptune forms a sextile to the Moon, emphasizing the creative nature of her work; a sextile to Saturn, showing the opportunity for the methodical planning in her work, as well as the tendency for circumstances to undermine her efforts; and a semi-square to the Node, indicating a lack of judgment where associates are concerned, as well as the desire to deceive others.

Progressions and Transits

Focusing on the Sixth House and its aspects, we find that at significant moments in each of their lives, the Moon by solar arc was in the Sixth House in both charts, forming powerful aspects to natal planets. In Mata Hari's chart, the solar arc Moon formed a trine to Uranus, and semi-square to Saturn. In Peggy Fleming's chart the solar arc Moon came to 0 degrees of Taurus, changing from the fire element to earth. It is in a separating sesqui-square to Pluto and applies to quincunx the Midheaven. Here is a case where a trine was not a good thing, as it set up the condition for sudden change that is reflected in the trial and guilty verdict for Mata Hari. For Peggy we do not see sudden change when she won her first title, but rather the adjustment to her new status as a champion, and we can see the inner stresses that led up to that competition.

Both individuals have progressed aspects to planets or points in the Sixth House. Mata Hari has solar arc and transiting Pluto forming a sextile to Neptune, while the progressed Moon forms a sesqui-square. Peggy Fleming has solar arc Venus applying to sextile the North Node. So while Mata Hari was in the throes of self-torment and anguish, caught in her own deceptions, Peggy Fleming was enjoying the love affair with skating that guided her entire career.

Both have aspects to the ruler of the Sixth, Mars. Mata Hari has solar arc Jupiter sesqui-square, while Peggy Fleming has the progressed Moon conjunct Mars. Mata Hari's flaunting of the accepted rules brought her to her conviction, while Peggy Fleming was vigorously pursuing here heart's desire to win at skating.

Even though Mata Hari was forty years old and Peggy Fleming was only eleven on the dates under consideration, both had momentous events in the career area. Mata Hari was convicted of espionage, culminating a life filled with excitement, travel, and intrigue. Peggy Fleming won her first skating championship, beginning what has been an outstanding career in the sport. Both ladies demonstrated intense drive and passion for life. Both have shown their creativity in more than one career path. Both have traveled widely (numerous Ninth House planets) in connection with their careers. It is also important to relate the Sixth House in all its facets to the Second and Tenth Houses. These relationships are considered in other chapters.

Summary

In order to gather pertinent information on your own charts, I have included an outline of the Sixth House factors to consider:

- sign on the Sixth House cusp
- house and sign placement of the ruler of that sign
- aspects of the ruler of the Sixth to the cusp of the Sixth and to planets
- closest aspect of the Sixth House ruler to another planet
- planets and points in the Sixth House, and aspects of planets in the Sixth to other planets and
- progressions, directions, and transits to the above planets and points.

Sixth House Sign: Places of Work

> *Aries:* Denmark, England, Germany, Iceland, Israel, Japan, Lithuania, New York City, New Zealand, Peru, Poland, Portugal, Spain, Syria, and Wales.
>
> Sandy places, laboratories, nuclear facilities, new construction sites, hillsides, ceilings, fireplaces and furnaces, and east walls and rooms.

Taurus: *Asia Minor, Australia, Cyprus, Florida, Holland, Ireland, Labrador, Louisiana, Maryland, Minnesota, New Guinea, Newfoundland, Persia, Poland, St. Louis, and South America.*

Entertainment businesses, restaurants, public gardens, bedrooms, dressing rooms, cultivated land, lawns, trees, dim rooms, low ceilings, dark closets, basements, tiled floors, and southeast walls and rooms.

Gemini: *Arkansas, Belgium, Eastern Canada, Colombia, Lower Egypt, London, Rhode Island, South Carolina, Tennessee, U.A.R., Venezuela, South Vietnam, Wales, West Virginia, and Wisconsin.*

Places of commerce or transportation, offices, pulpits, high hilly places, lofts, post offices, billboards, stairways, ladders, halls, schools, upper parts of rooms, filing cabinets, and southwest or west walls or rooms.

Cancer: *Africa, Amsterdam, Southern California, Central Canada, China, Holland, Idaho, New Hampshire, New York, New Zealand, Paraguay, Pittsburgh, and Wyoming.*

Residences, hotels, boats, beaches, docks, sheltered places, wells, fountains, ditches, canals, hydrants, kitchens, cellars, laundries, plumbing lines, and north walls or rooms.

Leo: *East Africa, Alaska, the Alps, Bohemia, California, Western Canada, Chicago, Colorado, Detroit, France, Western Los Angeles, Madagascar, Miami, Missouri, Oklahoma City, Oregon, Pacific Islands, Philadelphia, Sicily, and Zanzibar.*

Parks, playgrounds, yards, jungles, reservations, steep hillsides, natural fortresses, hot and humid places, forests, main entries, living rooms, dining rooms, out-of-reach locations, disorganized spaces, and east walls or rooms.

Virgo: *Western Alaska, Assyria, Boston, Congo, Greece, Hawaii, Los Angeles, Moscow, New England, Turkey, Uruguay, Virgin Islands, North Vietnam, Virginia, and West Indies.*

Level, productive land, gardens, cornfields, dairies and farms, barns, storehouses, closets, pantries, home offices, locked rooms, crooked hallways, and south walls or rooms.

Libra: *Argentina, Austria, Caspian Sea, China, Upper Egypt, Indochina, Japan, Miami, Northern India, Siberia, South Pacific Islands, and Tibet.*

Hillsides, meadows, areas with clear air, detached buildings, cleared fields, upstairs, airy rooms, alcoves, garrets, wardrobes and dressers, upper-level floors, and west walls or rooms.

Scorpio: *Algeria, Baltimore, Bavaria, Cleveland, East Indies, Korea, Manchuria, Milwaukee, Montana, Nevada, New Orleans, North Carolina, North Dakota, Oklahoma, Philippines, South Dakota, Tokyo, and Washington, D.C.*

Swamps, bleak places, drains, dumps, sewage treatment stations, drains, low wet ground, bathrooms and cleaning closets, medicine cabinets, mortuaries, cemeteries, and northeast rooms or walls.

Sagittarius: *Alabama, Arabia, Australia, Bolivia, Chile, Czechoslovakia, Delaware, Hungary, Illinois, Madagascar, Mississippi, New Jersey, Ohio, Pakistan, Singapore, Spain, Toledo, and Yugoslavia.*

Dignified offices, churches, courts, banks, large institutions, universities, high ground, estates, large sites, upper-level rooms, places to store ammunition, and southeast rooms or walls.

Capricorn: *Antarctic Ocean, Bulgaria, Connecticut, Georgia, India, Iowa, Lithuania, Macedonia, Mexico, New Mexico, Texas, and Utah.*

Remote or abandoned places, places where hard labor is performed, slums, deserts, barren fields, mines, mountain peaks, storage buildings or rooms, corners near the ground or floor, and south walls or rooms.

Aquarius: *Abyssinia, Arabia, Arizona, Cyprus, the Holy Land, Kansas, Long Beach, Massachusetts, Michigan, Russia, Sweden, and Wichita.*

Scientific laboratories, reclaimed land or buildings, near new buildings, modern architecture, areas with built-in equipment, unusual work places, and northwest rooms or walls.

Pisces: *Maine, islands in the Mediterranean, Nebraska, Normandy, Polynesia, Portugal, Sahara, Samoa, Southern Asia, Seville, Tripoli, and Vermont.*

Flood plains, lower ground, monasteries, retreats, rooms with low ceilings, small rooms, rooms with adequate furnishings, rooms with water, places of confinement, and northwest rooms or walls.

Sixth House Planets

Planets in the Sixth House reveal the kind of associates you find most cooperative, and the people who will frequent your work place, be they associates, clients, or visitors. The analysis of planets can be extended to any house, but specifically to the Second and Tenth where career is concerned. Knowing which planets are in the Sixth House can help a client:

- choose between jobs on the basis of the people they meet when they interview and tour a site
- use this information when they are in a position to hire subordinates or to interview peers
- learn to work with individuals in the work place who present challenges and
- develop an understanding of how associates tend to interact with each other.

Planets in the Sixth: People in the Work Place

Sun: The Sun in the Sixth House indicates strong, authoritative individuals. They are generally confident of their own skills and open and above board in their dealings with others. They are ambitious and desire recognition, so praising their successes is worth the effort, whether they be the boss, peers, or employees. They can brighten the work area both literally and figuratively. Associates tend to be men.

Moon: Whether male or female, work associates tend to have nurturing capabilities. They are generally receptive to new ideas and are willing to try any good idea. They have active imaginations and can usually be counted on to take an idea, flesh it out, and then sell it. They may tend to run in packs, and this is not a bad thing as long as they do not exclude key associates. They need an environment conducive to their work, yet attractive and safe.

Mercury: Mercurial coworkers combine the best of education and reason with a brilliance and versatility born of their changeable nature. These individuals observe and analyze, learning to discriminate between favorable and unfavorable forces. They make for skilled examination of every situation, but may not be reliable in the clinches, as they will dance away to the next situation in which their attention to every detail provides them with the fuel for their own advancement.

Venus: Socially refined to the last detail, Venus makes for courteous fellow employees. Mostly female, these individuals are cooperative team members who sincerely think of others as well as of themselves. They love to feel that they are part of the group. They understand the dynamics of personal interaction in the work place. Part of what makes them so good at this is their temperamental nature which often masks a keen appreciation for their companions.

Mars: These people are the driving force of action in the work environment. Constantly looking for a new venture, they dive into new projects and demonstrate their enthusiasm at every turn. They are impulsive and need the balance of someone who is more cautious, or at least more grounded. They enjoy working independently and are self-reliant. Their fearless attitude in the face of change can seem rash or even destructive. Above all, they are determined to succeed in their own right and not at the expense of others.

Jupiter: Optimism is the keynote of Jupiter in the Sixth House. Why not, when good fortune seems to follow them wherever they apply their energies. More interested in the processes involved in a project than the precise outcome, they are popular among their coworkers. They grasp opportunities with a keen sense of the potential, but can dissipate their energies and fail to achieve the highest level of wealth possible. They are promoters with a grand start who need the support of more responsible, serious types.

Saturn: Discipline is the keynote of Saturn in the Sixth. Fellow workers will be serious if they are anything at all, with a proper sense of restraint, terminal punctuality, and near reverence for the conventional. They are the ones who systems were invented for, as they thrive in situations where dutiful attention to detail will win out over exuberance. Saturn's seriousness can turn to pessimism if they forget that results can be measured and success can be manifested materially. They are usually patient.

Uranus: Uranus is anything but patient. Independent, nonconformist, always looking for something new and exciting, these people can be loose cannons in the work place. They can also be the source of intuitive insight into the way things really work. The willingness to consider the new becomes the ingenuity of the problem solver. They are friendly in a rather impersonal way, and are not the best repository of secrets.

Neptune: Neptune can be wise beyond all expectation, with a gift of imaginative genius, or it can be deceptive and self-indulgent, seeking only to satisfy warped and obsessive urges. Thus, such a person can be the inspiration for an entire work force or the most negative drag on the energies of others. Generally sensitive, they can be counted on to provide a unique impression of the intricacies of office politics. Such a person thrives where imagination is more important than precision, where intuition is supported by more logical individuals.

Pluto: "Off with their heads!" This can be the watchword of a tyrant Pluto or it can be the rejuvenation that a budding work force requires. These individuals drive others to change, to grow, and to master their abilities. They tend to drastic action from the beginning and may never learn to be moderate. They understand how things work on the deep inner levels of both the physical and the psychic planes. They make their own rules.

None: Even though people in the work environment are not represented by a planet in the Sixth House, they exist nevertheless. The empty Sixth House indicates a person who is fully able to work alone, and who may enjoy that much more than be surrounded by others. Even in a busy work environment, the individual will feel somewhat separate, and possibly isolated. Aspects to the Sixth House ruler will indicate how such a person interacts with the world where career is concerned.

Placement of the Sixth House Ruler

The location of the Sixth House ruler indicates where the energy for work comes from, or an area of the life that affects one's work environment. Mata Hari, for example, was energized by travel and did much of her work far from home. Peggy Fleming, on the other hand, was energized by the people around her, and she probably still does her best work in the company of her peers.

House of the Sixth House Ruler

First House: People in your work environment have a deep personal impact on you. They can be the source of the encouragement that pushes you to your full leadership potential.

Second House: Your actual work is the source of much of your income. It is also one strong factor in the development of your self-esteem.

Third House: You generally enjoy intellectual interchange with coworkers. Work relationships add to your own versatility and enhance your adaptability to the work situation.

Fourth House: Your work is likely to follow the path of older family members, or of individuals whose lives you most admire, as these people have similar beliefs and feelings to your own.

Fifth House: You bring confidence and creativity to your work environment, although you don't usually wave a flag to attract attention. You usually know when to make your move and have the self-assurance to do so.

Sixth House: You are likely to find the work conditions that suit your career rather easily. The people in the work environment are well suited to their tasks.

Seventh House: Significant others, especially business partners, will be a force in your work environment. Look to them for back-up in the clinches.

Eighth House: You are likely to see whole companies or divisions of companies come and go during your working years, and these cycles serve to stimulate your own career growth.

Ninth House: You find yourself positioned just off stage for many public scenes which impact your career. This is the place to be, as you avoid the direct conflict yet reap the benefits.

Tenth House: You have the direct connections you need in order to make career progress. You take a somewhat sober approach to your work.

Eleventh House: Circumstances over which you have no control will influence your work environment, often to your benefit. You are often on the spot to handle them quickly and capably when they arise.

Twelfth House: You work better when you have time in seclusion to develop your work strategy. Through careful planning you are able to maintain your composure when the heat is on.

Sign of the Sixth House Ruler

Aries: Your urge to assert yourself in the work environment can be a potent tool for change. Don't let it get you into trouble—curb any tendency toward egotism. Your enterprising attitude will take you far at work.

Taurus: You have a somewhat materialistic approach to your work, yet you can use this to increase production. Your interest in finances helps you to see the larger picture. Be thorough in your work habits.

Gemini: Even though your work may not depend on it, your manual dexterity is an asset. Avoid indecisiveness, maximize versatility. Writing may be a significant part of your work.

Cancer: Your work focuses on the nurturing quality—perhaps you fulfill the role of facilitator. You can be a bit timid in your work. Your generally sympathetic attitude and intuitive awareness are strong assets.

Leo: Leadership roles may come to you, as you demonstrate your capacity for management. There is no need to be overbearing in your attitude toward coworkers. Rather, demonstrate loyalty and generosity and you will go far.

Virgo: Your work benefits from discriminating awareness of new situations and people. You don't have to be overly critical—it is better to encourage an attentive attitude than to stimulate arguments.

Libra: You are the "schmoozer," the one who soothes ruffled feelings and maintains harmony among your coworkers. A little training will make you a skilled counselor.

Scorpio: You understand the undercurrents in the work environment, identify trends early, and see the possibilities for change. There is no room for sarcasm or secretiveness. There may be healing potential in your work.

Sagittarius: You bring broad-mindedness to your work and will do well not to bring personal religious beliefs that could interfere with your work. Yet your idealistic attitude and idealism can be very useful.

Capricorn: You find that your ambitions can be served by others in the work environment. You take an authoritative approach to your job. Avoid pessimism and consider taking the edge off as you review your peers and subordinates.

Aquarius: You seek a high degree of freedom in your work and thrive in a progressive environment. You sometimes have impractical ideas and must accept the fact that they cannot be put into motion.

Pisces: You may have a tendency to procrastinate about work tasks and should strive to accomplish your work in a timely manner. Your sensitivity becomes a plus in dealing with other people, either clients or coworkers.

Chapter Ten

Client Consultation: K. A.

K. A.: I have been taking classes to hone my natural psychic abilities. I am also trying to obtain the funds to take certification in hypnotherapy. About six years ago I had a nervous breakdown. I cannot handle stress, so these careers offer a path that is conducive for my continued progress toward recovery. I used to work for a big company and it was the conditions there that led to my illness. They promised to rehabilitate me, but are now reneging on that promise.

I need to know if I am truly working with the universe for the greater good. There are not too many roadblocks, just enough that I need confirmation that my insights are correct. In addition, my natal chart has all the planets in the bottom half of the chart. I was once told that it means I have lots of ideas and no ability to use them. Is this true?

S. C.: In light of your illness, your questions make perfect sense. You need to find a career that does not recreate the stress you had before. But first things first. Whoever told you that you have no ability to use your ideas was not a very good astrologer. Any concentration of planets such as you have indicates *where* your abilities are concentrated, not whether you have any. The concentration also indicates how you generally approach life and therefore can reveal suitable careers, or suitable areas within career fields.

Second, at the approximate time of your illness, you were experiencing several major stressful aspects which are now well past. There were opportunities you wanted to grasp in terms of work or business, and yet there were conditions that led you to disillusionment and disappointment, in yourself as much as in others. Those aspects are in the past.

To begin examining your chart, all of your planets are indeed in the north (bottom) half of the chart. In psychological terms, as an introvert you judge the world in terms of what events mean for you and you are not as responsive to others as the extravert. Life's activities tend to be measured on an internal, personally unique basis. In introversion one's thoughts refer more to the self, to what is within the individual. You seek to understand what life offers before you jump into it. If there is a real world for you, it is the inner world of ideas and subjective understanding. You tend to insulate yourself against the outer world in favor of the inner life.

It is evident that there are many successful introverts in the world, so this is not an inhibiting factor. Rather, it indicates how you will judge your personal successes. I also believe that the inner life is a rich resource of creative material.

You have seven planets in the eastern half of the chart. This is an indication that you have the potential to develop by increasing your skills and awareness. There is movement in the direction of greater personal control in your life than others experience. You like to be in command of situations and create your own circumstances. Even if you work for other people, you like to be responsible for your own work. You are able to exercise initiative and find ways to apply your will to projects. You like to see your projects grow and you put in the necessary energy for this to happen. You tend to measure success in terms of personal results.

Being self-motivated, for the most part, and being an introvert (measuring results on a personal evaluation scale), you were like a fish out of water in a big company. You need a calm work atmosphere in which you can listen to your inner voice. The fact that you are training your psychic ability is perfect for this. As you learn to trust that inner voice, you gain confidence and are able to interact with others without feeling the high degree of stress. But you have to determine the context in which you can work.

With the highest concentration of planets in the first quadrant (the sector that is both east and north) you tend to focus your attention on the self and persona (what you show to the world); your possessions (financial worth) and feelings (self worth); and how you express yourself to others and learn about your immediate environment. This is the area of life over which you have the greatest potential control, as you are the only one who even knows the true content of yourself. You are also the one who decides how to act toward others, and you are the source of your own personal motivation to learn and to communicate.

K. A.
Aug 01, 1955

OUTER RING
Directed Chart
Oct 13, 1996

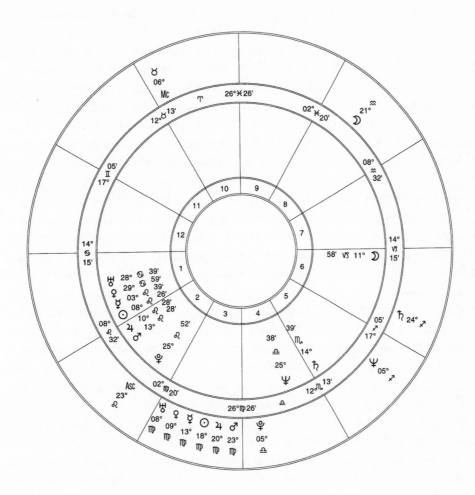

Geocentric
Tropical
Koch Houses

Figure 14. K. A.'s Directed Chart.

One more indicator of how you tend to operate will be helpful: With Mercury rising ahead of the Sun, and the Moon fast in motion (about 14 degrees per day when you were born), you tend to be ahead of yourself all the time. You seldom take time to stop and smell the roses, as you are already on to the next project. You will need to cultivate the usual, the normal, and the mundane to be successful in the work environment. You may struggle to learn meditation, as sitting still is actually rather painful. Even if you slow down to a pace you consider deadly, you will still go faster than most of the people around you. The cell phone and computers were made for you to keep track of the details and keep up to date as you rush through life. If you are honest about it, you can learn to enjoy life at other people's pace, at least part of the time. Sometimes we require a major wake-up call to get onto the proper path. Your illness was such a wake up call, and it is clear from your statements that you know this.

Now, I would like to consider the work environment in which you can work best. As you need to avoid stress, this is a vital concern. With Sagittarius on the Sixth House cusp, the best work environments for you include dignified offices, churches, courts, banks, large institutions, universities, high ground, estates, large sites, upper-level rooms, places to store ammunition, and southeast rooms or walls. I think we can disregard armories, but the other possibilities deserve consideration. You can focus on the words dignified, upstairs, and southeast rooms or the southeast corner of a building. It may seem silly to designate the work space so precisely, yet you will find that it is appropriate to do so. Perhaps you can recall a job where everything went really well, and you note that some of these characteristics were present. The southeast direction offers morning light, something you no doubt prefer with all of those planets rising. With planets below the horizon, you may find you can work best in the early morning hours, when other people are still sleeping. Many psychics find this to be true, as they can be clearer at that time of day.

A place on higher ground will suit your work energy. With Virgo on the Fourth House cusp, your home is well-placed on the ground floor, but work can benefit from a site with a view. If you work at home, you should choose a room in the southeast part of the house for your office. It is probably beneficial for you to see the sunrise.

Coming back to that word "dignified." You will find that stress is, in your view, often related to what you consider to be undignified. Perhaps certain tasks demand activities you feel silly doing. Or perhaps the hectic pace of a large company makes you feel that you are rushing about without finishing tasks to your satisfaction. Time pressure can make you feel a bit like the rabbit in Alice's dream. It's not that you can't bear to hear people say what's on their minds, it's that you choose not to yell or be yelled at. Manners are important. Diplomacy is always appropriate.

If you have thought of moving, some geographic locations which may be suited to your work include Alabama, Arabia, Australia, Bolivia, Chile, Czechoslovakia, Delaware, Hungary, Illinois, Madagascar, Mississippi, New Jersey, Ohio, Pakistan, Singapore, Spain, Toledo, Toronto, or Yugoslavia. These places respond specifically to what you need in the work environment, in one way or another. Please don't feel these are the only places you can live and work.

The work environment is the focus of the Sixth House in the chart, and the Sixth House indicates the attributes of the best work environment for you. Whether male or female, work associates tend to have nurturing capabilities. They are generally receptive to new ideas and are willing to try any good idea. They have active imaginations and can usually be counted on to take an idea, flesh it out, and then sell it. They may tend to run in packs, and this is not a bad thing as long as they do not exclude key associates. They need an environment conducive to their work, yet attractive and safe.

Leadership roles may come to you, as you demonstrate your capacity for management. There is no need to be overbearing in your attitude toward coworkers. Rather, demonstrate loyalty and generosity and you will go far. With Jupiter, the ruler of the Sixth in the Second, you understand the undercurrents in the work environment, identify trends early, and see the possibilities for change. There is no room for sarcasm or secretiveness. There may be healing potential in your work.

Perhaps the best planet in your chart is Neptune. The abilities of Neptune will be facilitated because it is well placed in the chart and forms strong aspects. The abilities associated with Neptune include psychic impressionability, subtlety, abstract thinking, musical talent, compassion, and spiritual wisdom. Neptune brings creativity in writing and the arts. The ability to bring metaphysical values into concrete practice is indicated.

Neptune is the planet usually associated with hypnosis and with psychic ability. You are right on the mark with your career objectives, as the best career is one that uses the abilities indicated by this planet. The down side is that there can be vagueness, confusion, and fear. You have experienced this side of Neptune, and now can focus on the clearer, more creative facets of its energy. It is important to embody your higher ideals in your work.

Pluto is also a candidate for best planet. The abilities associated with Pluto include facilitating transition, organizing group activities, revitalizing situations and a sixth sense in dealing with people. Pluto brings out your power. The ability to manifest creative transformation is indicated.

The Moon is in the Sixth House in Capricorn. It indicates that you can have a gloomy demeanor at times, and at your best seem rather reserved. You have the patience and endurance needed to sustain a career over the long haul, and you develop a deep interest in your profession as well as the actual work you do. You stick with it until you come out on top. It is possible that you hung in there a bit too long at the job you had when you became ill. Still, this is a valuable career trait.

The "lord" of the Sixth House is Jupiter, and Jupiter is found in the Second House in Leo. You are self-confident—you believe you can accomplish whatever you set out to do. When you have accomplished your goals, you can then become your own greatest admirer, and then you are not so attractive to others. Most of your plans involve other people, and you are a naturally optimistic leader. Courage can lead to strength of character, which will be recognized by others if you do the inner work. Fame then becomes an instrument for career advancement.

With the Moon in semi-sextile aspect to Saturn, your mission in life may center on the development of self control. Thoughtful or depressed periods define your growth. Sometimes you feel isolated and need to regroup in private.

The Moon is also quincunx Mars and Jupiter. Impulsive actions mark the cyclical flow of energy in your life. You tend to begin projects with tremendous energy. Rashness can cause problems that can be overcome through honest self-assessment and personal effort. You are lucky—in all areas. You get the best opportunities to come your way and you may achieve recognition suddenly. Hence you are generally optimistic. Both of these aspects indicate that you must make adjustments from time to time in order to remain energetic and optimistic. So while you need a work environment that is conducive to your mental and emotional health, an environment which you control fairly closely, you also need to cultivate the flexibility to adapt to circumstances. Clearly, a well-managed environment will result in fewer demands.

With Jupiter in square aspect to Saturn, you are often happiest when you are involved in secluded activities. Your patience, diplomacy, and sense of duty are exemplary. Your life is filled with challenges successfully met. It is important to remember this fact. Also, fortunate decisions mark the major turning points of your life. You have the ability to concentrate on a particular goal and thus will have successful results professionally. With the Sun conjunct Jupiter, you are generally blessed with good health and destined for success; you will gain recognition and accomplish much if you can avoid extravagance.

The current astrological climate indicates that you may come into contact with a woman who can be very influential in getting your hypnotherapy training under way. You may also meet someone who could be a coworker or partner in the future. You have the chance to learn easily, as at this time you can absorb information easily and develop practical methods for using your psychic ability as well. Your natal planets have moved by solar arc into the Third House, solar arc Venus is trine the Moon, and solar arc Mercury is sextile the Ascendant. Your awareness of self and others is at a high point (solar arc Ascendant sextile Neptune and conjunct Pluto), so your training should go smoothly. Transiting Pluto is trine Mercury and transiting Neptune is opposite Venus, giving you the creative healing ability you need for yourself, as well as for the career path you propose.

Two years from now you will have the Midheaven making a strong aspect to the Sun, one that indicates success in the pursuit of your personal objectives. You will, by that time, understand your personal mission more clearly and be on the road toward your career goals.

To summarize, I feel your career goals are consistent with your chart. You have seen the dark side of your being and dealt with it. Important considerations are the environment in which you choose to work, as the environment must be supportive of your powerful psychic energy. You may decide to work at home, either working on the phone or meeting clients there. If you have a job outside the home, it should have some of the characteristics I have mentioned: dignified atmosphere, southeast windows, upstairs or on higher ground. Your coworkers should be sensitive and nurturing in general. You clients, of course, may not have mastered these character traits. Allowing the next two years for development of therapeutic skills, you should be well-positioned to move ahead at that time.

Chapter Eleven

The Second House

The focus is on the Second House throughout this chapter. To gain a sense of a client's talents and skills, one must examine every facet of this house, its ruler, the planets there, and aspects to them and to the ruler. Here, as in other chapters, the emphasis is on the ultimate synthesis of a variety of factors into a useful model of the client's capacities in terms of vocation. The Second House is significant in vocational considerations because it deals with the following essential factors in work success and happiness:

- how one actually obtains money
- one's earning capacity
- the condition of one's self-esteem
- the accumulation of material things and
- one's attitude toward possessions.

Of the three houses associated with vocation, the Second House is the most personal and private. At the end of your life, all you have to take with you is your self-worth. Money, material possessions, and others' opinions will make no difference at all. What you think of yourself is all that you will have. Second House matters, such as moral growth, personal debts (other than those involving money), and self-esteem, are tremendously important issues. The question is: How do you maximize your potential, fulfill your higher mission, satisfy your daimon, obtain the money you need to live, enjoy your life, and enhance your moral growth—all within the confines of the natural talents you possess, in such a way that, at the end of your life, you are satisfied—personally satisfied—that you did well?

One chapter in one book cannot hope to answer all of these questions. I do, however, hope to provide some guidelines for measuring your natural talents, evaluating the ways for you to obtain money, examining your attitude toward material possessions, and improving your self-esteem. Then you will have some information to consider. You will be able to identify those factors you are aware of, and you will have an opportunity to meet some facets of yourself you have not previously acknowledged. You will be able to consider your life or the client's life in a fresh light. This is a very personal set of considerations, so be aware your interpretations may not be applicable to others, and should not be imposed upon them!

Your client may not see these issues the same way you do. When you are telling a client about the Second House, do so as a set of questions. How do you feel about these astrological factors? Which factors feel more important to you? In this way you help the client to approach his or her own understanding of what is most significant. That said, let us examine each of the points in the following outline, using the chart of J. P. Morgan for illustration. The approach to delineation of the Second House is identical to that of the Sixth and Tenth:

- sign on the cusp of Second
- placement of the ruler of the sign by sign and house
- aspects of the ruler to the Second House cusp and the planets in the Second
- the closest aspect of the Second House ruler to another planet
- planets and points in the Second House and aspects of those planets to other planets and
- progressions, directions and transits to the above planets and cusps.

Sign on the Second House Cusp

The sign on the cusp of the Second House tells about earning potential and self-esteem in several ways. First, the element reveals the natural style of earning. Second, the quality reveals the action involved. Third, the sign can tell a lot about how the individual masks his or her inner reality through the use of money and material things.

J. P. Morgan was one of the most impressive financial geniuses in history. From his first job as a banker's clerk, he was able to observe the 1857 financial crisis on Wall Street, and he learned from it by studying each phase of the situation as it unfolded.

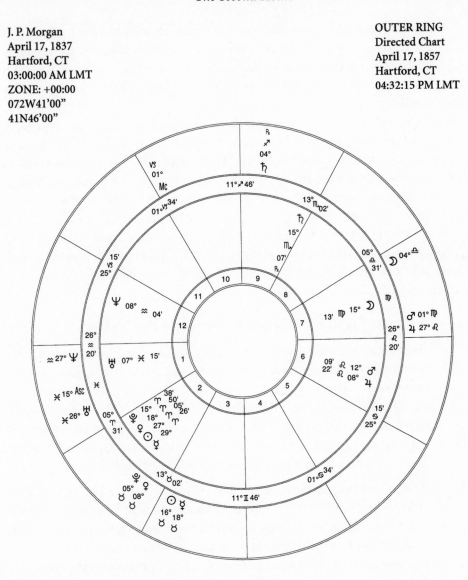

Figure 15. J. P. Morgan's Directed Chart.

J. P. Morgan was the single powerful individual who consolidated the myriad short railroad lines into one working entity, created huge business combines like U.S. Steel, and even bankrolled the U.S. government to pay its army. I will use his chart throughout this chapter to illustrate points about the Second House, beginning here with the ruler.

With Aries on the Second House cusp, J. P. Morgan was nothing if not creative in his approach to making money. There was an element of the game in his approach, and he wanted to be in a position to say, "*I am money.*" He was inspired, creative, ambitious, and aggressive in his accumulation of wealth, and his desire was difficult to satisfy. A strong sense of self-importance may have been justified, given his successful career, yet it may have disguised a need to appear larger than he felt.

The preceding chapter contained a list of the signs and their characteristics as they apply to creativity. That list can be applied to the Second House in general, as self-esteem, a Second House matter, is closely tied to the successful and fulfilling uses of one's energies.

Second House Sign: How Money Comes to the Native

Aries: Money comes most easily through self-assertion. Even if it would come from other sources, the native is impatient, and may feel compelled to create cash flow directly. Courage and resourcefulness make such acquisition of cash possible. The desire to be on the offensive may develop into a series of careers, or at least of projects. Money will be more satisfying if it is earned as a result of personal activity, and more so if that activity is somewhat aggressive in nature. There is likely to be an edge on all moneymaking activities.

Taurus: Persistent and consistent effort is likely to produce money, even if the actual source is indirect. Thus, even the management of inherited money will be best accomplished through somewhat industrious attention to the task. Patience may be required where stock trading or real estate transactions are concerned. The comforts and niceties of material possessions are valued and there is a conservative attitude toward liquidating any possessions. This is sometimes seen as a tendency to hoard material things.

Gemini: Money comes most easily to you through communication. Activities that focus on the creative, versatile communication skills will pay the largest financial dividends. You can be a student, a mediator or intermediary, or a writer, and you may be something of a jack-of-all-trades, with more than one career before it's all said and done. It is important to develop a depth of sensitivity to get the most from life's experiences. It is also helpful to be clear about one's own direction, as it is easy to fall into the habit of learning whatever is necessary at the moment to succeed, without much thought to the long-term value of the skills being learned. Still, you generally ends up with a nicely rounded resume of skills which, though not critical to particular tasks, certainly make them more fun and easier to accomplish.

Cancer: Even within the changeable nature of fortunes there is a prudent attention to finances. Money comes from nurturing activities. These range from farming to family enterprises to all areas of food service. The focus of attention in any of these endeavors is emotional harmony. Caution may make the fortune grow somewhat more slowly than is absolutely necessary, but it prevents the dissipation of wealth that frivolous behavior causes. Too close of a grip on money, on the other hand, prevents the establishment of a comfortable home and secure future.

Leo: Confidence and ambition are the hallmark of this placement. It is essential that all income be from fair business practices, as dignity must be maintained throughout the career. However, one can be somewhat cruel and still be fair. It is better to be generous but not overly so, authoritative but not harsh, determined but not stubborn, in dealing with coworkers, clients, or the public in general. These are the qualities of leadership that increase income. Faith in oneself is essential if you expect others to have faith in you.

Virgo: Service professions are associated with Virgo because this sign reflects the care and attention that good service demands. Money will come through any activity that is based on moral clarity and personal dependability. There is a tendency to keep things beyond their usefulness with this placement. Perhaps this stems from worry about the future. A willingness to study all facets of the financial situation will prevent significant losses. In the final analysis, it is how things turn out that is of greater concern than how you got there.

Libra: Money and material things will come most easily through cooperative endeavors or actual partnerships. You could go out on your own, but you don't want to be the only one—you are a social person and measure your self-esteem in terms of relationships to a large extent. Because you are able to integrate many perspectives into your world view, you may have fingers in many pies. Guard against a tendency to fritter your money away. You will do well in handling other people's finances as you are honest in your dealings and adaptable to their requirements. Your greatest talent lies in weighing the possibilities—you may need your partner to make the final decisions.

Scorpio: There is some mystery about where the money comes from with Scorpio on the Second. It will seem that there is nothing, and then the needed cash magically appears. Some people think that this happens through magic. You know that creativity and secret plans, along with devotion to your set goals, are the reason for your success. Your desires can lead to excess, yet you can be the most trustworthy of individuals. Avoid any cruelty or sarcasm in your dealings, but maintain a frank, straightforward attitude where money is concerned. Bold action is sometimes needed to make the most of career situations.

Sagittarius: You take a philosophical attitude toward money, wherever it comes from. The source can be the philosophy, law, or religion. It can just as well be from breeding horses. It is the attitude that matters. You appreciate the duality of nature and know this extends into the financial realm. Don't be too gullible when others present moneymaking schemes, and don't indulge every personal whim. Instead, capitalize on your open-minded and high-minded approach to life.

Capricorn: You need to find the line between caution and fear—and remain on the side of caution. Your ambition and patience see you through to achieving your highest financial aims, but only if you avoid materialistic selfishness. Honesty serves best in the long run. You understand your duty in any career situation and are efficient in your pursuit of career goals. Money challenges you to find its best uses, and you often reinvest rather than spending. You are somewhat secretive about money matters.

Aquarius: Whereas you know that money is an artificial means to engaging in commerce, you still like to have it. You want the newest and the coolest, yet you are willing to part with material objects to move on to something different. Your tastes are unconventional, so your home or office may not suit anyone but you. You use your intuition to manage financial affairs and thus are able to build and retain a degree of comfort. Then you may exchange your security for a metaphysical journey that satisfies your inner being more (go figure).

Pisces: You are unselfish to a fault—you may end up with very little in your effort to help family, friends, or coworkers. This idealism may be seen as indulgent or even silly by others. You serve yourself best when you temper compassionate acts with well thought out plans that have practical underpinnings. You are receptive to new ideas but are patient and devoted to the task once you choose your direction. Money probably will always flow through your hands, so it's a good thing you don't depend on material possessions to establish your self-worth.

Placement and Sign of Second House Ruler

The placement of the ruler of the Second House can indicate where one's money actually comes from. Mars, the ruler of J. P. Morgan's Second House, is in the Sixth. The indication is that his money came directly from his own work environment—he earned his money. With Jupiter conjunct Mars, there were large quantities of money. With Mars in Leo, money came through leadership, self-reliance, and the will to create. So he is an active factor in the obtaining of money and material things.

House of Second House Ruler: Sources of Income

First House: One earns money primarily through one's own efforts, physical activity, and one's personality.

Second House: Money comes mainly through one's own efforts, and involves movable or liquid goods.

Third House: Personal enterprise, education, communication, writing, and transportation are the most likely sources of income.

Fourth House: Income may come from land, property, or family. Work at home is another possibility.

Fifth House: Creative effort is involved in the earning of money. Speculation, entertainment industry, and buying and selling are other possibilities.

Sixth House: Diet and health industries are likely sources of income. In addition, animals or foreign trade are possibilities.

Seventh House: The marriage or business partner provides the major income. Dealings with others through contracts also generate money.

Eighth House: Banking on contracts involving other people's investment will generate cash. In addition, occupations connected with death, illness, or surgery are good.

Ninth House: Religion, education, travel, and the legal professions will produce money for the native.

Tenth House: Public life or politics are good sources of income. You may end up at the very top and receive honors as well.

Eleventh House: Working within organizations or groups will provide good income. You will also receive money through circumstances beyond your control.

Twelfth House: Hard battles, secret sources, and scheming may contribute to your income. Oddly, enemies may be the source of money as well.

Sign of Second House Ruler: Sources of Income

Aries: Self-assertion, initiative, and personal power are the most likely ways to earn a living.

Taurus: Production of some kind is needed. Self-esteem is a critical part of the work dynamic as well.

Gemini: Mental effort or manual dexterity are good ways to earn a living.

Cancer: Construction and food industries allow you to put your feelings into your work successfully.

Leo: Leadership, self-reliance, and the will to create bring substantial income.

Virgo: Service, or work which requires a studied effort, are likely income sources.

Libra: Partnership, fine arts, or businesses involved with beauty are good income sources.

Scorpio: Any of the healing arts are good careers. The military and occupations related to sex provide moneymaking potential as well.

Sagittarius: Philosophical pursuits will offer the potential for income. These include teaching, legal professions, and religious endeavors.

Capricorn: Appointed or elected positions are very possible.

Aquarius: Humanitarian activities are potential careers. In addition, unconventional occupations are possible for you.

Pisces: Mystical work is possible. Fated contacts with others result in job positions for you, so your psychic or intuitive senses play a part in finding the right job.

Second House Ruler's Aspects to Second House Cusp and Planets

If the ruler of the Second House forms an aspect to the cusp or to planets in the Second House, then the conscious connection to Second House matters is strong. With no aspect, the connection is there because of rulership, but it is indirect and therefore less of a compelling force in the individual's life. With no connection the individual gets and uses money, for example, but it is not the driving force behind that person's activities. Self-esteem is important, but it is not as important as other considerations.

When the connections are there, then self-esteem, moral principals, and the actual flow of cash and material goods hold an immediate place in daily considerations. The nature of the planets and aspects involved delineates the nature of these concerns.

Mars trines Pluto and Venus in the Second House in Morgan's chart. The Mars/Pluto trine suggests the mighty effort he made in his career. He concentrated his force on making big deals, and his great ambition was rewarded. His self-esteem was bolstered with each success. Whereas he may have been cruel in his dealings with this aspect, biographers have not been terribly unkind in this respect. The Venus/Mars trine has a wider orb, but no doubt came into play. This trine reflects the passion Morgan had for making money and for other Second House matters. He surrounded himself with beautiful things, most notably antique miniatures and illuminations. He also is reported to have passionately loved his first wife, who was an integral part of his life.

Closest Aspect of the Second House Ruler

The closest aspect of the Second House ruler indicates the most compelling energy where Second House matters are concerned. The aspects and the planets involved show where one's thoughts and feelings go, and how they flow. For example, a conjunction between energetic Mars and communicative Mercury would indicate much "traffic" concerning money, material things, and self-esteem. The conjunction would put considerations in a spotlight, making them very visible. A square between economical Saturn and expansive Jupiter would indicate thoughts and feelings involving structure and process, or perhaps a strong focus on business-oriented questions and less focus on personal issues. The focus of the square would be challenging.

Mars' closest aspect in this case is the square to Saturn in the Ninth House. Ordinarily this aspect would indicate a destructive energy, and one to be respected, if not feared. J. P. Morgan exhibited immense endurance, pulling deals together that no one else would have attempted. There may have been periods of relative weakness or ruthlessness. Saturn in the Ninth indicates a strong sense of justice and prudence , which Morgan exercised in his dealings that affected the lives and livelihood of others.

Second House Planets and Aspects

Planets in the Second House indicate the energies available for accumulating money and material things. They also indicate the moral direction of the individual and the path toward development of self-esteem. With four planets in the Second House, J. P. Morgan certainly had his life focused solidly on money and other Second House matters. He has a variety of energies that he could apply to making and spending money. Venus in the Second imparts a love of luxury and artistic things and constancy of affection. Pluto reflects Morgan's strong desire, even urgency, to acquire possessions. It focuses attention on the rhythm of loss and gain, and Morgan never let that focus waiver. The Sun indicates that his very individuality was involved in money and material things. He had a material outlook, great endurance, and a strong sense of his soul's purpose as well. He studied situations closely (Mercury), listened to others, and used his intellect to advantage. He observed the market, followed its downswing, learned not only what others tend to do in a weak market, but also how he could take advantage of it. He exercised sound judgment and then leapt into action with his whole being.

There are numerous aspects to the four planets in the Second House:

- Sun: conjunct Mercury, septile Uranus, and sextile the Ascendant
- Mercury: septile Uranus, and sextile Ascendant
- Venus: biquintile the Moon, quintile Neptune, conjunct Pluto, and septile the Ascendant and
- Pluto: quincunx the Moon, trine Mars, quincunx Saturn, trine the Midheaven, and septile the Ascendant.

Each of Morgan's Second House planets forms a septile, indicating the strong influence of fate or karma in Morgan's life. The Ascendant and Uranus in the First House are both powerful forces in Morgan's decision-making process. His success record is due not only to his ability to analyze a situation, but also to his intuitive sense of when to take action and how to convince others to put their money into his deals.

Pluto forms a Yod with Saturn and the Moon (Pluto quincunxes the Moon and Saturn, and the Moon and Saturn are sextile), drawing two more energies into the Second House pattern. Morgan used the force of his personality to resolve problems among his partners, and to convince them to go along with him. When sheer force was not enough, he used his deep philosophical understanding of finance, gained through attentive study, to explain his plans. This Yod includes three of the five closest aspects in the chart. Morgan was probably faced with decisions of this nature in childhood, long before he was in a position to apply the knowledge and philosophy to the financial world.

Venus forms a quintile to Neptune and a biquintile to the Moon. While these aspects are not as close as those in the Yod, they are close enough to form a tight pattern that indicates the creative nature of Morgan's activities. The soul of his dealings lay in the partnerships he formed. Those relationships were adaptable, but they were also necessary. Without his partners' money, the huge deals for which Morgan is famous could not have concocted. This configuration confirms that he had charm. He could have become susceptible to the charms of others if he had not the force of personality and directed intention shown by the Second House planets. He used his visionary talent in the material world instead of letting it take him off into romantic bliss.

The Sun and Mercury sextile the Ascendant, while Pluto and Venus trine the Midheaven. Thus, the angles are drawn into the Second House picture as well. Morgan made his own opportunities throughout his career. These were no accident: his studious attention to the market provided him with the ability to recognize opportunities when they arose. Pluto and Venus trine the Midheaven are strong indicators of the powerful forces that surged around Morgan.

Progressions, Directions and Transits

When aspects occur by progression, direction or transit, the tendencies present in the moment will support or contradict those present in the birth chart. Thus people experience periods of change that seem quite different from their typical approach to life. Generally, the progressed or directed planet making an aspect indicates the nature of the energy being injected into the person's physical, mental, emotional or spiritual sphere. Whatever the birth potential, the progression shows that potential being activated in a certain way. Transits indicate energies that are coming into the picture in the form of events or conditions to be acted upon. The transits often trigger the energies indicated by progression and direction. All of this depends on the potential in the birth chart. Thus a fabulous combination by progression and transit brings something fabulous only in relation to the birth potential, and only to the extent that the individual is able to grasp the opportunity or respond to the challenge.

J. P. Morgan: Solar Arc Progressions

Let's take a look at the solar arc direction for the year 1857 in Morgan's chart: the solar arc Ascendant trines Saturn and opposes the Moon; solar arc Neptune sextiles the Sun; solar arc Venus squares Jupiter and Neptune; solar arc Jupiter trines the Sun; and solar arc Jupiter enters the Seventh House. Of these aspects Neptune sextiles the Second House Sun, solar arc Jupiter trines the Sun, and Venus (in the Second House natally) squares Jupiter and Neptune. The number of aspects indicates that this is a big year in Morgan's life; the two aspects directly related to the Second House indicate the potential for events related to income, material things, and self-esteem.

By transit Jupiter, Pluto and Mars are in the Second on Morgan's birthday. During this year Saturn transited to square Pluto, Venus, Sun and Mercury in the Second House and trine Saturn in the Ninth. Jupiter conjuncts all the Second House planets and opposes Saturn. Uranus squares the Ascendant in June. These squares to Second House planets indicate the action. J. P. Morgan's life certainly took a definite turn during this year, with his financial situation changing dramatically. This was the year he took a job as bank clerk with the man who would eventually become his partner. At age twenty J. P. Morgan took a giant step toward his destiny as a financier.

Mata Hari and Peggy Fleming

Mata Hari has no planets in her Sagittarius-ruled Second House. Jupiter is in the First House and is square to Mercury, square to Uranus, and opposes Pluto. Thus her acquisition of money depends on travel or distant connections, and with Jupiter in the First, she is directly responsible—personally active—in the acquisition of money. It probably comes to her in large sums (Jupiter). With Jupiter square Uranus and Mercury (and Uranus in the midpoint of Jupiter/Mercury), she used her quick wit and easy conversational ability to convince people to tell her the secrets she sought. The same aspect indicates the unusual style that attracted her informants to her in the first place. This combination suits her choice of name—Mata Hari means "eye of the dawn" or "eye of the day."

Peggy Fleming also has Sagittarius on the Second House cusp, and Jupiter is in the Second. Jupiter trines the Moon, Saturn and Pluto, forming a Grand Trine. Money or self-esteem come to her in large amounts, based on her creative ability (Moon in the Fifth) and her will and power (Pluto). She demonstrated that she could manage the intense practice and travel schedules involved in competitive skating. She radiates her charm in the most public venues (television), while Mata Hari came to use her talents in the most secretive of all possible careers.

When Peggy Fleming won her first championship in 1960, she had transiting Uranus in the midpoint of natal Moon/Jupiter, forming a Grand Trine. It was her golden opportunity, as the conditions were right for her to shine. Mata Hari had solar arc Jupiter in the midpoint of Mercury/Mars, forming sesqui-squares to both. For her, it was the end of her career, her trial for espionage in July of 1917. Looking back to February of 1917, transiting Pluto was semi-square to Mercury and Mars at the time she was arrested for spying. It is interesting that the planet that governs the Second House in both charts can indicate the beginning of one career and the end of the other. Note that the day she won her first titles was not the first day Fleming ever skated: it was the first time she knew she could be the best. The day Mata Hari was found guilty was not the last day she had a thought about espionage, but it marked the end of her career possibilities.

Second House Cusp Sign: Self-Esteem

Aries: You have a stormy nature where self-esteem is concerned. It is important to you to be the first with the most, and you want this all the time. You also want to have security where money is concerned. These two urges are not always compatible. You will find that when you become one-sided in your attitudes about financial matters, you feel weakened. Use your energy and courage to help you to move ahead, and avoid vindictive behavior that may hurt you as much as it does your opponent. You will learn to appease your desires without demanding satiation, and you can learn economics from experience.

Taurus: Money comes most easily through determined and persistent effort. You have the capacity for patient work habits and thrifty spending habits, and these qualities, when cultivated, will make for success in financial matters. You may have a tendency toward attachment, even possessiveness, that prevents the smooth flow of material goods into and out of your environment. Fulfillment of your sensual appetites and general enjoyment of pleasures gives your self-esteem a boost. Material things will be more satisfying if you learn to share them generously.

Gemini: You have a tendency to worry about financial matters and you are impatient to move from one moneymaking scheme to the next. Alert to the many factors involved in financial management, you can adapt to changing situations with creative responses and resourcefulness. Sometimes you appear to be emotionally unattached to your money, yet your thoughts often return to active consideration of ways to handle things differently. Material considerations will prosper when you generally think through your decisions and then take decisive action, open to the positive results you expect.

Cancer: You can be tight-fisted with your money or you can be cautious, but it is important to understand how the difference plays out in your financial management scheme. You can appear timid with spending, and yet you are self-indulgent at times, causing your finances to have significant ups and downs. You are usually prudent where money is concerned, and have an edge because your intuition tells you what is around the corner. Material matters prosper when you purchase a few items for dramatic effect, while keeping the background elegantly plain. You will find that less is truly more relaxing and rewarding.

Leo: Ambitious and persistent in the accumulation of wealth on some scale, you can appear selfish to others. Sometimes you indulge to the extreme, but usually your spending impulses are guided toward a few substantial dramatic pieces that have lasting value in the bargain. It would be a mistake to devote your entire life to gaining wealth, as this tends to isolate you from others who, at the very least, you want to be close enough to admire you. Self-esteem is enhanced by financial success; it also thrives when you are generous with your well-deserved material comforts.

Virgo: Money comes to you via practical management. You consider the details of all financial matters and manipulate the material realm with precision. Just as your emotional security is based on being honest with yourself, your material security is grounded in honest dealings with others. You can be overly self-critical when finances don't go the way you planned. You can be skeptical of other people's management abilities, seemingly egotistical in your analysis of their errors in judgment. Material matters prosper through your usually balanced approach to the practical considerations.

Libra: You gain through partnerships of all kinds, including business, marriage, or even play. If you occasionally find yourself depending on someone for your material well-being, you may feel out of harmony and impatient with your dependence. Your desire for material harmony usually keeps you from extravagant expenditures that add nothing to your self-esteem, yet you enjoy the romance of occasional frivolity. Your money is always more satisfying when you are certain you came by it fairly and when you are able to share it impartially.

Scorpio: You can be aggressive in the pursuit of money and material things. Once you have them, you tend to hold on to them with a certain determination. Yet you also are able to make major sacrifices when the chips are down. The balance of these factors makes you a trustworthy individual where money is concerned. You may occasionally indulge to excess, or rebel by spending when you should be saving. You are able to recognize those rare situations when throwing money at a problem can actually be helpful. Money is more satisfying where you don't hoard it jealously, but spend it creatively.

Sagittarius: You can be gullible where money is concerned. When people appeal to your indulgent side, they can take you for a financial ride that you will not soon forget. Your material well-being, and your self-esteem too, are best served by a cheerful earning style, coupled with a philosophical view of the value of money. You can earn money through athletics or an adjunct business. Study of the history of economics and money can give you the theoretical base you need to offset any lack of restraint. Be magnanimous, not frivolous, and finances will thrive.

Capricorn: Generally cautious where money is concerned, you can become pessimistic and even secretive in your dealings. However, your systematic approach to financial management will prove successful over time, and your industrious work habits pay off in the end. Money and material things will make you happier if you place your faith in yourself and not in them.

Aquarius: Cooperative efforts provide the strongest source of income for you, and they also enhance your self-esteem. You need to work with people, not exploit them, to get the most benefit. Occasionally, you can be impetuous, even rebellious, and this can cause upsets in your material world. Scientific and metaphysical fields both have the earning potential that you need. Your knowledge of how people think is another moneymaking tool. Sometimes people find you too detached from your feelings. The material side of life will flow best if you use your intellect to consider how your actions will feel later, both to you and to others.

Pisces: Money comes most easily through sources that appeal to your sense of universality. Thus it is important to believe in the work you are doing, and to find that part of the work that meets with your approval on an idealistic level. Your mystical understanding can be a significant aid in the pursuit of material security, as you see past the supposed requirements to what you truly need to be happy. You may have an impractical streak that needs some objectivity. You deal best with your material world when you work with sympathetic people and avoid situations that distress your sensitive nature.

Planets in the Second House

Sun: Qualities that help you to achieve material success include candidness, confidence, will power, dignity, loyalty, determination, self-consciousness, boldness, generosity, and ambition. The Sun deals with form and personality at the most basic level, the soul and consciousness on the intermediate level, and with life energy on the highest spiritual level.

Moon: Qualities that help you to achieve material success include sensitivity, magnetism, romance, protectiveness, a sense of rhythm, flexibility, and imagination. The Moon influences you by transmitting thoughts and feelings to the inner recesses of your mind. Not so much an active energy as a conduit, it reveals the less conscious activities of mind and serves to illuminate the hidden side of your personality. You have the ability to act when the time comes, based on higher spiritual principles.

Mercury: Qualities that help you to achieve material success include reason, discrimination, precision, analytical ability, resourcefulness, efficiency, refinement, versatility, and clear expression. Mercury is important to you on the practical level because it reflects: first, it reflects what you know through your own communication; second, its role as mediator is key to vocation. How you respond to outside influences is governed by how you hear your inner spiritual voice. Material matters may aggravate you until you adjust your outward expression to suit your inner spiritual mission.

Venus: Qualities that help you to achieve material success include artistic and musical ability, gentleness, rhythm, courtesy, charm, sociability, awareness of the relationships among things, and cooperation. Venus serves to reveal the harmony of your thoughts and actions and relationships. Things themselves simply exist—it is your intelligence that brings them together in meaningful ways. Personal values form the core of your material success. Finances improve as you develop a gentleness of style.

Mars: Qualities that help you to achieve material success include courage, independence, definiteness, enthusiasm, frankness, boldness, devotion to a task, determination, and assertiveness. The urge to accomplish and build must be expressed through your work in order to build self-esteem. Your war for self-mastery may be waged in the material world, but the courage to do so is already deep within you. Financial matters prosper as you learn to assert your desires and work enthusiastically to achieve your goals.

Jupiter: Qualities that help you to achieve material success include generosity, expansiveness, broadmindedness, optimism, idealism, understanding, vision, and confidence. You have a natural inclination to receive and spend. How these two things balance each other determines the state of your self-esteem to a large degree. Thus training your natural talents can result in ample security, along with plenty of fun. Material success comes to you, perhaps more than once in your lifetime.

Saturn: Qualities that help you to achieve material success include caution, sincerity, attention to details, punctuality, self-discipline, patience, diplomacy, endurance, and compassion. Your understanding of how things work is often the key to increased financial security as well as higher self-esteem. Your skills allow you to work within an existing structure while envisioning the future. Material matters will be more successful when you exercise patience with your work, with other people, and most of all with yourself.

Uranus: Qualities that help you to achieve material success include innovativeness, independence, originality, the ability to change, a sense of adventure, intuition, and a scientific approach to tasks. You may experience sudden changes in fortune during your life. Changes in self-esteem may seem just as sudden, but are based on the growth of personal beliefs over time. The ability to bring thinking and intuition together is a powerful tool in your work. Financial security comes with the development of foresight and the application of scientific method in your work.

Neptune: Qualities that help you to achieve material success include sensitivity, responsiveness, subtlety, abstract thinking, the ability to inspire others, and sympathy. You are impressionable where the material world is concerned, and you are able to read beyond the obvious into the true nature of a situation. You also can sometimes avoid the truth by clouding the issue. You have the capacity to understand your own approach to personal, interpersonal, and spiritual devotion. Money is more satisfying when you use it, instead of allowing it to use you.

Pluto: Qualities that help you to achieve material success include will and will power; candidness, zeal, understanding of the life/death cycle, interest in group activities, the capacity to allow ideas to ferment, awareness of your sexual nature, the ability to be indifferent, the ability to regenerate, and passion in all things. You have a forceful and powerful nature through which you establish your self-worth both in terms of material things and in terms of spiritual growth. You have an uncanny knack for selecting the finest antiques and the best value for the dollar.

None: The main focus of your life is not on earning money, but on doing something meaningful with it. You measure meaning in terms of self-esteem for the most part. However, you feel better about yourself when you are surrounded by material things that show your sense of self to the world.

Summary

Second House considerations help us to see how these areas of our lives develop. The natal chart shows the potential. Progressions, directions, and transits indicate times when issues of money and self-esteem are likely to be foremost in our minds, and when events occur to shape our understanding of material existence.

The more connections to the Second House, the more energy the individual expends on Second House issues. J. P. Morgan is an example of an individual whose life was focused on the uses of money, the collection of valuable material goods, and probably personal consideration of moral and ethical issues. The typical chart will not have this intense focus. However, even without a single planet in the Second, each of us has to face financial considerations and moral issues, as we develop self-esteem through our own efforts and with the help of others.

Remember, there are plenty of very successful people who have no planets in the Second House, including Della Reese, Marilyn Monroe, Saint Bernadette, Yoko Ono, Ernest Hemingway, and even Al Capone, not to mention George Washington, John Quincy Adams, William Henry Harrison, John Tyler, James Polk, Zachary Taylor, Franklin Pierce, Ulysses S. Grant, Theodore Roosevelt, William Taft, Woodrow Wilson, Calvin Coolidge, Herbert Hoover, Franklin Roosevelt, Harry Truman, John F. Kennedy, Lyndon Johnson, Richard Nixon, and Bill Clinton.

Chapter Twelve

Client Consultation: Linda

Linda: I was born on August 31, 1960. Even though I have had lady luck with me throughout my life, it has not helped me with the choice of my career. I have been doing a lot of searching in my astrological chart to find out which of my areas of interest would be the best career for me. I am into arts and crafts, including woodwork, Christmas dolls, painting canvases, and sewing. I would say that anything handmade that is creative is my thing. I also enjoy horticulture, writing, astrology, and doing research for people. What I am not into are rules and conventions. Which direction should I take that will be like a hobby, yet also make a financially rewarding and honest living? And, of course, if you can tell me more about myself, I would love it.

S. C.: With such a wide range of interests, it can be frustrating to try to find the one thing that can help you to earn a living. In order to zero in on the finances, I will consider all the factors relating to the Second House in your chart. I will also include other factors as needed to answer your questions.

With Libra on the Second House, money comes to you in two ways: first, you gain through partnerships of all kinds, including business, marriage or even play. Second, you can earn money through artistic pursuits. If you occasionally find yourself depending on someone for your material well being, you may feel out of harmony and impatient to get through it. Your desire for material harmony usually keeps you from extravagant expenditures that add nothing to your self-esteem, yet you enjoy the romance of occasional frivolity. Your money is always more satisfying when you are certain you came by it fairly and when you are able to share it impartially.

You have Neptune in the Second House. Qualities that help you to achieve material success include sensitivity, responsiveness, subtlety, abstract thinking, the ability to inspire others, and sympathy. You are impressionable where the material world is concerned, and you are able to read beyond the obvious into the true nature of a situation. You also can sometimes avoid the truth by clouding the issue. You have the capacity to understand your own approach to personal, interpersonal, and spiritual devotion. Money is more satisfying when you use it, instead of allowing it to use you.

Venus, the ruler of the Second House, is in the First. This indicates that you are a good source of your income, and you are the person to safeguard your material security. In the process, you find that you are the principal factor in development of self-esteem as well. With Venus in Virgo, your personal finances are often directly connected to the financial condition of others, and your work may involve handling other people's money. You are reliable in this because you treat their resources as carefully as your own.

The aspects made by Venus and Neptune describe how you operate in the financial area. The Moon squares Venus. You have intensity in your emotional life, which can produce conflict. It can also develop into strong emotional understanding. Use your sense of harmony to overcome emotional conflicts, especially with women. Venus also squares Jupiter. You will be known for the extent of your kindness. You will meet successful women who affect the major transitions in your life. Don't waste your expansive emotions on frivolous activities.

The Sun sextiles Neptune. You are far more sensitive to your environment than most people. Without careful attention to your choices, you make emphasize weaknesses in your physical body. Increased psychic awareness that helps you to make the most of your possibilities.

Mercury also sextiles Neptune. You have a vivid fantasy life which is connected to some form of psychic activity. You are seldom surprised by changes and see them as openings for further insight.

Jupiter forms a semi-square to Neptune. The richness of feelings in your life is the result of your close connection to the psychic realm. A lack of spiritual rigor can be matched by a lack of physical strength; working with both will help you to avoid instability.

Linda
Aug 31, 1960

MIDDLE RING
Directed Chart
Aug 01, 1997

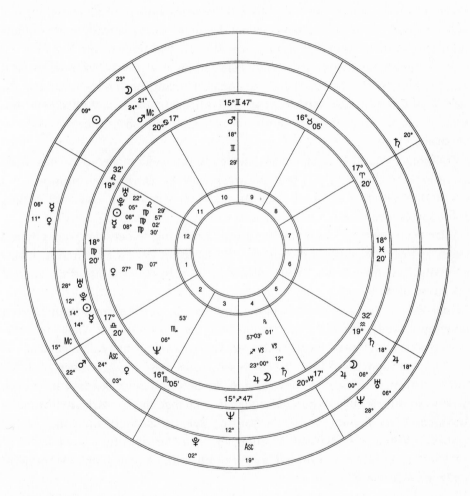

OUTER RING
Transit Chart
Aug 01, 1997

Geocentric
Tropical
Koch Houses

Figure 16. Linda's Directed and Transit Chart.

With Neptune sextile Pluto, you are a highly sensitive person and can develop your psychic gifts steadily throughout your life. You are aware of events before they occur. Your age group peers share this tendency.

The Midheaven forms a biquintile to Neptune. Unconscious talents provide landmarks for otherwise undefined objectives. They reveal how your less conscious side is responding to the outer realities of career demands. You are already aware of these abilities, and can depend on your inner voice to help you guide them.

At this time several astrological factors are coming into play. By solar arc Venus is sesqui-square Mars. You experience passionate relationships and you can use the physical tension to moderate between self and other. Irritability is reflected in tactless communication. Your sensuality gets you into relationships; other qualities will sustain them.

Transiting Neptune has past the trine to Venus. You would prefer to live in a world of illusion and can make this your life work. You idealize love relationships. You become known for your good taste. As this is a past aspect, you have already absorbed its energy and can move forward with it.

Solar arc Neptune is semi-sextile Saturn. You struggle between your physical desires and your higher aspirations. Careful listening to Spirit can result in tiny pricks of conscience instead of major disasters caused by material dissatisfaction that gets out of control.

Transiting Uranus is squaring Neptune. You have the potential for developing your psychic gifts because you can set aside your "ordinary" consciousness. While you sometimes experience confused psychic states, you can achieve spiritual enlightenment.

Transiting Jupiter will conjunct the Sixth House cusp on December 12, 1997. While this transit does not involve and of the Second House factors I have been discussing, it is significant because it signals a change in the work environment. Fortunate turns in your life are the stuff of legends. Occasionally you miss the opportunity, but generally you seek independence and adventure. You need to be ready to make a move, and should lay the groundwork between now (summer of 1997) and December.

Venus has moved to conjunct Neptune by solar arc. You would prefer to live in a world of illusion and can make this your life work. You idealize love relationships and can be devastated when they end. Know that a new one is just around the corner, or that your current relationship is due for renewal at a higher level. As this aspect involves the ruler of the Second and a planet in the Second, there is a very strong focus on change in terms of how you make money.

Solar arc Neptune opposes the Midheaven at this time. You may experience a decided lack of ego-consciousness. There can be an opening to larger mystical and intuitive understanding which is indeed not grounded in personal ego, but rather is indicative of awareness which transcends the present. These unusual mental states include indecision, self-deception, wrong ideas, and aimlessness, as well as the more constructive altered states. There can also be supernatural or psychic awareness emerging. You experience the lack of direction in other people and can learn from it without getting lost yourself. You may benefit from a partner who helps to define the long-term goals. Uncertainty is the keyword for this combination. You must work hard to manifest the higher qualities of psychic awareness. The strength gained from contemplative practice of meditation can provide more consistent mental focus that compensates for dreaminess and aimlessness. As you move into the twenty-first century, you will find better ways to work with uncertainty, thereby relieving any depression and mental disturbance which this planet can bring. Then psychic awareness will become a source of depth and strength. The prerequisites are the trained capacity for mental focus and a grounded connection to the material world. Definition in the physical realm balances the lack of definition coming from Neptune combinations.

With Neptune so strong in your chart, and ruler of the Seventh House, I feel you would do well to find a partner who could act as an agent for you to sell the wonderful things you make. You might even want to consider traveling to fairs to sell your work. There are those little shops set up in malls before Christmas where you could see the dolls and other things. There might be stores that showcase the work of many people. Specialty toy store might sell the dolls. You could advertise in specialty magazines—these ads are usually not very expensive. The partner you seek probably already has expertise in these types of ventures.

I also feel you may want to consider offering classes. Many people want to develop their creative talents, and you have the potential for teaching many different subjects. You could teach in a craft shop, perhaps, or offer continuing education classes at a college. You could organize classes for children for weekends or in the summer, focusing on development of creativity. You could work in clinical settings where occupational therapy or art therapy are needed (you could partner with a therapist if licensing is a problem).

The strong influence of Neptune as discussed above suggests that you have psychic ability. I don't know how this fits into your financial picture at this time, but you may want to consider developing astrology or other psychic talents into money-making possibilities.

Neptune encourages the imagination, which is a strong asset for a writer. Have you thought of writing for publication? It could be part of the creative package. If you have published, you might consider teaching creative writing.

The point is, your source of income is unusual. It may be that money comes from a number of different places. If you follow the above approach, you can focus on work that will allow you:

- to use your creative side
- to do a lot of your work in private
- to connect with people of similar interests
- to build a group of students, clients, and outlets
- to start part time and increase the hours as the business grows
- to assure the element of honesty in all your dealings and
- to integrate your many interests into a career, and build on your self-esteem.

Chapter Thirteen

The Heliocentric Chart

Now that we have examined the geocentric birth chart in detail, we return to the original question: If vocation is calling, then who calls? While the geocentric chart has delineated the nature of the calling and how it may manifest in the world, we still need to identify with the Spirit of that calling. The heliocentric chart provides us with the tools we need to do this.

The heliocentric chart is a mandala that describes the role of Spirit in one's life. As it is centered in the Sun, the heart of the solar system, it reveals something of the nature of Mind as the *solar logos*, mentioned by Tibetan and theosophical astrologers. From this perspective the planets always move in direct motion. There are no seasons as we experience them on Earth. Instead any seasonal effects come from the cycles of the planets and result from the aspects they form as they follow their orbits. The planets are displayed against the background of the zodiacal signs, and planetary energies can be understood in the context of the signs. In this discussion the tropical zodiac is used, but an argument could be made for using a sidereal zodiac. I personally find that the tropical zodiac and its metaphors work very well to describe the nature of spiritual mission for individual charts.

The position of Earth in the heliocentric chart has powerful significance. From the heliocentric perspective, all of humanity resides in the degree occupied by Earth. This means that all people born at a particular moment share essentially the same spiritual impulse, as seen from the Sun's point of view. The richness of human diversity reflects the richness of Spirit—each of these individuals develops a unique personality while drawing on the same spiritual impulse.

The speed of the orbits of the inner planets from the heliocentric perspective is greater than from the geocentric point of view. This means that while all births in a particular moment share in Spirit. While no planet moves as fast as the Moon in the geocentric chart, the moment still changes quickly in the helio chart. For example, Mercury's orbital period is just under eighty-eight days. This means that in one day, Mercury travels a little over four degrees. Venus travels about 1.6 degrees. In one day the relative positions of Mercury and Venus could change by as much as 2.4 degrees. The outer planets are considerably slower. I use rather small orbs when examining an individual's heliocentric chart, as the changes are subtle. I also consider Sabian symbols for heliocentric planets.

Planets in Heliocentric Charts

The following descriptions indicate the nature of the planets and the signs in the heliocentric chart. They do not change in their nature from the geocentric chart, but they do have an expression that is relatively free from personal considerations of ego. Thus they show us a higher expression of their energy, an expression consistent with theosophical teachings and transpersonal psychology.

Mercury: Mercury reflects your role as mediator. Mediation occurs not only in conflict resolution between or among people; it is an internal psychic function as well. It serves as the messenger of the fullness of Spirit. Communication in this sense is not limited to voice or writing which are tied to personality. Communication can include psychic and intuitive connections; it can include channeling; it can include direct transmission, mind to mind, from other people or from other galaxies.

In the heliocentric chart Mercury can be in any relationship to Earth. From the Sun's perspective Mercury is not limited in its effective range, and provides a metaphor for the broadest potential to mediate among the planets. This is an important point. From the geocentric viewpoint Mercury's widest angular distance from the Sun is about 30 degrees. The only aspects formed are the conjunction and semi-sextile. By contrast Earth and Mercury can form oppositions, squares, or any other aspect.

From the spiritual perspective of the solar logos, communication can be perfectly clear, perfectly complete in its range, and perfectly whole. Mediation then becomes the joyful carrying of messages from one planet to another, without the limitations of ego. This level of communication is beyond the mortal experience of self and others, yet holds a fascination for us and provides a worthwhile objective for our aspirations.

Venus: Venus helps to define the role of interdependence in your life. It also indicates your use of concrete knowledge in the pursuit of your mission. Concrete knowledge does not stop at the scientific definitions of things, nor is it limited to the scientific approach to understanding the relationships between people and things. It also includes a felt sense, an inner awareness of the right relationships between things. The placement of Venus in the heliocentric chart shows the natural direction of expanded consciousness for the individual, and can indicate one's spiritual mission in regard to group responsibility.

Venus, like Mercury enjoys a fuller range of position in the heliocentric chart. Therefore the potential for concrete knowledge is less limited in the heliocentric view. To the extent that concrete knowledge concerns the relationships between and among things, the heliocentric Venus focuses on the relationships, not on dependence or interdependence.

Venus has been cast as the alter ego of Earth. From the geocentric perspective, Venus is behind the attraction between the sexes and the resulting attachment. From the heliocentric perspective, Venus is not attached to Earth at all, but free to seek out knowledge through the full range of experience indicated by the aspects.

Earth: Earth represents the direction in which intelligent activity will most likely move. Earth is obviously where you, the individual are; thus Earth represents the human capacity from the perspective of the Sun. You will relate to the energy of the Sun through the sign Earth falls in and your life's mission will tend to involve this sign and its opposite. You tend to mobilize your intelligence through the sign that Earth occupies in the heliocentric chart.

Mars: Mars indicates the direction that your devotion takes. Mars is energetic, even aggressive at times. At other times Mars' energy is directed into

thoughtful devotional activities, quieter but no less energetic. The placement of Mars in your heliocentric chart reflects the energy and passion
that you employ when dealing with higher spiritual goals. Mars is an agent
for change, providing the energy for movement in thought and action.
Your energy is activated through the sign Mars occupies and thus indicates
where you will direct your activities.

The position of Mars in the heliocentric chart pinpoints the way in which an
individual becomes aware of his highest potential. Once you see the more
objective, purer devotional path that is available to you, based on the sign of
Mars in the heliocentric chart, you can adapt the direction of your physical
energy in terms of your career to suit. This is one way to align your spiritual
devotion with your material career path.

Jupiter: Jupiter indicates the path toward fusion of heart and mind, which
is the subjective purpose for manifestation. This is perhaps the most central
experience of wisdom that you will ever have. Your life's processes can be
defined by the placement of Jupiter in the heliocentric chart. The expansive
process of your mind and spirit relishes the richness to be found through
synthesis of love and wisdom into spiritual understanding.

The profusion of Jupiter's moons is one expression of the paradox of synthesis. We seek to resolve paradoxes and find that this can only be done
when we transcend ego. Love and wisdom often don't seem to mix well, but
understanding lies in the melding of these facets into a single jewel of spirit.

Saturn: Saturn is the lord of karma—the imposer of retribution and the
cause of all repayment of debts. This is the first of two indications of Saturn in
the heliocentric chart—that we accumulate debts and responsibilities on the
path toward resolution of difficulties. The second indication of Saturn's place
in the chart is that the power of indebtedness is ended when we have freed
ourselves from the accumulation of karma. It is through the exercise of intelligent activity—that is, the use of what we know and how we employ that
knowledge—that we even begin to approach the freedom we seek.

Saturn also reflects the structure of your mind. You approach structure in all
areas of your life through the sign Saturn occupies. In the geocentric chart
Saturn indicates the best path for career to take; in the heliocentric chart it
shows the best path for understanding a higher spiritual purpose. Intelligent

activity emerges when we understand that karma is both the result of our actions and the actions that grow out of our decisions. Intelligent activity is the application of mind to the pursuit of both material and spiritual goals.

Uranus: The search for equilibrium in your life reaches beyond the limits of this plane of manifestation, seeking to integrate the experiences of body, mind, and spirit into one profound experience of unfolded consciousness. This level of integration occurs when the soul and the personality are brought into alignment through accident or through ritual experience. Thus ritual is a valuable path for you as you develop a sense of equilibrium. Uranus tends to bring upset and abrupt change. Incorporation of ritual into your daily life and awareness of the form of ritual can provide a suitable vehicle for traveling life's sometimes bumpy road. You can develop a fuller sense of the value of ritual through the sign Uranus occupies.

Uranus rules the occult path. Occult here means hidden. The appropriate spiritual or material path is hidden only when we are unable to perceive it on the appropriate level. Ritual is used to open or to keep open the channel through which correct perception enters awareness. I once thought that occult studies were impossible. I have come to replace that belief with an attitude of openness to psychic or intuitive experiences, as well as a willingness to actively consider evidence of that kind, and even to act on that evidence without any so-called practical evidence.

Neptune: Psychic awareness is indicated by the placement of Neptune in your heliocentric chart. The focused nature of this awareness is to become aware through extraordinary means and to experience freedom of your feelings. Your higher vision is based on your examination of the essential duality of physical manifestation. One side of the duality is the desire or passionate nature; the other side is the innate quality of compassion that comes from another level of experience. The sign Neptune occupies colors the awareness of this essential duality.

Desire is one quality that drives us to strive for the highest possible career goals. The quality of that desire determines the nature of our path, as we can either trample others in the desire to reach the top, or bring others along with us as we search for success. Right relationship to others, for me, includes the psychic sensitivity to their path, as well as to my own.

Pluto: Your path to transformation lies in the death of personal traits that limit you and the desires that drive you. The sign Pluto occupies indicates the most direct way to actively engage will to guide your personal power. How to best mobilize your own efforts to maintain or achieve harmonious results from all important endeavors is a function of how you integrate power and will to act as a human being. You have the choice of how you implement your will. The power of the universe acts for and with you through a sharing of will between your personality and higher mind.

The death of personality and desire are eventual outcomes when we harness our personal power and will. This power can bring the change and darkness of coercive force; it also brings the shamanistic experience of death that marks the healer and the seer alike. The heliocentric chart positions Pluto in a degree very near to its geocentric position; the slight difference reflects the small shift of consciousness necessary to achieve powerful material and spiritual goals.

Signs in Heliocentric Charts

Just as the planets have similar qualities in both geocentric and heliocentric charts, the signs are the same as well. The planets still travel through the background of the zodiac, and are colored by twelve expressions of the elements and modalities. However, because of the heliocentric perspective, the signs take on a more hidden spiritual quality (hence the term esoteric as it is applied to astrology). The following brief descriptions focus on the meanings ascribed to the signs in esoteric astrology.

Aries: Two profoundly significant realities of being are expressed here. First, Aries mirrors the movement into incarnation. This movement includes the desire to manifest in the material world and requires an effort of will. Second, this sign implies a desire to cooperate with a larger plan. Thus it indicates both the will to manifest individually and the culmination of individual experience because of the desire to return to the ultimate source. "The secret of Aries is the secret of beginnings" (Bailey, *Esoteric Astrology,* 387).

Taurus: Taurus focuses the desire to express through personality. This expression of the bull can become stubbornness, or it can exemplify purposeful progress. The coexistence of physical form and spiritual will illuminate our individual desires as well as the powerful idealism of the larger sphere of life. "The secret of Taurus . . . is revealed in the blinding energy of light (through) the sudden removal . . . of world glamour" (Bailey, 388). Here we can learn to avoid the limitations of personality and embrace the boundless possibilities of Spirit.

Gemini: The desire to manifest in the world is found in Gemini. This placement addresses the creative passion as it expresses procreatively. The child is a physical example of the synthesis of opposites. Gemini also produces the energy needed to evolve in consciousness to a higher expression. Planets here experience two truths: their energy uses the mind to mediate within the personality, and also communicates between the personality and the soul. "The secret of Gemini is the mystery of the relation of Father, Mother and Child," (Bailey, 388) a mystical expression of the power of love.

Cancer: Physical human instinct includes a desire and need to nurture the body and mind. At the same time there is a profound instinctual drive to discover meaning, so much so that at some point life without meaning becomes intolerable. Just as physical life is breathed into us, so is the life of the spirit instilled within us. "The light of substance . . . is . . . awaiting the stimulation coming from the soul light" (Bailey, 239).

Leo: Planets here show the energies you use for the unfolding of spiritual consciousness within your personality. Mature self-consciousness includes awareness of these two components of your being and how they interweave to produce what we call life. In our daily activities we seldom think of this profound reality of existence; as we grow in conscience we develop an affinity for the "heart of the Sun," sensitizing ourselves to our higher mission.

Virgo: The nurturing capability of the material can develop on the path to higher spiritual realization. You have deep experiences that reveal the light to you. You have the capability of unified understanding of the feminine principle in all its expressions, embodying it in the mental, emotional, and physical manifestations. Outer attention to detail reveals your inner understanding of unity.

Libra: Heliocentric planets in Libra show the testing of opposites. Energies are weighed and balanced here, and understanding begins to form about the profitable uses of polarity. Harmony is not only expressed through balance and symmetry, but through intentional asymmetry as well. Knowing how to work with this concept allows you to achieve new levels of energy.

Scorpio: Planets in Scorpio indicate fierce testing on the spiritual and material planes. The planetary energies are subjected to physical, mental, and spiritual demands which leave us changed forever. While duality is part of all experience, there is a struggle in Scorpio which tests even the nature of opposites. This spiritual battle challenges you to rise above merely material considerations.

Sagittarius: The process of linking form and soul is essential when heliocentric planets occupy this sign. Without this step the soul would not attach to the body and life independent from the mother would not be possible. This deep mystery occurs metaphorically while the Sun is sinking to its lowest point of the year, suggesting that the mysteries of life dwell in the dark recesses of consciousness.

Capricorn: The most complete understanding of the laws of karma and dharma are embodied in planets here. Just as Capricorn deals with the path of work, it also reveals the conclusion of that work. You experience those endings in connection with new beginnings as well, moving into a new cycle each time you complete the old one. Intellect becomes a principle factor, as you utilize concrete knowledge in your pursuit of intelligent activity.

Aquarius: Planets here seek the melding love and wisdom into a working unity. Your sight is always set on the masses and not the individual, your goals and work tend to be global, in thought and in action. Ritual provides an avenue for working with others. By honoring your human connection to form, you are able to help people to move forward. It is through the use of ritual that you are able to resolve difficulties between people, as ritual affords the possibility of acknowledging conflict while encouraging movement toward solution.

Pisces: Heliocentric planets in Pisces work through sensitivity on both the material and spiritual planes. At times you feel limited or even imprisoned in your body, yet you are able to use your physical manifestation to communicate about subjects of the soul. You continually face the possibility of raising your human desires to a higher level of spiritual expression; through such activity you sympathetically raise your fellow beings as well. You grasp the meaning of polarity in human experience, opening the door to future progress.

In a world where many of us are searching for deeper meaning in our lives, the heliocentric chart provides a map of our personal relationship to the larger mind of the Solar Logos, God, or the Universal Mind. It provides a glimpse of what our power and potential truly are, freed from the limitations of ego and emotion to a large extent. Where vocation is concerned, the geocentric chart provides a wealth of specific information about how to act—how to go about establishing a viable, satisfying vocation. The heliocentric chart complements that perspective with a complementary view of your creative spiritual path.

The best vocational guidance comes from an understanding of the spiritual mission and how it expresses through your daimon—your individual spirit. If you have never used heliocentric charts, now may be a good time to incorporate them into your astrological techniques, as they open a rich vein of ore for the vocational astrologer as they reveal the spiritual underpinnings of personality and drive.

Lincoln and Darwin: Virtual Twins

Charles Darwin and Abraham Lincoln were born within two hours of each other on different continents and into utterly different circumstances. Yet they had many things in common. Both became famous in their chosen vocations. Their heliocentric charts are virtually identical, as are their geocentric charts, with the exception that the Midheavens differ by about 61 degrees.

In the geocentric chart Lincoln has Virgo at the Midheaven and no planets in the Tenth House. We must look to Mercury to find the career direction he will most likely take. His life as a politician is based on the placement of Mercury in the Third House. He was able to move people by his words. Mercury conjunct Pluto indicates the power that he brought to his efforts to convince others of his opinions. The helio Mercury promised tension where communication is concerned—a tension that maximizes the use of power and will (helio Mercury sextile Pluto), while at the same time holding the wisdom and love of the cause in plain view (Mercury semi-square Jupiter).

Darwin's natal chart has Scorpio at the Midheaven with Saturn and Neptune in the Tenth House. His career focused on research into the causes of the varieties of life. As he examined the variations, he came to understand that this structure came from an evolutionary process over millennia. In his case the Mercury sextile to Pluto in the helio chart indicates a career in which words are the outcome—his publication of his theories was an end result of his studies. Compare this to Lincoln, for whom the spoken word was the means to his political goals.

There is no surprise that these two famous men share the ability to express their power. We would not remember them if they had not done so. The point of astrological interest is that one heliocentric aspect—one element of their spiritual mission—can be expressed so differently. Compare the Gettysburg Address, a speech marking a step in the process toward reunification of the Union, to *The Origin of Species*, the end result of a life's work. Both have had lasting impact on the world; both have the innate power of the Pluto aspect; each is designed to fulfill a very different purpose.

We have seen throughout this book that the planets reflect very different expressions in different charts, different signs, and different houses. In each chapter there have been examples, both historical and contemporary, to illustrate each astrological factor. It is significant to note that mission as viewed from the heliocentric perspective is capable of being expressed through the multiplicity of human personalities, as in the case of Lincoln and Darwin.

Summary

The created universe, from its beginning, has embodied basic goodness as an essential of being. This quality has not dwindled, nor will it do so in the future. The aim of vocational astrology is to place yourself or your clients in the best possible position to apprehend that basic goodness and to manifest it openly in your life. Astrologers have the capacity to look into the lives of their clients, opening doors to understanding of spiritual mission and its place in ordinary vocation. Hopefully, some of the techniques in this book will help you to understand your personal vocation and also facilitate your work with others.

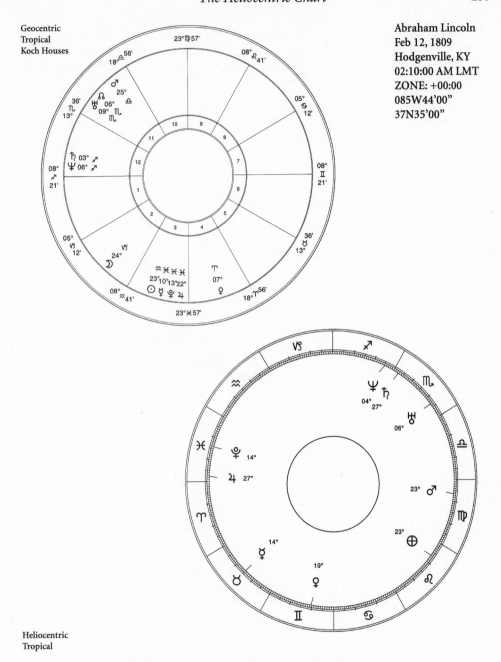

Abraham Lincoln
Feb 12, 1809
Hodgenville, KY
02:10:00 AM LMT
ZONE: +00:00
085W44'00"
37N35'00"

Figure 17. Abraham Lincoln's Heliocentric Chart.

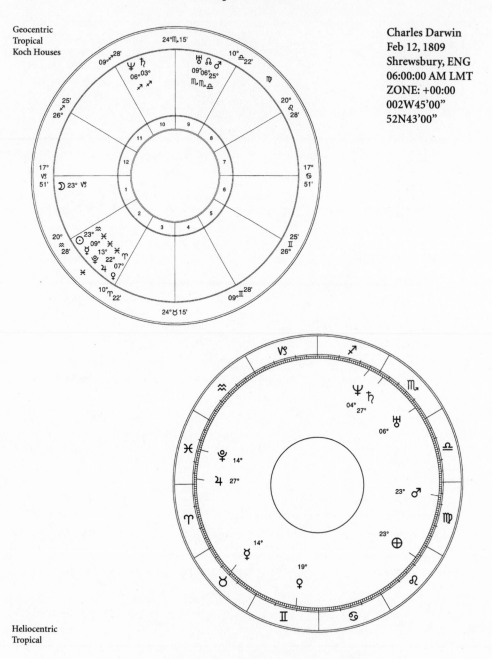

Figure 18. Charles Darwin's Heliocentric Chart.

Appendix

Planets as Dispositors

A dispositor is a planet which, through sign rulership, gives its disposition to another planet. For example, Mars gives its disposition to any planet in Aries. The dispositor can give its disposition to a planet indirectly as well. For example, if Mercury is in Aries and Jupiter is in Virgo, then Mars gives its disposition to Mercury directly and to Jupiter indirectly. A final dispositor is a planet which is found in its own sign.

In some charts there will be more than one final dispositor, and in some charts there will be none. This is because there may be more than one planet in its own sign, and there may be no planet in its own sign as well. In these cases three conditions occur:

- mutual reception, in which two planets are in each other's sign, such as Mars in Gemini and Mercury in Aries
- rings, where three or more planets are in each other's signs, such as Mars in Gemini, Mercury in Taurus, and Venus in Aries or
- combinations of final dispositors, mutual receptions, and rings are also possible.

The dispositor shows how a person tends to formulate policies, make decisions, and take action. In mutual receptions there are two usual approaches which take turns; in rings there are three or more possibilities.

Sun: When the final dispositor, there is tremendous drive for significance. Pride is a factor in all of the person's activities. Power is also a primary consideration for this individual. Thought processes will focus on how to achieve power and how to control the environment. Such a person can become self-centered. However, the Sun's drive for significance is not a bad thing in itself, but personal considerations are at the top of the list.

Moon: The Moon as dispositor indicates an individual who makes decisions based on intuitive or emotional considerations. The home and family are major factors in the decision-making process as well. Such a person will have behaviors that can be traced to other family members. The "gut" reaction is significant, as are other internal processes. Something has to feel good or feel right for this person to take action.

Mercury: Rational thought is the focus of the decision-making process for Mercury. Practical considerations are also key to taking action. Often the decisions are tied to ideas and therefore are not totally grounded in reality, and this could be problematic. On the other hand, the rational approach is held in high esteem in our society and logic is a powerful tool in the career venue.

Venus: General policies and specific actions are based on social considerations for the most part. Harmony may be sought to the exclusion of other considerations, yet decisions tend to work out in the end. These individuals are on a rather straight and narrow path ethically and will not tolerate moral missteps. Elegance or beauty are added considerations.

Mars: Action is the keynote, action is the process, and action is the outcome for Mars. This can lead to disasters, but you do find out quickly. No time wasted here. Such an individual is first into the new venture and first out, as he or she is on to the next new thing. Such an individual is well placed in a career where quick decisions are a plus.

Jupiter: If Jupiter is the dispositor, the thought processes are fully engaged before decisions are made. Not one to be pushed, such an individual considers all the angles from a philosophical perspective. Action is confident, and tends to be very consistent with the individual's character. Good will is valued by the Jupiter dispositor.

Saturn: With Saturn as dispositor, life takes on a cautious, even serious tone. Security issues are in the forefront. Such an individual makes a good teacher or trainer, as they keep all the factors in mind and teach theoretical principles as well as workable procedures. Discipline can become a limitation; structure is paramount for Saturn.

Uranus: Intuitive insight drives the Uranus dispositor. Such a person is able to see through the daily detail to the heart of a process. These people appear to be unpredictable, but they are actually marching right in step with their own drummer. These people rarely find themselves trapped by circumstances because freedom is a primary concern.

Neptune: The Neptune dispositor provides deep wells of strength that arises almost unbidden when the chips are down. This is ideal for artists, musicians, and designers of all kinds. Subtle capabilities like intuition and psychic awareness are naturally a fact of life for people with Neptune as dispositor. Whole generations with Neptune in Pisces will have a mystical side to their thought processes.

Pluto: Another generational influence, people with Pluto as dispositor see control as a primary consideration. Personal will power is key. While the Pluto cycle is quite long, we see the influence of the dispositor through mutual receptions and rings in every generation. When the desire for control becomes self-control, then the Pluto dispositor is at its most powerful.

Bibliography

Bailey, Alice. *Esoteric Astrology*. New York: Lucis Pub. Col., 1951.

Bennet, E. A. *What Jung Really Said*. New York: Schocken Books, 1967.

Clement, Stephanie. *Consciousness and the Midheaven*. Tempe, AZ: American Federation of Astrologers, 1994.

Crowley, Aleister. *The Book of Thoth*. York Beach: Samuel Weiser, 1974.

Ebertin, Reinhold. *Combination of Stellar Influences*. Aalen: Ebertin Verlag, 1972.

Hillman, James. *The Soul's Code: In Search of Character and Calling*. New York: Random House, 1996.

————. *The Myth of Analysis: Three Essays in Archetypal Psychology*. New York: Harper Colophon, 1972.

Lewi, Grant. "Your Job and Astrology." *American Astrology Magazine* 3, no. 5 (July 1935).

Moacanin, Radmilla. *Jung's Psychology and Tibetan Buddhism*. London: Wisdom Publications, 1986.

Myers, Isabel Briggs and Peter B. Myers. *Gifts Differing: Understanding Personality Type.* Palo Alto: CPP Books, 1980.

Penfield, Marc. *2001: The Penfield Collection.* Seattle: Vulcan Books, 1979.

Rodden, Lois. *Profiles of Women: A Collection of Astrological Biographies.* Tempe, AZ: American Federation of Astrologers, 1979.

Rudhyar, Dane. *Astrology and Personality.* Santa Fe: Aurora Press, 1990.

Young, Arthur. *The Reflexive Universe.* Mill Valley, CA: Robert Briggs Assoc., 1976.

Index

LOOK FOR THE CRESCENT MOON

Llewellyn publishes hundreds of books on your favorite subjects! To get these exciting books, including the ones on the following pages, check your local bookstore or order them directly from Llewellyn.

ORDER BY PHONE

- Call toll-free within the U.S. and Canada, 1–800–THE MOON
- In Minnesota, call (651) 291–1970
- We accept VISA, MasterCard, and American Express

ORDER BY MAIL

- Send the full price of your order (MN residents add 7% sales tax) in U.S. funds, plus postage & handling to:

  Llewellyn Worldwide
  P.O. Box 64383, Dept. K144–9
  St. Paul, MN 55164–0383, U.S.A.

POSTAGE & HANDLING
(For the U.S., Canada, and Mexico)

- $4 for orders $15 and under
- $5 for orders over $15
- No charge for orders over $100

We ship UPS in the continental United States. We ship standard mail to P.O. boxes. Orders shipped to Alaska, Hawaii, the Virgin Islands, and Puerto Rico are sent first-class mail. Orders shipped to Canada and Mexico are sent surface mail.

International orders: Airmail—add freight equal to price of each book to the total price of order, plus $5.00 for each non-book item (audio tapes, etc.).

Surface mail—Add $1.00 per item.

Allow 4–6 weeks for delivery on all orders.
Postage and handling rates subject to change.

DISCOUNTS

We offer a 20% discount to group leaders or agents. You must order a minimum of 5 copies of the same book to get our special quantity price.

FREE CATALOG
Get a free copy of our color catalog, *New Worlds of Mind and Spirit*. Subscribe for just $10.00 in the United States and Canada ($30.00 overseas, airmail). Many bookstores carry *New Worlds*—ask for it!

Visit our website at www.llewellyn.com for more information.

Twelve Faces of Saturn
Your Guardian Angel Planet

Bil Tierney

Astrological Saturn. It's usually associated with personal limitations, material obstacles, psychological roadblocks and restriction. We observe Saturn's symbolism in our natal chart with uneasiness and anxiety, while intellectually proclaiming its higher purpose as our "wise teacher."

But now it's time to throw out the portrait of the creepy looking, scythe-wielding Saturn of centuries ago. Bil Tierney offers a refreshing new picture of a this planet as friend, not foe. Saturn is actually key to liberating us from a life handicapped by lack of clear self definition. It is indispensable to psychological maturity and material stability—it is your guardian angel planet.

Explore Saturn from the perspective of your natal sign and house. Uncover another layer of Saturnian themes at work in Saturn's aspects. Look at Saturn through each element and modality, as well as through astronomy, mythology and metaphysics.

1–56718–711–0
6 x 9, 360 pp. $16.95

ASTROLOGICAL TIMING OF CRITICAL ILLNESS
Early Warning Patterns in the Horoscope

Noel Tyl
Foreword by Mitchell Gibson, M.D.
Introduction by Jeffrey Wolf Green

Now, through master astrologer Noel Tyl's work, astrology has a thoroughly tested method with which to understand and anticipate the emergence of critical illness: from the natal horoscope, throughout development, and within the aging process. Astrologers can use Noel Tyl's discovery to work with people to extend life as much as possible, to live a full life, and to do it all with holistic understanding.

Tyl painstakingly researched more than seventy cases to test his patterning discoveries Your analytical skill will be alerted, tested, and sharpened through these very same cases, which include notables such as Carl Sagan (bone cancer), Betty Ford (breast cancer), Larry King (heart attack), Norman Schwarzkopf (prostate cancer), and Mike Wallace (manic depression), and many, many others.

1–56718–738–2
7 x 10, 288 pp., charts   **$19.95**

To order, call 1–800–THE MOON
Prices subject to change without notice.

Pluto, Vol. II
The Soul's Evolution Through Relationships
Jeffrey Wolf Green

From the great mass of people on the planet we all choose certain ones with whom to be intimate. *Pluto, Vol II* shows the evolutionary and karmic causes, reasons, and prior life background that determines whom we relate to and how.

This is the first book to explore the astrological Pluto model that embraces the evolutionary development and progression of the Soul from life to life. It offers a unique, original paradigm that allows for a total understanding of the past life dynamics that exist between two people. You will find a precise astrological methodology to determine the prior life orientation, where the relationship left off, where the relationship picked up in this lifetime, and what the current evolutionary next step is: the specific reasons or intentions for being together again.

In addition, there are chapters devoted to Mars and Venus in the signs, Mars and Venus in relationship, Mars and Pluto in relationship, and Pluto through the Composite Houses.

1–56718–333–6
6 x 9, 432 pp. $17.95